DIMENSIONS
OF PRIVATE LAW

Categories and Concepts
in Anglo-American
Legal Reasoning

STEPHEN WADDAMS

CAMBRIDGE
UNIVERSITY PRESS

PUBLISHED BY THE PRESS SYNDICATE OF THE UNIVERSITY OF CAMBRIDGE
The Pitt Building, Trumpington Street, Cambridge CB2 1RP, United Kingdom

CAMBRIDGE UNIVERSITY PRESS
The Edinburgh Building, Cambridge, CB2 2RU, UK
40 West 20th Street, New York, NY 10011–4211, USA
477 Williamstown Road, Port Melbourne, VIC 3207, Australia
Ruiz de Alarcón 13, 28014 Madrid, Spain
Dock House, The Waterfront, Cape Town 8001, South Africa

http://www.cambridge.org

© Cambridge University Press 2003

First published 2003

Printed in the United Kingdom at the University Press, Cambridge

Typeface Adobe Minion 10.5/13.5 pt. *System* LaTeX 2_ε [TB]

A catalogue record for this book is available from the British Library

ISBN 0 521 81643 2 hardback
ISBN 0 521 01669 X paperback

CONTENTS

PREFACE

Organization of ideas in Anglo-American private law has been beset with difficulties – linguistic, philosophical, jurisprudential, rhetorical, and historical. This study, though not a history of private law (by period or by topic), is historical in perspective: attention is directed to the past (from the eighteenth century to the recent past), and to the failure of any organizational scheme or of any single or simple explanation either to describe the law that preceded it, or to supply a workable guide for decisions thereafter. This failure suggests that the interrelation of legal concepts has involved a greater complexity than can be captured by organizational schemes, maps, or diagrams, or by any single explanatory principle.

Since the nineteenth century it has been common to make distinctions in respect of Anglo-American law between public and private law, and within private law between property and obligations, and within obligations among contracts, torts, and unjust enrichment. Legal issues and rules have been supposed to belong to one of these subcategories, and the rules applied to determine the result in particular cases. But this scheme has failed to account for many actual judicial decisions, a failure that led, in the twentieth century, to scepticism of formal explanations of law, to alternative explanations, and in turn to counter-reaction.

This study approaches these questions not by proposing any new all-embracing explanation, or by seeking to impose a single pattern on all of private law, but by proceeding from the particular towards the general. From this direction it will be seen that many important legal issues have not been resolved by being initially allocated exclusively to a particular subcategory, but by simultaneous application of several or all of the concepts mentioned in the last paragraph. The plan of the study is not schematic but progressive, considering first a particular dispute – that between the two principal opera houses in mid-nineteenth-century London for the services of Johanna Wagner – and then proceeding to a number of other legal issues that have similarly resisted classification. In the light of these issues we turn to the interrelation of obligations, then to the distinction between obligations and property, and finally to that between private right and public policy. This progression from particular to general, like the method of legal thinking it describes, shows why it has been so difficult to reverse the process and to impose the general upon the particular.

I am grateful to the University of Toronto for research leave, to the Killam Program at the Canada Council for the Arts, and to the Social Sciences and Humanities Research Council of Canada for research funds. I am grateful also to many friends, colleagues, and students who read the drafts and made helpful comments, and to Stephanie Chong, Adam Taylor, Craig Lockwood, Megan Ferrier, and John Sawicki for valuable research assistance.

Stephen Waddams
Toronto, 2002

TABLE OF CASES

1

Introduction: the mapping of legal concepts

> The more effectually to accomplish the redress of private injuries, courts
> of justice are instituted in every civilized society, in order to protect the
> weak from the insults of the stronger, by expounding and enforcing
> those laws, by which rights are defined, and wrongs prohibited.[1]

With these words William Blackstone introduced readers of the *Commentaries on the Laws of England* to the topic of private wrongs. Blackstone did not offer a definition of private law, nor is such a definition to be found in any authoritative source. Anglo-American law has claimed many merits, but linguistic and conceptual precision are not among them.[2] Private law, as the term is used in this study, is concerned principally with the mutual rights and obligations of individuals.[3] Like other legal concepts, the term takes its meaning partly from what it excludes, notably public international law, constitutional law, local government law, administrative law, criminal law, military law, and taxation.

Many attempts have been made to explain the relation to each other of categories (organizing divisions) and concepts (recurring ideas) in private law, leading, since Blackstone's time, to a great variety of suggested maps, schemes, and diagrams; none of these has commanded general assent or has fully explained the actual decisions of the courts. In this study a number of legal issues will be examined in which the interrelation of fundamental concepts has been crucial. It will appear that the concepts have, when looked at from the standpoint of these legal issues,[4] operated not in isolation from each other, but cumulatively and in combination, and that their relation

---

[1] W. Blackstone, *Commentaries on the Laws of England* (4 vols., London, 1765–9), vol. III, p. 2.
[2] D. J. Ibbetson, *A Historical Introduction to the Law of Obligations* (Oxford, 1999), p. 294.
[3] But it includes corporations, and government agencies in many of their relations to citizens.
[4] See K. Greenawalt, 'From the Bottom Up' (1997) 82 *Cornell Law Review* 994, G. Samuel, 'Classification of Obligations and the Impact of Constructivist Epistemologies' (1997) 17 *Legal Studies* 448, 465 ('the view from the bottom').

to each other is fully captured neither by the image of a map nor by that of a diagram. Often a legal obligation has been derived not from a single concept, but from the interaction of two or more concepts in such a way as to preclude the allocation of the legal issue to a single category.

A desire for precision and order naturally leads to a search for clear categories and good maps, but such a search, if pressed too far, may be self-defeating, for material that is inherently complex is not better understood by concealing its complexity. Schemes that have failed to account for the inherent complexity of the law have not been conducive to good intellectual order, and have engendered both academic scepticism and judicial resistance. The latter has an immediate complicating effect since judicial opinions are part of the data, as well as sometimes the effect, of organizational schemes. Oliver Wendell Holmes, abandoning earlier attempts to reduce the law to tabular form,[5] said in 1881 that 'the life of the law has not been logic: it has been experience',[6] and this was echoed in England by Lord Halsbury's statement that 'every lawyer must acknowledge that the law is not always logical at all'.[7] Very similar views were current a century later. 'There are many situations of daily life,' Lord Wilberforce observed, 'which do not fit neatly into conceptual analysis.'[8] Other twentieth-century judges have similarly warned against 'the temptation of elegance',[9] against 'that well known ailment of lawyers, a hardening of the categories',[10] against 'a preoccupation with conceptualistic reasoning',[11] and against reasoning that is 'legalistic', 'formalistic', or 'mechanical'.[12] Where judges have used the phrase 'strict logic' it has usually been for the express purpose of rejecting it.[13]

---

[5] See F. Frankfurter, 'The Early Writings of O. W. Holmes Jr' (1931) 44 *Harvard Law Review* 717. O. W. Holmes, *The Common Law*, ed. M. D. Howe (Boston, 1963 [1881]), 'Introduction', p. xxii.

[6] Holmes, *The Common Law*, p. 1. See p. 221 below.

[7] *Quinn* v. *Leatham* [1901] AC 495 at 506, HL.

[8] *Woodar Investment Development Ltd* v. *Wimpey Construction UK Ltd* [1980] 1 WLR 277 at 283, quoted with approval in *Alfred McAlpine Construction Ltd* v. *Panatown Ltd* [2001] 1 AC 518, HL, at 535 (Lord Clyde), and 588 (Lord Millett, dissenting).

[9] R. Goff, 'The Search for Principle' (Maccabean lecture, 1983), repr. in W. Swadling and G. Jones (eds.), *The Search for Principle* (London, 1999), p. 313 at p. 318.

[10] Lord Nicholls in *Attorney General* v. *Blake* [2001] 1 AC 268, HL, at 284, echoing J. P. Dawson, 'Restitution or Damages' (1959) 20 *Ohio State Law Journal* 175 at 187.

[11] *Lister* v. *Hesley Hall, Ltd* [2002] 1 AC 215 at 224.

[12] *Dobson* v. *Dobson* [1999] 2 SCR 753 at 778, 174 DLR (4th) 1 at 19; *Bazley* v. *Curry* [1999] 2 SCR 534 at 551, 558, 563, 174 DLR (4th) 45 at 58, 63, 67; *Jacobi* v. *Griffiths* [1999] 2 SCR 570 at 581, 174 DLR (4th) 71 at 79, *Fairchild* v. *Glenhaven Funeral Services Ltd* [2002] 3 WLR 89, HL, at 96, 98.

[13] P. S. Atiyah, *Pragmatism and Theory in English Law* (London, 1987), pp. 11–13.

Such sentiments do not establish that legal categories and concepts are non-existent, or that reason is unimportant, but they do show that the courts, in attempting to accommodate 'life in all its untidy complexity',[14] have in many cases not derived their conclusions from pre-existing conceptual schemes or maps. The future might, no doubt, be different: historical evidence cannot exclude the possibility of future attainment of greater order and precision (though it might be relevant to an assessment of its probability). Neither can evidence drawn from one legal system exclude the possibility of greater order and precision in others.[15] This study is restricted to Anglo-American law and to its fairly recent past. It does not and cannot establish that in the future, or in other systems, or in an ideal system, things might not be ordered differently.

The idea of mapping, in relation to law, like many metaphors, owes its attraction partly to its indeterminacy: there is no consensus on what is to be mapped (facts, cases, issues, rules, reasons, categories, or concepts), on what is to be located on the map when drawn, or on whether the map is governed by the shape of the terrain, or vice versa. Use of the metaphor is so ingrained as to be to some degree inevitable, for any set of ideas may be said, in a sense, to have its map. Blackstone himself employed a mapping metaphor, writing that 'an academical expounder of the laws . . . should consider his course as a general map of the law, marking out the shape of the country, its connexions and boundaries, its greater divisions and principal cities: it is not his business to describe minutely the subordinate limits, and to fix the longitude and latitude of every inconsiderable hamlet'.[16] The map that Blackstone offered to his readers, however, was very different from maps proposed in the nineteenth and twentieth centuries:

> Now, as municipal law is a rule of civil conduct, commanding what is right, and prohibiting what is wrong; or as Cicero, and after him our Bracton, has expressed it, *sanctio justa, jubens honesta et prohibens contraria* [a just ordinance, commanding what is right and prohibiting the contrary]; it follows, that the primary and principal objects of the law are RIGHTS, and WRONGS.

---

[14] Goff, 'The Search for Principle', note 9 above, p. 318. See W. M. C. Gummow, 'Unjust Enrichment, Restitution, and Proprietary Remedies', in P. D. Finn (ed.), *Essays on Restitution* (Sydney, 1990), p. 47 at p. 50.

[15] Other systems have complexities of their own in relation to the issues discussed in this study. See F. H. Lawson, *A Common Lawyer Looks at the Civil Law* (Ann Arbor, 1955), pp. 58–61, 82, 112, 161–3, 205–6; G. Samuel, 'Property Notions in the Law of Obligations' [1994] *Cambridge Law Journal* 524 at 527, 541.

[16] Blackstone, *Commentaries*, vol. I, p. 35.

In the prosecution therefore of these commentaries, I shall follow this very simple and obvious division: and shall in the first place consider the *rights* that are commanded, and secondly the *wrongs* that are forbidden by the laws of England.[17]

Blackstone then went on to divide rights into 'rights of persons' and 'rights of things', and wrongs into 'private wrongs' and 'public wrongs', supplying titles for each of his four volumes.[18] Despite the enormous success of the *Commentaries*,[19] this scheme gained little following. It depended too much on doubtful verbal parallels and antitheses,[20] and it omitted divisions that later came to be thought to be of fundamental importance, notably the distinctions between public and private law,[21] and within private law between property and obligations, and within obligations between contractual and other kinds of obligation.[22] Peter Birks, the editor of *English Private Law* (2000) planned originally to base the work on Blackstone's scheme, but 'That hope rather quickly faded. It became evident that it was impossible to base an enlightening account of modern English law on Blackstone's scheme.'[23]

---

[17] *Ibid.*, p. 118.   [18] *Ibid.*

[19] For fluctuations in Blackstone's reputation, see S. F. C. Milsom, 'The Nature of Blackstone's Achievement' (1981) 1 *Oxford Journal of Legal Studies* 1, J. W. Cairns, 'Blackstone, an English Institutionalist: Legal Literature and the Rise of the Nation State' (1984) 4 *Oxford Journal of Legal Studies* 318 at 318–19, 341, P. Birks, 'Rights, Wrongs and Remedies' (2000) 20 *Oxford Journal of Legal Studies* 1 at 4–5.

[20] The primary division between 'right' and 'wrong' depends on a dual meaning in the English language of the word 'right' ('that which is just', and 'an interest protected by the law'). In many languages these concepts are expressed by different words. So, Blackstone's French translator found it necessary to add, after 'what is right' in the first line ('ce qui est juste') the words 'et de droit', and, before the word 'RIGHTS' in the fourth line, the words 'ce qui est juste et ce qui est injuste'. N. Chompre, *Commentaires sur les lois anglaises* (Paris, 1822), pp. 207–8. It has also been pointed out that the contrast is in a sense false, because the extent of 'rights' depends on what the law treats as 'wrongs': J. Austin, *Lectures on Jurisprudence: the Philosophy of Positive Law* (4th edn, London, 1873, repr. 1996), pp. 751–2, G. Jones, *The Sovereignty of the Law* (Toronto, 1973), p. xxvi. Blackstone's editor, Edward Christian, went so far as to call the expression 'rights of things' a 'solecism', and his French translator agreed (Chompre, *Commentaires*, p. 209).

[21] Jones, *Sovereignty of the Law*, p. xxv. Blackstone distinguished between private and public *wrongs*.

[22] These distinctions were known in Roman law, G. Samuel and J. Rinkes, *Law of Obligations and Legal Remedies* (London, 1996), pp. 64–5, 73, and some of them were used by Hale, whom Blackstone said he 'principally followed', W. Blackstone, *An Analysis of the Laws of England* (London, 1756), p. vii, Cairns, 'Blackstone, an English Institutionalist', note 19 above, at 340–2, A. W. B. Simpson, 'The Rise and Fall of the Legal Treatise', in *Legal Theory and Legal History* (London, 1987), p. 273 at pp. 281–2.

[23] P. Birks (ed.) *English Private Law* (Oxford, 2000), 'Introduction', p. xlix.

Blackstone's purpose was not to set out an ideal or a universal legal system with which to contrast English law,[24] but to describe an existing institution. The matter to be mapped was English law as it was and as it had been, and so his 'general map of the law' was more akin to the plan of an existing building than to a map of geographical territory. Blackstone himself made striking use of architectural metaphor. In a private letter of 1745 he described fifteenth-century English law as resembling 'a regular Edifice: where the Apartments were properly disposed, leading one into another without Confusion; where every part was subservient to the whole, all uniting in one beautiful Symmetry: and every Room had its distinct Office allotted to it'.[25] In the *Commentaries*, Blackstone likened remedial law to a gothic castle,[26] and he reverted to the architectural metaphor in the concluding words of the *Commentaries*, calling on legislators 'to sustain, to repair, to beautify this noble pile'.[27]

Though Blackstone's primary purpose was not to subject English law to critical analysis,[28] his work paved the way for others to do so.[29] Blackstone's scheme had found no explicit place for contract law. In the *Commentaries*, aspects of contracts formed part of rights of persons (employment) and of rights of things (transfers of property), general contract law being assigned to a chapter of the book on private wrongs entitled 'Of injuries to Personal Property', and very briefly treated.[30] In 1790 the first English treatise on contract law[31] gave conceptual unity to the topic, and in 1806 a treatise on *Obligations* by Blackstone's French contemporary Robert Joseph Pothier was published in English translation. So unfamiliar to English readers was the idea of a law of obligations that the translator found it necessary to add

---

[24] W. Holdsworth, *History of English Law* (16 vols., London, 1903–66) vol. XII (1938), pp. 734–5; A. Watson, 'The Structure of Blackstone's Commmentaries' (1988) 97 *Yale Law Journal* 795 at 810; M. Lobban, *The Common Law and English Jurisprudence 1760–1850* (Oxford, 1991), pp. 18, 40.

[25] Blackstone to Richmond, 28 Jan 1745, repr. in (1919) 32 *Harvard Law Review*, 975–6.

[26] Blackstone, *Commentaries*, vol. III, p. 268.

[27] *Commentaries*, vol. IV, p. 443.

[28] D. Kennedy, 'The Structure of Blackstone's Commentaries' (1979) 28 *Buffalo Law Review* 205 suggests a hidden conservative purpose.

[29] S. Milsom, *Historical Foundations of the Common Law* (London, 1969), p. xii, showing that Blackstone, by offering the first description of 'the system as a whole', paved the way for Bentham to attack it.

[30] Blackstone, *Commentaries*, vol. III, pp. 157–8.

[31] J. J. Powell, *An Essay upon the Law of Contracts and Agreements* (London, 1790). See P. S. Atiyah, *The Rise and Fall of Freedom of Contract* (Oxford, 1979), p. 103.

to the title, calling it *A Treatise on the Law of Obligations or Contracts*.[32] The modern reader might naturally suppose that the purpose must have been to enlarge the meaning of 'contracts', but the translator explained that his purpose was in fact to enlarge the meaning of 'obligations' beyond the restricted meaning (i.e., penal bond) that it had in contemporary English legal usage:

> To an English reader the name of the principal treatise would have conveyed a more extensive idea, if the term *Contracts* had been substituted for that of *Obligations*, as we are familiar with the latter term, in a more confined application of it; but the object of the treatise is, to comprize the general doctrines which relate to the obligations between one individual and another, as well for the reparation of injuries, as for the performance of engagements. The principles applicable to obligations resulting from contracts, however, constitute the leading subject of the author's attention, and the reference to other topics may be considered as subordinate and incidental.[33]

Pothier did indeed devote the vast bulk of the treatise (573 pages of 578 in Evans' translation) to contractual obligation, but he was notably concerned that his account should be conceptually complete. He divided obligations into 'contracts' and 'other causes of obligations', and though he devoted only five pages to these 'other causes' he took care to divide them in their turn into 'quasi contracts' (one and a half pages), 'injuries and neglects' (two and a half pages) and a residual class called 'of the law' (one page), consisting of obligations derived directly from natural or positive law. Pothier's works were highly influential in England.[34] In 1822 it was said by Best J (later Chief Justice of the Common Pleas) that

> The authority of Pothier is ... as high as can be had, next to the decision of a Court of Justice in this country. It is extremely well known that he is a writer of acknowledged character; his writings have been constantly referred to by the Courts, and he is spoken of with great praise by Sir William Jones in his

---

[32] R. J. Pothier, *A Treatise on the Law of Obligations or Contracts*, trans. W. D. Evans (London, 1806). The words 'treatise' and 'contracts' appear in italics on the title page, allowing for 'Law of Obligations' to be read as the true title.

[33] *Ibid.*, p. 82 (translator's introduction).

[34] A. W. B. Simpson, 'Innovation in Nineteenth Century Contract Law' (1975) 91 *Law Quarterly Review* 247, repr. in *Legal Theory and Legal History* (London, 1987), p. 171, D. Lieberman, *The Province of Legislation Determined: Legal Theory in Eighteenth-century Britain* (Cambridge, 1989), p. 110, G. Samuel, *The Foundations of Legal Reasoning* (Maastricht, 1994), p. 72, Ibbetson, *Historical Introduction*, p. 220.

Law of Bailments and his writings are considered by that author equal, in point of luminous method, apposite examples, and a clear manly style, to the works of Littleton on the laws of this country.[35]

The demarcation of contract law from other bases of obligation had far-reaching implications, including a division between property and obligation, and divisions among different classes of obligation. It also implied that the contract law of a particular legal system was a manifestation of a universal order, with which, therefore, it might be critically contrasted and compared. This attitude is well illustrated by Charles Addison's preface to his *Treatise on Contracts* (1847), where he said that English contract law was not 'a mere collection of positive rules' or 'founded upon any positive or arbitrary regulations, but upon the broad and general principles of universal law'. He added that 'the law of contracts may justly indeed be said to be a universal law adapted to all times and races, and all places and circumstances, being founded upon those great and fundamental principles of right and wrong deduced from natural reason which are immutable and eternal', and went on to compare English writings, to their disadvantage, with 'the elaborate and elegant works of Pothier'.[36]

This approach gave to contract law a high conceptual significance that had been absent from Blackstone. But attempts to subordinate English contract law to a single classifying concept, such as consent, have not succeeded. Actual consent to be bound has been neither sufficient nor necessary in Anglo-American contract law: not sufficient, because it is ineffective in the absence of a bargain or a formality; not necessary, because contractual words and conduct are given effect according to the meaning reasonably ascribed to them by the promisee, not that actually intended by the promisor.[37] Thus, an offer may be effectively accepted even though the offeror has intended to withdraw it. On this last question the authority of Pothier was expressly rejected by an English court in 1880, relying on American law:

> I am aware that Pothier and some other writers of celebrity are of opinion that there can be no contract if an offer is withdrawn before it is accepted, although the withdrawal is not communicated to the person to whom the offer has been

---

[35] *Cox* v. *Troy* (1822) 5 B & A 474 at 480–1.
[36] C. Addison, *A Treatise on the Law of Contracts and Rights and Liabilities ex contractu* (London, 1847), preface, pp. iv, v, vii.
[37] A passage in *Smith* v. *Hughes* (1871) LR 6 QB 597 at 607 (Lord Blackburn) has been very frequently quoted to this effect.

made. The reason for this opinion is that there is not in fact any such consent by both parties as is essential to constitute a contract between them. Against this view, however, it has been urged that a state of mind not notified cannot be regarded in dealings between man and man, and that an uncommunicated revocation is for all practical purposes and in point of law no revocation at all. This is the view taken in the United States: see *Tayloe* v. *Merchants' Fire Insurance Co.*[38] ... This view... appears to me much more in accordance with the general principles of English law than the view maintained by Pothier.[39]

English contract law, as Blackstone's scheme reminds us, had developed by treating breach of contract as a species of wrong, associated with injury to property. The nineteenth century produced a large number of treatises on English contract law,[40] and though the delictual and proprietary associations of the subject were neglected they were not altogether buried: the primary right of the promisee remained a right to compensation for loss caused by wrongdoing, overlaid on the earlier concepts of covenant and debt, and supplemented by the power of the court of equity, where it thought it appropriate, to decree specific performance, to issue injunctions, and to declare and enforce trusts. These delictual and proprietary associations have been an obstacle to schematic classification because they preclude a sharp demarcation between contractual and other sources of obligation. Such a demarcation would have required the abandonment, as a central concept, of breach of contract as a wrong, the abolition of covenant and debt, the abolition of equity as a source of contractual obligation, the dissociation of contract from property, and the substitution of a primary legal obligation of fulfilment of contracts, as in some other legal systems. Simultaneous changes of this magnitude could scarcely have been achieved without codifying legislation.

Most of the nineteenth-century treatises did not struggle with the precise relation of contracts to other kinds of obligation, but Anson (1879), like Pothier, did. Anson's attempt to reconcile conceptual completeness with the actual structure of English contract law led him to allocate to entirely separate categories the initial obligation to perform a contract and the

---

[38] 50 US 390 (1850).
[39] *Byrne & Co.* v. *Leon Van Tienhoven & Co.* (1880) 5 CPD 344 at 347 (Lindley J).
[40] See Simpson, 'Innovation', note 34 above, at 177, mentioning Comyn, Lawes, Colebrook, Chitty, Fox, Addison, Leake, Pollock, Anson, Plumtre, and Ball.

obligation to pay compensation for loss caused by breach.[41] Anson recognized also that the obligation to pay a judgment could not readily be accommodated under other headings; neither could matrimonial obligations, nor obligations arising from trusts. He thus found it necessary to postulate six categories of obligation: contract, delict, breach of contract, judgment, quasi-contract, and miscellaneous.[42]

Anson's scheme, despite the very high repute of his book, and though carried through seventeen editions over fifty years,[43] attracted no following. Nor was any similar scheme adopted. Halsbury's *Laws of England* (1907–17) organized the law alphabetically under 164 titles, with no title for 'public law', 'private law', 'property', 'obligation', 'quasi-contract', or 'unjust enrichment'.[44] The highly influential *Smith's Leading Cases* (12th edition, 1915) succeeded in arranging much of English private law in the form of annotations on sixty judicial decisions.[45] The general tendency of English lawyers at this time was to think in terms of two general categories only of personal obligation, namely contract and tort, and this tendency was assisted by comparisons with Roman law, by curricula of legal education, by a statutory provision on costs in county courts,[46] and by the prevailing desire for clarity, predictability, and certainty in the law. Though this was the general tendency, it did not receive the approval of the two most prominent contemporary English academic writers. F. W. Maitland, in a study published posthumously in 1909, after referring to the divisions of Roman law, said that 'The attempt to distribute our personal forms under the two heads of contract and tort was never very successful or very important.'[47] Frederick Pollock, writing at about the same date, pointed out that 'Since about the middle of the 19th century there has been a current assumption

---

[41] Pothier had drawn attention to this distinction, but did not perceive the obligations as parallel: *Obligations*, p. 106, where the obligations are called 'primary' and 'secondary'. The distinction is also accepted by N. J. McBride, 'A Fifth Common Law Obligation' (1994) 14 *Legal Studies* 35.

[42] W. Anson, *Principles of the English Law of Contract* (Oxford, 1879), pp. 7–8.

[43] J. C. Miles and J. L. Brierly (eds.), *Anson's Law of Contract* (17th edn, Oxford, 1929), pp. 7–8.

[44] Earl of Halsbury [H. S. Giffard] (ed.) *Laws of England* (31 vols., London, 1907–17).

[45] J. W. Smith, *A Selection of Leading Cases on Various Branches of the Law* (12th edn, London, 1915; 13th [last] edn, 1929).

[46] County Court Acts, 1867, 30 & 31 Vic., c. 142, s. 5, and 1888, 51 & 52 Vic., c. 43, ss. 62–5. See *Bryant* v. *Herbert* (1877) 3 CPD 389: 'One may observe there is no middle term; the statute supposes all actions are founded either on contract or on tort' (Bramwell LJ, at 390). It should be noted that Bramwell LJ was here construing the statute, not commending the dichotomy.

[47] F. W. Maitland, *The Forms of Action at Common Law* (London, 1968 [1909]), p. 61.

that all civil causes of action must be founded on either contract or tort, but added flatly, 'there is no historical foundation for this doctrine.'[48] Nevertheless the tendency to think in terms of only two categories went so far as to lead the House of Lords in 1914 to subordinate the category of quasi-contract (obligations imposed by law for the avoidance of unjust enrichment) to that of contract. Viscount Haldane said expressly that 'so far as proceedings *in personam* are concerned the common law of England really recognizes (unlike the Roman law) only actions of two classes, those founded on contract and those founded on tort'.[49] This was an over-simplification of earlier law, for the links between contract and quasi-contract in English law had been largely procedural. As Lord Wright pointed out in 1942, referring to the decision of Lord Mansfield in *Moses* v. *Macferlan*[50] nearly 200 years earlier, 'Lord Mansfield does not say that the law implies a promise. The law implies a debt or obligation which is a different thing.'[51] More substantially, Viscount Haldane's conclusion tended to suppress the very important concept of unjust enrichment.

The revival of unjust enrichment has been one of the most important developments of the twentieth century in Anglo-American private law. The American Law Institute's *Restatement of Restitution* (1937) was welcomed in England by Lord Wright,[52] who took the opportunity of expanding his views in the *Fibrosa* case (1942):

> It is clear that any civilized system of law is bound to provide remedies for cases of what has been called unjust enrichment or unjust benefit, that is to prevent a man from retaining the money of or some other benefit derived from another which it is against conscience that he should keep. Such remedies in English law are generically different from remedies in contract or in tort, and are now recognized to fall within a third category of the common law which has been called quasi-contract or restitution.[53]

Lord Wright was anticipating a little, as reforming judges – and indeed academics – sometimes do, with the phrase 'are now recognized', but within the

---

[48] *Encyclopaedia Britannica* (11th edn, 29 vols., Cambridge, 1910–11), vol. 27, p. 64.
[49] *Sinclair* v. *Brougham* [1914] AC 398 at 415.
[50] (1760) 2 Burr 1005.
[51] *Fibrosa Spolka Akcyjna* v. *Fairbairn Lawson Combe Barbour Ltd* [1943] AC 32 at 62. This had earlier been pointed out by H. Maine, *Ancient Law* (London, 1931 [1861]), p. 305.
[52] Lord Wright of Durley, *Legal Essays and Addresses* (Cambridge, 1939), ch. 2.
[53] [1943] AC 32 at 61.

comparatively short period of fifty-three years, led by academic writers,[54] the House of Lords came to accept this view.[55]

In one sense, this development may be viewed as a victory for the law of unjust enrichment and for the influence of academic writing.[56] But Lord Wright's language, rejecting the notion of two categories only, and advocating 'a third category', had the effect of entrenching a particular view of categories. The notion of three categories may be superior, from a historical perspective, to that of two, but it directs attention away from the question of whether it is necessary or desirable to think in terms of exhaustive and mutually exclusive divisions.[57]

Some modern writers have accepted the threefold division,[58] but there are still many kinds of obligation that cannot be comfortably fitted within it. For this reason, some have proposed 'trust' or 'fiduciary relationship' as a separate category.[59] Others, following Pothier and Anson, have admitted a residual or 'miscellaneous' class,[60] but the need for it points to the limitations of this kind of diagrammatic classification.[61] First, the contents of the residual class are potentially very large – 'a huge and various assortment

---

[54] R. Goff and G. Jones, *The Law of Restitution* (London, 1966), P. Birks, *Introduction to the Law of Restitution* (Oxford, 1985), A. Burrows, *The Law of Restitution* (London, 1993).

[55] *Westdeutsche Landesbank Girozentrale v. Islington London Borough Council* [1996] AC 669, HL.

[56] See A. Burrows, *Understanding the Law of Obligations* (Oxford, 1998), p. 112, P. Birks, 'The Academic and the Practitioner' (1998) 18 *Legal Studies* 397.

[57] Samuel and Rinkes, *Law of Obligations and Legal Remedies*, p. 65, warn that categorization may lead to the law's becoming 'dogmatic and positivistic'.

[58] A. Burrows, 'Contract, Tort and Restitution – a Satisfactory Division or Not?' (1983) 99 *Law Quarterly Review* 217, and 'Dividing the Law of Obligations' in *Understanding the Law of Obligations*, pp. 1, 2, though accepting (p. 3n.) that 'there are undoubtedly obligations that fall outside this tripartite division'.

[59] D. Walker, *The Oxford Companion to Law* (Oxford, 1980), p. 898 (s.t. Obligation, Law of), E. Weinrib, 'The Juridical Classification of Obligations', in P. Birks (ed.), *The Classification of Obligations* (Oxford, 1997), p. 37, Gummow J in *Roxborough v. Rothmans of Pall Mall Australia, Ltd* (2001) 76 ALJR 203 at 216 (but omitting unjust enrichment as a category).

[60] P. Birks, *English Private Law* (Oxford, 2000), p. xli (contract, wrongs, unjust enrichment, other events). Elsewhere he has called the first class 'consent' and has included in it obligations arising from conveyances, trusts, and wills. See *English Private Law*, p. xlii, and P. Birks, 'Equity in the Modern Law: An Exercise in Taxonomy' (1996) 26 *Western Australian Law Review* 1 at 10; P. Birks, 'Unjust Enrichment and Wrongful Enrichment' (2001) 79 *Texas Law Review* 1769, at 1771. See also P. Birks, 'Definition and Division: A Meditation on *Institutes* 3.13', in Birks, *The Classification of Obligations*, p. 1. Conveyances, trusts, and wills are treated separately from contracts in *English Private Law*.

[61] Birks has called it 'a sort of cheat', 'Equity in the Modern Law', note 60 above at 9.

of rights.[62] When the number of specimens that has to be classified as 'sui generis' is indeterminate and far larger than the number of primary 'genera', doubt is cast on the primacy and distinctiveness of the named classes.[63] Secondly, most of the kinds of obligation called 'sui generis' have not been *distinct* from the three primary classes, but have contained elements of two or more of them, often combined with elements of property and public policy. Thirdly, the admission of a residual class deprives the scheme of all excluding power: to establish, in response to a claim, that there is no obligation derived from contract, tort, or unjust enrichment is inconclusive, because it leaves open the possibility that there is another unnamed and hitherto unidentified kind of obligation that may lead to similar or analogous legal consequences.[64] It is equally difficult to reconcile a miscellaneous category with the image of a map: the notion of a limitless and permanently unknowable residual territory demonstrates the limits of the mapping metaphor in its application to law. Bentham thought that a map of the law could admit no '*terrae incognitae* [unknown lands]'.[65]

'Legal history', it has been said, 'is the study of legal change.'[66] The image of mapping, and sometimes also the idea of schematic classification, imply a stability that cannot easily be reconciled with changes that have occurred in every aspect of private law in its recent history. For certain purposes it has been found necessary to maintain that the judges merely declare and do not make the law, but this is generally recognized as a fiction: the

---

[62] Birks, *ibid.*, at 10. It would be possible to create a very long list. It will be sufficient for present purposes to mention matrimonial and quasi-matrimonial obligations, family support obligations, child custody rights, trusts, equity, fiduciary obligations, obligations arising from wills, restrictive covenants, liability for unauthorized acts of agents, breach of warranty of authority, tracing, obligations pursuant to judicial orders, maritime salvage, maritime liens, general average contribution, use of confidential information, bailment, detinue, bills of exchange, letters of credit, estoppel, profits derived from wrongs, rights to burial, intellectual property, obligations arising from statute, and various other cases discussed in chapters 3 and 4 below. Many of these have been called 'sui generis'.

[63] See p. 229 below, M. Bryan, Book Review (1999) 21 *Adelaide Law Review* 151 at 154, D. Wright, 'Wrong and Remedy: A Sticky Relationship' [2001] *Singapore Journal of Legal Studies* 300 at 305.

[64] Discussions of promissory and proprietary estoppel in relation to contract are a prime example of this. See chapter 4 below.

[65] See Lieberman, *The Province of Legislation Determined*, p. 272, also pp. 262–3, noting Bentham's insistence that classification should be methodical and exhaustive, and his express reference to Linnaeus, and at p. 290, noting Bentham's lack of success in applying these ideas to law.

[66] J. Baker, 'Why the History of English Law Has Not Been Finished' [2000] *Cambridge Law Journal* 62 at 63.

law can change and has changed in many important respects.[67] When, as frequently, a legal question appears to be governed by a pre-existing rule, or when, in respect of a novel situation, an imposition of liability is sought and rejected, the conclusions may seem to be derived from the omission of the relevant obligation in pre-existing maps or schemes. The omission is practically certain, because the maps will have been drawn, and the schemes devised, to accommodate precisely those obligations formerly recognized. But, for the same reason, where liability is *imposed* in novel circumstances the conclusion cannot be derived from a pre-existing map. As we shall see in the next few chapters, the conclusion in such cases has often been supported by the cumulative weight of a number of legal concepts operating concurrently.

A related problem is the absence of uniformity in the reasoning and conclusions of judges, both within particular jurisdictions and from one jurisdiction to another. Thus in *White* v. *Jones*,[68] to be discussed in chapter 3, where loss was caused to an intended beneficiary by a lawyer's failure to prepare a will in due time, the three majority judges and the two dissenting judges all took different approaches. A differently constituted panel of English judges could very well have reached the opposite conclusion, as has indeed occurred on this question in other common law jurisdictions. This diversity also tends to impede a close analogy between judicial reasoning and the mapping of geographical territory.

A serious obstacle to classification has been the institutional divisions in the history of the English courts. The prime example of this is equity, which was separately administered in England until 1875, and until later in other Anglo-American jurisdictions. It has often been said that a century and a quarter after the Judicature Acts law and equity should be integrated. This may be a desirable aspiration, but it has not proved easy to achieve, and in the context of the present discussion this is hardly surprising. The concepts and terminology of equity were quite different from those of the common law, and this was just what gave equity the power to supplement and correct the law without directly overturning it. Equitable concepts, therefore, cut across legal categories, and cannot easily be fitted to concepts derived from the common law.[69] Justice Gummow has said that 'one result

---

[67] See chapter 10 below.   [68] [1995] 2 AC 207, HL. See chapter 3 below.
[69] See G. S. Alexander, 'The Transformation of Trusts as a Legal Category, 1800–1914' (1987) 5 *Law and History Review* 303.

of the leavening effect of equitable thoughts and concepts upon the civil law is an apparent untidiness of general structure'. He added that 'this marks as doomed any attempt at neat systemization'.[70] There are other examples besides equity. The law of maritime salvage has been found difficult to classify, and this is partly because it was administered, in England until 1875, by a separate court applying a body of law entirely distinct from the common law. Naturally the law of maritime salvage cannot be easily fitted into any category derived from common law, or even from common law together with equity. Again, the law of matrimonial obligations fell, until 1858, within the jurisdiction of the ecclesiastical courts, which felt no kind of pressure to explain the law in terms of common law concepts. This is part of the reason why matrimonial obligations, though falling strictly within most definitions of private law and of the law of obligations, were not shown on nineteenth-century maps and why it remains difficult to fit these obligations into categories derived from other parts of the law.[71]

Another obstacle to conceptual organization has been the complexity of the relation between facts and law. The facts of a case are defined in relation to legal principles, but the principles themselves are formulated in relation to facts, real or hypothetical. Facts may be stated at countless levels of particularity, and legal issues and legal rules may be formulated at countless levels of generality.[72] No map or scheme could possibly classify all imaginable facts, for there is no limit whatever to the number of facts that may be postulated of a sequence of human events. The selection of legally relevant facts is a matter not of empirical investigation but of judgment, and not wholly separable from the formulation of the applicable legal rule. Facts are selected and marshalled to fit perceived rules of law, but the rules themselves change in response to facts, often by deploying concepts and categories that had not formerly been supposed to be applicable. Thus, in the dispute between the two opera houses for the services of Johanna Wagner (1852–3), to be discussed in the next chapter, Wagner, having agreed to sing for Lumley exclusively, proposed to sing instead for Gye. Such a breach of contract had formerly been categorized as giving rise solely to an action against the contract breaker for damages at common law. But in response

---

[70] W. M. C. Gummow, *Change and Continuity: Statute, Equity and Federalism* (Oxford, 1999), p. 70.
[71] Matrimonial obligations are classed in *English Private Law* (2000) as part of the law of persons together with company law, a conjunction traceable to Blackstone and, more remotely, Gaius.
[72] This point is further developed in relation to the *Lumley* cases in chapter 2 below.

to the facts of this particular dispute several new legal rules emerged: the Court of Chancery issued injunctions restraining Wagner from singing and restraining Gye from engaging her services, and the Court of Queen's Bench decided that Gye might be directly liable to Lumley in tort. The facts previously categorized as belonging to 'common law', 'damages', and 'contracts' belonged, after 1853, also to 'equity', 'injunctions', and 'torts'. The malleability and interaction of facts, rules, concepts, and categories has thus inhibited a close analogy between the application of legal rules and the use of geographical maps.

Another instance is reliance on gratuitous promises. It is usually stated as a rule of contract law that gratuitous promises are not enforceable, but this rule does not, as we shall see,[73] determine the result where a promise is made to convey land on which the promisee then makes valuable improvements. To one who knows how Anglo-American courts have dealt with such cases, the added facts import several additional legal concepts, notably reliance, wrongdoing, unjust enrichment, equity, estoppel, and property. But these concepts have themselves developed partly in response to facts such as those just envisaged. It is certainly important to analyse the concepts and to distinguish them from each other, but their relation to each other and to the facts cannot conveniently be depicted by a diagram or map. Geoffrey Samuel, drawing on mediaeval sources,[74] has put this point by saying that the law *arises out of* fact,[75] thereby indicating that legal rules do not have an independent stable and timeless existence, as conceptual maps and diagrams tend sometimes to imply.

It is to this lack of stability that Edward Levi alluded when he wrote (1949) that 'the classification changes as the classification is made'.[76] The contents of a class take their legal significance from the class, but the class takes its meaning from its contents, and every addition alters the class. One consequence is a lack of correspondence between the names of legal categories and the ideas suggested by them. Thus, many instances of liability studied as part of contract law do not involve 'contracts' in any ordinary sense of the word: the body of law so called has been concerned with promises (as much as with agreements) and with reliance or expectations

---

[73] See chapter 4 below.

[74] D. Kelley, 'Clio and the Lawyers: Forms of Historical Consciousness in Mediaeval Jurisprudence' (1974) 5 *Mediaevalia et Humanistica* (NS) 25 at 35.

[75] G. Samuel, 'Ex Facto Ius Oritur' (1989) 8 *Civil Justice Quarterly* 53 at 64, 65, 69.

[76] E. Levi, *An Introduction to Legal Reasoning* (Chicago, 1949), p. 3.

(as much as with consent or will), and with utility (as much as with morality). A substantial part of what is called tort law does not depend on wrongdoing or fault in any ordinary sense: tort liability has been imposed in respect of conduct that is blameless, and indeed admirable.[77] Unjust enrichment has supported liability where there is no enrichment in the ordinary sense of the word,[78] and where the appellation 'unjust' signifies only that there is a legal obligation to make restitution. The corollary is that there are agreements, wrongs, and unfair benefits that do not give rise to legal obligations. Thus, while tort means wrong, it also means 'that conduct to which the law attaches liability'. The meanings are different but in an uncodified system they cannot be entirely dissociated, because where a new question has arisen for decision the perception of the defendant's conduct as wrong, though not legally conclusive, has been influential. Similarly the terms contract, property, equity, and unjust enrichment carry both general and specifically legal meanings. The perceptions that conduct is wrong, that an agreement has been broken, that reasonable expectations have been disappointed, that something belonging to another has been taken, that the defendant has done something unfair, or that a benefit has been unjustly retained, while not in themselves legally conclusive, have been highly relevant. Moreover, as the instances examined in the following chapters will show, they have often been intertwined, and influential across categories, so that the perception of unjust enrichment (in its general sense) has influenced findings of proprietary interests, of torts, and of breaches of contract.

A related difficulty is linguistic. Writers define their own terms, so (for example) the propositions that gratuitous promises are not contracts, or that tortious liability arises only from fault, or that profits derived from wrongs are not unjust enrichments, may be made true by definition, but then the propositions tell the reader nothing about past or present law, but only that, in the writer's opinion, contract, tort, and unjust enrichment are not, respectively, the appropriate names for those instances of liability.

Legal principles concerned with unjust enrichment were earlier known to the common law as quasi-contract, and after publication of the American Law Institute's *Restatement of Restitution* (1937) as restitution. Since 1990, Peter Birks has argued in favour of renaming the subject 'unjust

---

[77] This is discussed in chapter 5 below.

[78] For example, the receipt of services that turn out to be of no actual value to the recipient.

enrichment'.[79] There are many good reasons for this view, but hope of achieving an exact correspondence between the legal and the ordinary meanings of the phrase is not among them.[80] Whether such a correspondence is theoretically possible, whether precision in law is attainable, and whether the alternatives to precision have undesirable social or political consequences are not questions that can be conclusively answered by historical evidence. But an examination of the past does show that Anglo-American law has in practice accommodated a high degree of imprecision without abandoning reasoned argument or intellectual attention to influential concepts.

One of the reasons for Birks' rejection of 'restitution' as a name was that the terms 'contracts', 'wrongs', and 'restitution' were not parallel in that restitution alone indicated a legal response.[81] This point may be taken a step further: even where 'restitution' is replaced by 'unjust enrichment', the terms 'contracts' and 'wrongs' are not parallel, because the *making* of a contract is not comparable to a tort or wrong. It is the *breach* of contract that provokes a legal response and that might be considered parallel to 'wrong'.[82] Nor, because of the delictual and proprietary origins of English contract law, can contract and wrongdoing be visualized as entirely separate sources of obligation. No easy resolution of these anomalies has been found. Alternatives might be to substitute 'breach of contract' for 'contract', or on the other hand to substitute some phrase like 'obligations arising from various circumstances in which the law requires compensation to be made for harms' for 'wrongs', but both have difficulties. The first alternative would tend to subsume 'breach of contract' under 'wrongs', casting adrift the primary obligation to perform a contract, while the second would tend to reduce the major divisions to 'contractual' and 'non-contractual' obligations – a dichotomy that would certainly be logical, exhaustive, and mutually exclusive, but one that would leave open all distinctions among non-contractual obligations. Such a scheme has been used in some other

---

[79] P. Birks, 'Misnomer', in W. Cornish and others (eds.), *Restitution Past, Present, and Future* (Oxford, 1998), p. 1.

[80] Nor has Birks entertained any such hope. He writes of 'looking downward to the cases', P. Birks, *Introduction to the Law of Restitution* (Oxford, 1985), p. 23.

[81] See P. Birks, 'Equity in the Modern Law' (1996) 26 *Western Australian Law Review* 1 at 8, and in other writings, subordinating 'contract' to a wider concept of 'consent'.

[82] This is pointed out by Birks, 'Equity in the Modern Law', note 81 above, at 16, and in 'Rights, Wrongs, and Remedies' (2000) 20 *Oxford Journal of Legal Studies* 1 at 22 and 27.

legal systems, and was proposed in 1889 for Anglo-American law,[83] but gained no following.

A major problem for any scheme of classification of private law has been the relation between property and obligation.[84] Sometimes property has been thought of as inherently separate from obligations. Thus a distinction has often been made between ownership and obligation,[85] which corresponds in some measure to the distinction between rights 'in rem' and rights 'in personam'. These expressions, however, have lacked consistent meaning in Anglo-American law, and often both have been applicable simultaneously. It is not likely that any of the opinions that have been held of the relation of property to obligation can be shown to be exclusively correct as an explanation of past judicial decisions. Each captures a different aspect of a complex interrelation, for property rights have been simultaneously both the cause and the effect of obligations. As we shall see, equitable remedies pose particular problems in this context, for they have often given what is effectively a proprietary remedy for breach of a personal obligation.[86]

Legal decision-making requires the statement of relevant facts, the identification of a legal issue, and the formulation and application of a legal rule. These steps are interrelated, and each requires the use of judgment. Every legal proposition, in the courtroom, in the lecture room, or in an academic journal, is implicitly tested by an appeal to judgment: it is always an effective answer to any legal proposition to show that, however logical it may at first seem, it would lead to consequences agreed by speaker and listener, or by writer and reader, to be intolerable. This is not to say that unstructured judgment dissolves all other considerations. Judgment has not been wholly unfettered, but neither has it, in practice, been very narrowly constrained: in the instances considered in this study it has been guided by several concepts often operating cumulatively and in combination with each other, but it is not reducible to any one of them alone. A prominent

---

[83] J. P. Bishop published, in 1889, a work entitled *Commentaries on the Non-Contract Law*; see J. McCamus, 'Unjust Enrichment: Its Role and Its Limits', in D. W. Waters (ed.), *Equity, Fiduciaries and Trusts, 1993* (Toronto, 1993), p. 131. The Quebec Civil Code of 1992 recognizes two classes only: 'an obligation arises from a contract or from any act or fact to which the effects of an obligation are attached by law' (art. 1372).

[84] Birks, following Gaius, calls it a 'first division', 'Rights, Wrongs, and Remedies', note 82 above, at 21.

[85] Sometimes stated as a distinction between 'owning' and 'owing', which is euphonious, but does not convey the meaning intended.

[86] C. Rotherham, *Proprietary Remedies* (Oxford, 2002), and see chapter 9 below.

nineteenth-century English judge said that 'I confess that when I am sought to be driven to a conclusion which appears to me unreasonable and unjust, I at once suspect the validity of the premises'.[87] Twentieth-century English judges have said, in similar vein, that 'one cannot but feel that the reasoning which leads to results so unjust and anomalous must be fallacious',[88] and that 'I confess I approach the investigation of a legal proposition that has results of this character with a prejudice in favour of the idea that there may be a flaw in the argument somewhere'.[89] The phrases 'I confess' and 'one cannot but feel' acknowledge a tension between strict logic and general judgment, to be resolved by preferring the latter: 'coherence', another judge said, 'must sometimes yield to practical justice'.[90] Justice Benjamin Cardozo in *The Nature of the Judicial Process* (1921) also emphasized the scope for individual judgment:

> We like to picture to ourselves the field of the law as accurately mapped and plotted. We draw our little lines, and they are hardly drawn before we blur them... [The judge] must balance all his ingredients, his philosophy, his logic, his analogies, his history, his customs, his sense of right, and all the rest, and adding a little here and taking out a little there, must determine, as wisely as he can, which weight shall tip the scales.[91]

A closely related question is the interaction between private law and public policy, a question complicated by varying meanings of the latter phrase. From one point of view there is an identity of meaning, because protection of property, enforcement of contracts, redress of wrongs, and avoidance of unjust enrichment *are* public policies, but 'policy' is often used to denote the residual or overriding sense of justice between the parties mentioned in the last paragraph, and 'public policy' often indicates enlargement or restriction of liability because of anticipated salutary effects on the future behaviour of others. The extent to which, as a matter of theory, such considerations are proper to the judicial role is debatable: if every question were to collapse into unstructured policy, private law would lose all appearance of coherence and stability.[92] Despite attempts to minimize this feature of private

---

[87] Lindley LJ in *In re Holford* (1894) 3 Ch 40, CA, at 45.
[88] *Wertheim v. Chicoutimi Pulp Co.* [1911] AC 301, PC, at 307 (Lord Atkinson).
[89] Devlin J in *St John Shipping Corp. v. Joseph Rank Ltd* [1957] 1 QB 267.
[90] *Williams v. Natural Life Ltd* [1998] 1 WLR 830 at 837 (Lord Steyn).
[91] B. Cardozo, *The Nature of the Judicial Process* (New Haven, 1921), rep. 1963, pp. 161–2.
[92] E. Weinrib, *The Idea of Private Law* (Cambridge, Mass., 1995).

law, an examination of the actual past decisions of Anglo-American courts shows that considerations of public policy have directly and often decisively influenced almost every aspect of private law, both in the enlargement and in the restriction of liability.[93] There have been practical as well as theoretical reasons for minimizing public policy: a working legal system must be able to resolve minor disputes without examining from first principles speculative questions of economics, politics, and philosophy, and it need not be emphasized that most judges and lawyers have been unfit, both by temperament and by training, for such tasks.[94] The potentially far-reaching effect of public policy has been concealed to some extent by the doctrine of precedent, which, so long as the policy in question remains unquestioned, has permitted instances after the first to appear rather as applications of positive legal rules established by prior authority than as independent assessments of policy.[95] But it is evident that public policy can alter and that it has altered during the past two centuries, with consequent radical changes in the law.[96] It is difficult to accommodate on a map of private law concepts the idea of constantly changing and potentially overriding policy.

The relation of judge-made law to legislation must also be borne in mind. There is a natural and long-established tendency to think of public policy as belonging to the realm of legislation, and of judge-made law, in Lord Mansfield's bold neoclassical phrase, as 'the common law, *that works itself pure* by rules drawn from the fountain of justice'.[97] But a strict separation has not been maintained, for legislation has often sought to do justice between individuals, many legal questions have required joint application of legislation and judge-made principles, legislation often gives implicit recognition to previously judge-made law, and when one common law jurisdiction is compared with another, or when the same jurisdiction is compared at different times, parallel solutions are often to be discerned in legislation and judge-made law.

One of the consequences of the fluidity and interrelatedness of legal concepts is that it has not been possible to allocate a dispute, in advance of

---

[93] Discussed in chapter 10 below.
[94] J. Smillie, 'Formalism, Fairness, and Efficiency: Civil Adjudication in New Zealand' [1996] *New Zealand Law Review* 254.
[95] See p. 193 below (Parke, B).
[96] For example in respect of cohabitation between unmarried persons, or in respect of contracts that are racially discriminatory. See pp. 200–1 below.
[97] Arguendo in *Omychund* v. *Barker* (1744) 1 Atk 21, 33–4 (emphasis in original). See p. 192 below.

its resolution, to one concept or discrete set of principles to the exclusion of others. Thus cumulation and concurrence of claims have been permitted and in practice encouraged,[98] and election between inconsistent remedies may be postponed to the latest possible stage.[99] A claim for misuse of trade secrets, to take one example, commonly invokes concepts of property, contract, wrongdoing, unjust enrichment, and breach of fiduciary duty.[100] It has not proved possible to allocate such a dispute to one of these concepts to the exclusion of the others, or to say that one is primary and that others are subordinate, secondary, subsidiary, or supplemental.[101]

The variety of maps produced since Blackstone's time shows that precision in legal map making has been elusive. Nineteenth-century views differed sharply from Blackstone's, notably on the question of the unity and prominence of contract law. More recent writers have differed from both, and among themselves. It is not that one view is necessarily more accurate than another, for each may properly emphasize different aspects. Thus, Blackstone's treatment of contracts, puzzling to most modern readers, has been praised by a distinguished twentieth-century legal historian for emphasizing the distinctions among different kinds of contract.[102] Moreover, schemes of classification usually – perhaps always – have a rhetorical component, in that they are calculated not only to describe, but to persuade readers of the merits of the view favoured by the writer.[103] Legal writers are participants in the debates they describe, as well as observers.

The relation of classification to actual historical evidence has been little noticed or examined. Proposed accounts of Anglo-American law have usually been in part derived from and in part imposed upon historical materials, the reader being invited to understand the past in the light of the account, and then to apply the account to past, present, and future as a universal

---

[98] Cf. *J. Nunes Diamonds Ltd* v. *Dominion Electric Protection Co.* [1972] SCR 769, effectively overruled in *Central Trust Co.* v. *Rafuse* [1986] 2 SCR 147, *Queen* v. *Cognos Inc.* [1993] 1 SCR 87.

[99] *United Australia Ltd* v. *Barclays Bank Ltd* [1941] AC 1, HL, *Johnson* v. *Agnew* [1980] AC 167, HL.

[100] See *Cadbury Schweppes Inc.* v. *FBI Foods Ltd* [1999] 1 SCR 142, 167 DLR (4th) 577.

[101] See chapter 8 below.

[102] Milsom, 'Blackstone's Achievement', note 19 above, at 7.

[103] That this point may have been overstated by Blackstone's critics (see J. Bentham, *A Comment on the Commentaries and A Fragment on Government*, ed. J. H. Burns and H. L. A. Hart (Oxford, 1977), pp. 404–12, Lieberman, *Province of Legislation Determined*, pp. 66–7, Kennedy, 'Structure', note 28 above, and Watson, 'Structure', note 24 above) does not mean that it has no force.

criterion of right judgment. Past instances that tend to favour the account have been adduced in its support, and those that do not apparently conform have been 'explained' so as to fit (where this is possible), or condemned (where it is not) as marginal, insignificant, anomalous, or unprincipled. But this method tends to elide an important distinction – that between historical and non-historical propositions about law. As the issues examined in the following chapters will show, non-conforming instances have in the past been neither infrequent nor unimportant, and cannot therefore by measurable criteria be called marginal or insignificant; whether they can be called anomalous or unprincipled depends on the independently persuasive force of the principles to which it is asserted that they ought to have conformed, something that cannot be tested by historical evidence – for example, principles of ethics, utility, logic, elegance, or conformity with a philosophical or political system or with other legal systems ancient or modern. A proposed principle might, if it enjoyed such justification, and if the justification, standing alone, were adjudged sufficiently persuasive, be used to condemn what had been inconsistent with it in the past; but then the past, with non-conforming evidence thus excluded, could not at the same time be adduced as independent proof in support of the principle, for this would be to select the evidence by assuming what it was supposed to prove. An account of private law might possibly be supported entirely on non-historical grounds, such as those just mentioned or others, but then the account would not necessarily reflect past or present law. On the other hand accounts that do claim to be descriptive of or supported by past or present law must reckon with the evidence of what the law has actually been.

2

Johanna Wagner and the rival opera houses

The twin cases of *Lumley* v. *Wagner*[1] (1852) and *Lumley* v. *Gye*[2] (1853), decisions respectively of the courts of Chancery and Queen's Bench, were perceived in their time, and indeed have been perceived ever since, to have determined crucial issues of fundamental importance in English private law. The then very recent Common Law Procedure Act of 1852,[3] putting an end to the forms of action, had opened the question of organization and classification of concepts, and required the common law courts to give new thought to the description and explanation of private law.[4] Contract, wrongdoing, unjust enrichment, property, and public policy were all involved in these cases and interrelated in a complex way, and the relation between fact and law was crucial in several respects.

The background of these cases was a fierce rivalry between two London theatres, Her Majesty's Theatre, Haymarket, managed by Benjamin Lumley, and the then fairly new Royal Italian Opera, Covent Garden, managed by Frederick Gye. Hector Berlioz probably had this rivalry in mind when he wrote (1852) that 'a manager of a London opera house is a man who carries about a barrel of gunpowder and cannot put it down because he is pursued with flaming torches. The poor devil runs as fast as his legs will carry him, falls down, gets up again, leaps over ditches, palings, streams, and bogs, knocks down everything he meets, and would trample on the bodies of his father or his children if they got in his way.'[5]

A fuller account appears in S.Waddams, 'Johanna Wagner and the Rival Opera Houses' (2001) 117 *Law Quarterly Review* 431.
[1] (1852) 1 De G M & G 604, 21 LJ Ch 898, 16 Jur 871, 19 LT 264.
[2] (1853) 2 El & Bl 216, 22 LJQB 463 (demurrer) and (1854) 18 Jur 468n., 23 LT 66, 157, 23 LJQB 116n. (verdict).
[3] 15 & 16 Vic. C. 76, J. H. Baker, *An Introduction to English Legal History* (2nd edn, London, 1979), p. 60.
[4] G. Samuel and J. Rinkes, *Law of Obligations and Legal Remedies* (London, 1996), pp. 11, 78, 80.
[5] H. Berlioz, *Evenings with the Orchestra* (1852), trans. J. Barzun (1956) (repr. Chicago, 1973), p. 113.

The rivalry had been the cause of earlier litigation. There had been a dispute (with the interests of the parties effectively reversed[6]) in 1847, involving Jenny Lind, who, having signed first with another theatre, broke her contract and later sang at Her Majesty's, and was held liable for damages (£2,500, later settled for £2,000) for breach of contract. Lumley, who was alleged to have taken advantage of Lind's breach of contract in order to meet the competition from the new opera house at Covent Garden,[7] had made a very handsome profit out of the transaction, even after indemnifying Lind and paying her fee.[8] This earlier case, suggesting both that the ordinary remedy of damages for breach of contract was ineffective in these circumstances and that the real dispute was between the rival employers, must have been in the minds of the judges when they came to deal with Lumley's cases against Wagner and Gye four years later.[9] It is significant that Lind's case appeared to raise no legal point of interest, and was not reported in any law reports, whereas the Wagner dispute, on very similar facts, interested all the law reporters and produced two leading cases.

Johanna Wagner[10] was, like Jenny Lind, a star performer. Lumley, who had profited so handsomely from Lind's London appearance, confidently anticipated equal success with Wagner, and witnesses at the trial said that 'the Wagner fever' was 'quite as violent' as 'the Lind fever'.[11] The history of the negotiations was complex, and shows the extraordinary efforts of the two rival houses to secure Johanna Wagner's services. She was first in contact with Gye, but in November 1851 she entered into an agreement with Lumley, for £1,200 for a three-month engagement.

---

[6] Alfred Bunn, who had originally engaged Lind, assigned his interest in the contract to Covent Garden: D. Nalbach, *The King's Theatre, 1704–1867: London's First Italian Opera House* (London, 1972), p. 106.

[7] *Bunn v. Lind*, The Times, 23 Feb 1848, 7f, counsel's argument ('It was necessary to the very existence of Mr Lumley that he should get her').

[8] An indemnity was admitted by Lumley, *Reminiscences of the Opera* (London, 1864), p. 163. Nalbach, *The King's Theatre*, p. 106, also states that an indemnity was promised and that Lumley paid Lind £5,600 for the season of 1847. The amount of damages awarded against Lind was £2,500 (later settled for £2,000), but the takings of the theatre in 1847 for 39 nights of her performances were stated to be the enormous sum of £45,924, 6s. The Times, 22 Feb. 1854, 10g.

[9] The cases were linked in The Times, 3 May 1852, 5f ('Scandals like the Lind and Wagner squabbles...'), and by H. F. Chorley, *Thirty Years' Musical Recollections* (1862) (repr. New York, 1926), p. 312.

[10] 1826–1894 (*The New Grove Dictionary of Opera*, ed. Stanley Sadie (London, 1992), vol. IV).

[11] The Times, 22 Feb. 1854, 10d.

By the terms of the agreement, Wagner was to commence her engagement on 1 April 1852, and Lumley was to make an advance payment of £300 on 15 March. On 6 February, Wagner requested a postponement of the starting date to 15 April, and Lumley assented, no mention being made by either party of changing the date for payment of the advance.[12] By February, Johanna Wagner and her father, Albert, were regretting their bargain, having formed the view that they could have obtained a much better price for Johanna's services.[13] Moreover, they were changing their opinion of the comparative merits of the two theatres. Lumley's financial position was now unstable, and on 13 March he was arrested for debt.[14] The date of 15 March came and went without payment of the £300. Gye now wrote twice to Wagner (9 and 30 March), ostensibly to enquire whether her engagement with Lumley was firm, and, deducing from the absence of a reply that there might be doubt about this, he travelled to Germany and made her a very attractive offer: £2,000 for a two-month engagement, with £1,000 payable in advance. Wagner told him that Lumley was in default of payment of the sum due on 15 March and that she therefore considered herself free, and she accepted Gye's terms, repudiating her contract with Lumley.

Johanna Wagner arrived in London with Gye, and her debut was announced for 24 April at Covent Garden.[15] But Gye's victory was short-lived. On 23 April Lumley obtained a temporary injunction from a Vice-Chancellor (Sir James Parker) to restrain her from appearing. The injunction was continued by the Vice-Chancellor on 10 May, and an appeal was dismissed by the Lord Chancellor (Lord St Leonards) on 26 May. Just as Gye's victory was short-lived, so also was Lumley's, for in the end Wagner did not sing at either theatre, and the 1852 season was a disaster for Lumley, and for Her Majesty's theatre, which closed from 1853 to 1855, Lumley attributing the closure largely to Johanna Wagner's defection.[16] Lumley eventually lost his legal action against Gye for damages, so in the end

---

[12] *The Times*, 24 April 1852, 8b, and 21 Feb. 1854, 9d.
[13] Letter of A. Wagner to J. Bacher, 21 Feb. 1852, in Lumley's first affidavit, reproduced in 19 LT 128.
[14] Lumley stated in his affidavit that this was on account of his having made himself liable as guarantor of another's debt. He spent three days in custody and the obligation was paid in full: affidavit of May 5, PRO C31/861.
[15] *The Times*, 21 April 1852, 8d.
[16] Lumley, *Reminiscences of the Opera*, p. 335; *Dictionary of National Biography*, s.n. Benjamin Lumley.

Lumley, Gye, Wagner, and the opera-going public – everyone in fact except the lawyers – were all losers.

Few modern lawyers, asked to recall the facts of the cases, would mention Lumley's omission to make the advance payment originally promised for 15 March. Yet it was this omission that caused Wagner to accept Gye's proposal, and, though held by three courts for different reasons to be legally inconclusive, it eventually proved to be crucial. The Vice-Chancellor, revealing a surprising ignorance of the common law, and of the obvious purpose of an advance payment,[17] said that non-payment would not, as a matter of law, entitle Wagner to terminate the contract, that is that it was not a condition precedent. In the higher Chancery court this last question was determined as a matter of law in Wagner's favour, but Lord St Leonards found another reason for reaching the same conclusion as the Vice-Chancellor: this was that Lumley had in fact paid the money to his agent (Joseph Bacher) for transmission to Wagner in good time, and that she had been informed of this. He thought that Wagner had deliberately evaded receipt of the money in order to escape from the contract: 'I think it is entirely her own fault, and that she intended, as far as she could, to prevent the money being paid in order to escape the liability of performing the contract.'[18]

Lord St Leonards, seeking to derive the facts from the affidavits, relied very heavily on Bacher's statement that he had written to Albert Wagner on 10 March offering to pay the £300, deducing that the statement must be true because Bacher would not take the risk of swearing falsely to the contents of a letter that might be produced to contradict him. But when it came to the trial, Bacher's evidence on this point was shaken and Lumley's counsel pressed an alternative argument that, even if Bacher had not tendered the money on 10 March, the time for payment had been impliedly extended to and beyond 5 April by a letter written, in French, by Albert Wagner to Lumley in March saying 'if you send the bill of exchange, be good enough to address it either at this time to Berlin, or from (*dès*) the 2nd of April, to Hamburgh, to Engel & Co, Ferdinand Street, where we shall remain some time'.[19] Lord Campbell directed the jury that they could find that

---

[17] To cover travel expenses and to give security for Lumley's counter-performance. Parker V-C also made the point that the time for payment had been impliedly extended, 5 De G. & Sm. 511–12. See p. 27 below.

[18] 19 LT 267.

[19] 19 LT 128. There was a dispute as to whether '*dès*' meant 'not later than', or 'after', and expert evidence was adduced both in the Chancery court and at the trial on this point. Lord

the time for payment had been impliedly extended, and it seems likely that this was the basis for the jury finding that the contract remained in force on 5 April.[20] Thus, the fact that the advance money had not been paid on 15 March – apparently an important breach of Lumley's obligation – was held by three judges not to be legally conclusive, and for three quite different and inconsistent reasons: in the Vice-Chancellor's court because it was found not to be a condition precedent, in the Lord Chancellor's court because it was found as a fact that Bacher had offered to pay by his letter of 10 March, and (when Bacher's evidence on this point was later shaken) in the common law court because the time for payment might have been impliedly extended to and beyond 5 April, and it was for the jury to say whether this had occurred.[21] This successive variety of reasons shows how a fact, apparently relevant, may be made irrelevant by framing of the legal issues, or by findings of other facts. But ultimately Lumley's omission did turn out to be crucial, because at the trial Gye said that he honestly believed that Wagner was free to terminate her engagement with Lumley on this ground, and his defence succeeded.

The substantial issue in the Chancery courts was whether the court, not having jurisdiction (as was conceded) to order Wagner to sing for Lumley, might nevertheless order her not to sing for Gye. It is reasonable to assume that the notorious earlier case of Jenny Lind was in the Lord Chancellor's mind.[22] There Lumley had profited handsomely by Lind's breach of contract. In the later dispute, where Lumley was the aggrieved party, Lord St Leonards evidently considered that a law that permitted such a result was gravely defective: the real dispute was between the two opera houses, and a money remedy against Johanna Wagner personally would be wholly inadequate to protect Lumley's legitimate interest. Lord St Leonards said that 'men are not suffered by the law of this country to depart from their contracts at their pleasure, and to leave the party with whom they have broken their contract to the mere chance of what a jury may give in point of damages',[23] a probable reference to the jury award (£2,500) in *Bunn* v. *Lind*. He linked this point to a striking comment on public policy:

Campbell's opinion was favourable to Lumley on this point, *Morning Chronicle* 22 Feb. 1854, 11c (interruption of Gye's counsel), and 23 Feb. 7f (direction to jury).

[20] *The Times*, 23 Feb. 1854, 12c.   [21] *Ibid.*

[22] The connexion was commonly made; see note 9 above.   [23] 19 LT 265.

I have always thought that you may attribute a great deal of the right and fair dealing which exists between Englishmen to the exercise of that power [i.e. of specific performance] in this Court... This Court enforces where it can, a literal performance, and it is that literal performance which is here called a specific performance, which I believe has tended to that good faith which exists perhaps to so great a degree in this country, and certainly to a much greater degree than in many others.[24]

Even when allowance is made for the prevailing mood of national self-congratulation, this is very strong: it has not generally been thought that English law is to be distinguished from other systems by its greater readiness to decree specific performance, nor that this feature of contract law has been crucial to the national character. There is probably an implicit reference here to Albert Wagner's comment in a letter to Bacher that 'England is only to be valued for the sake of her money',[25] – a comment widely and indignantly reported in the English press.

Putting these points together, it is clear that Lord St Leonards formed a hostile view of Johanna Wagner's and her father's and Gye's actions and motives. He perceived the real dispute as being between the rival opera houses, and the existing state of the law (exemplified by *Bunn v. Lind*) as most inadequate to protect Lumley's interests: if Wagner sang for Gye, irreparable damage would have been done; an award of damages against Wagner by a common law court at some future date would almost certainly be too little and too late; even if a jury were prepared to award adequate damages (which he evidently thought doubtful), Wagner might be unable to pay, or might very probably be beyond the jurisdiction of the English courts. In short, as one of Lumley's counsel had put it, 'to suppose that Lumley could be properly compensated by damages through an action at law was farcical'.[26] An injunction against Wagner was therefore perceived to be the only practicable way of protecting Lumley's legitimate interest against Gye. Gye had agreed to indemnify Wagner against all costs and damages, and he conducted, and was perceived to conduct, the defence. He was named as a defendant, and the injunction was issued against him personally, as well as against Wagner, although no purely contractual principle justified such an order, and, as the common law then stood, Gye had committed no legal wrong.

But the common law on this point was about to change. The decision in *Lumley v. Wagner* might be said to amount, in practical effect, to a decision

[24] *Ibid.*   [25] 19 LT 128.   [26] *The Times*, 27 May 1852, 6e.

that Gye (on the facts stated in the affidavits) was to be treated as a wrong-doer, and *Lumley* v. *Gye* gave the imprimatur of the common law court to the same conclusion. Lumley brought an action against Gye claiming damages of £30,000. The declaration (statement of claim) stated that Gye, knowing of the contract with Lumley, had 'wrongfully and maliciously en-ticed and procured' Johanna Wagner to break her contract. This was a novel claim, and Gye demurred. Under a procedure authorized by the Common Law Procedure Act, the Court of Queen's Bench determined, before any evidence was heard, whether, assuming the facts alleged in the declaration to be proved, Lumley would be entitled to succeed.

The court of Queen's Bench, by a majority of three to one, decided the issue on the demurrer in Lumley's favour. As in the Chancery courts, the majority emphasized the inadequacy of a contractual action against Wagner, and again it is likely that they had in mind Jenny Lind's case – one of the judges in *Lumley* v. *Gye* had presided at the trial in *Bunn* v. *Lind* – and that they were mindful of the fact that Johanna Wagner was likely to be outside the jurisdiction of the English courts, and without the means of paying large damages. Crompton J said, of the contractual action, that 'the servant or contractor may be utterly unable to pay anything like the amount of the damages sustained entirely from the wrongful act of the defendant: and it would seem unjust, and contrary to the general principles of law, if such wrongdoer were not responsible for the damage caused by his wrongful and malicious acts'.

Coleridge J, in a very vigorous dissent, argued that a rule that anyone was guilty of a tort who advised another to break a contract was far too wide:

> None of this reasoning [about liability for encouraging torts] applies to the case of a breach of contract: if it does I should be glad to know how any treatise on the law of contract could be complete without a chapter on this head, or how it happens that we have no decisions upon it. Certainly no subject could be more fruitful or important; important contracts are more commonly broken with than without persuaders or procurers, and these often responsible persons when the principals may not be so.[27]

Lumley v. *Wagner* is 'a contract case', whereas *Lumley* v. *Gye* is 'a tort case'. Very rarely are the two discussed together. But when they are consid-ered together it can be seen that the concepts of breach of contract and of

---

[27] 2 El & Bl 250.

wrongdoing equally affected both, and that considerations of unjust enrichment, property rights, and public policy were also in play. These considerations were interrelated, and not derived from separate sources as though
lying apart from each other on a pre-existing map or scheme.

No previous case, as was recognized at the time,[28] had imposed tortious
liability in like circumstances, nor was *Lumley* v. *Gye* afterwards followed
until nearly thirty years later.[29] We may reasonably ask, therefore, what it
was about the particular case that led the court to think that tortious liability
was appropriate. The answer is that it was a cumulation of considerations.
The court had the example of *Bunn* v. *Lind* before its eyes: that was a
case where the law had shown itself most inadequate, and had permitted a
handsome profit to be made from breach of contract, encouraging a kind of
cut-throat competition in the theatre business that was in no one's interest.
The Court of Chancery had given an injunction, rightly, as the common law
judges probably thought, for this had been the only way to prevent Gye from
profiting from his own wrongdoing at the expense of Lumley's legitimate
business interests. If the injunction had been rightly granted, Gye's conduct
must be, legally speaking, wrongful; it was not in the public interest for the
law to permit persons to profit from wrongdoing as he sought to do.

Though neither *Lumley* v. *Wagner* nor *Lumley* v. *Gye* would normally
be considered 'a property case', proprietary concepts were nevertheless influential in both. It was vigorously argued by Gye's counsel in the Queen's
Bench that in order to succeed 'the plaintiff must have a property in the thing
taken away' and that 'the breach of contract is a wrong between the plaintiff
and Johanna Wagner alone, and against her he may maintain an action on
the contract, but not of tort'.[30] That this argument was weighty is shown
by its success with the dissenting judge, Coleridge J, who distinguished old
cases of seduction of wards and of servants on the ground that they in
effect recognized a kind of proprietary right, and were not to be extended
to independent contractors like Johanna Wagner. That the argument was

---

[28] The majority conceded this in effect. Crompton J held that 'the parties are in the relation
of employer and employed, or master and servant *within the meaning of this rule* [emphasis
added]. And I see no reason for narrowing such a rule, but I should rather, if necessary, apply
such a reasoning to a case "new in its instance but not in the reason and principle of it"' [citing
Keeble v. *Hickeringill*, 11 East 573] 2 E & B 754. In *Barber* v. *Lesiter* (1859) 7 CBNS 175, 185,
and *Lynch* v. *Knight* (1861) 9 HLC 577, 586–7, *Lumley* v. *Gye* was cited in argument for the
proposition that the absence of precedent was not conclusive against creation of a new cause
of action.

[29] *Bowen* v. *Hall* (1881) 6 QBD 333.   [30] 22 LJQB 466 (Willes).

insufficiently weighty is shown by its failure to persuade the other judges in the Chancery and the Queen's Bench: the willingness of the one court to grant an injunction against Wagner *and against Gye*, and the willingness of the other to hold Gye liable in tort reflected a perception that the benefit of Wagner's services in London for the three-month period belonged, as between the two managers, to Lumley rather than to Gye. A link between equitable remedies and proprietary interests has often been made by the courts,[31] and modern commentators have developed it, suggesting that one mark of what might reasonably be called a property interest is an interest that the law protects by injunction.[32] In the Queen's Bench Erle J said that 'he who maliciously procures a damage to another by violation of his right ought to be made to indemnify'.[33] The crucial phrase here, 'by violation of his right', suggestive of entitlement, has proprietary connotations.

Anson, writing in 1879, suggested that *Lumley* v. *Wagner* might be re-garded as creating a right *in rem* (a phrase again suggestive of proprietary interest[34]), and he doubted the correctness of the decision for just this reason:

> The case stands alone (it was decided in 1853) and no reported attempt has since been made to bring an action for a like case. But it is important to bear in mind that a considered judgment of the Court of Queen's Bench has laid it down that a contract confers rights *in rem* as well as *in personam*; that it not only binds together the parties by an obligation, but that it imposes upon all the world a duty to respect the contractual tie.[35]

Pollock, writing in 1886, also thought that *Lumley* v. *Gye* introduced for the first time in this context a 'real right', and 'an element analogous to ownership or possession', concepts that he, like Anson, found objectionable:

> When a binding promise is made, an obligation is created which remains in force until extinguished by the performance or discharge of the contract. Does the duty thus owed to the promisee constitute the object of a kind of real

---

[31] See *Rose* v. *Watson* (1864) 10 HLC 672, 678, 683; *Tailby* v. *Official Receiver* (1888) 13 App Cas 523, HL; *Re Wait* [1927] 1 Ch. 606, CA.

[32] G. Calabresi and A. D. Melamed, 'Property Rules, Liability Rules and Inalienability: One View of the Cathedral' (1972) 85 *Harvard Law Review* 1089; L. Kaplow and S. Shavell, 'Property Rules Versus Liability Rules: An Economic Analysis' (1996) 109 *Harvard Law Review* 715.

[33] 2 El & Bl 233.   [34] See chapter 9 below.

[35] W. Anson, *Principles of the Law of Contract* (London, 1879), p. 199. See R. Bagshaw, 'Can the Economic Torts be Unified?' (1998) 180 *Journal of Legal Studies* 729 at 735, quoting Anson's second edition, accepting the proposition as established after *Bowen* v. *Hall*, note 29 above.

right which a stranger to the contract can infringe, and thereby render himself liable *ex delicto*? In other words, does a man's title to the performance of a promise contain an element *analogous to ownership or possession*? The general principles of the law... seem to call for a negative answer. It would confuse every accustomed boundary between real and personal rights, dominion and obligation, to hold that one who without any ill will to Peter prevents Andrew from performing his contract with Peter may be *a kind of trespasser* against Peter... Yet there is some show of authority for affirming the proposition thus condemned...[36]

And Pollock went on to discuss *Lumley* v. *Gye* indicating that he could not accept all its implications.

Another way of putting Lumley's argument would be that he had a legitimate business interest in having his contractual arrangements with singers respected, at least where they were reasonable and for a short term. Any trade association of theatre managers would have had, as its first item of business in 1852, the restraint of the most extreme forms of cut-throat competition, and such a measure would (if challenged as a restraint of trade) probably have been upheld as reasonable. The business of presenting operas in a musical marketplace where audiences were primarily attracted by individual performers could not reasonably be carried on without some kind of assurance that contracts with the principal singers were firm, at least for limited periods. Works had to be translated, permissions obtained, costumes and scenery prepared, the cast assembled, rehearsals held, performances advertised, and tickets sold. Evidence at the trial showed that Lumley 'had embarked considerable capital in the undertaking', and had made a public announcement that Wagner would be singing at his theatre.[37] Moreover, the theatre's reputation and the value of its goodwill were at stake; it stood to lose large amounts, difficult to quantify, if Wagner failed to sing, and still more if she conferred a corresponding gain on the rival theatre.[38]

The factors mentioned in the last paragraph touch directly on an important question of public policy,[39] that is, the public interest in free

---

[36] F. Pollock, *The Law of Torts* (London, 1887), pp. 450–51 [emphasis added].
[37] *The Times*, 21 Feb. 1854, 9f.
[38] Lumley's claim against Gye was for damages of £30,000, 20 LT 103, *The Times*, 10 Feb. 1854, though Lumley, *Reminiscences of the Opera*, p. 333, gave the figure as £20,000.
[39] For other examples of the influence of public policy on private law, see M. Lobban, *The Common Law and English Jurisprudence 1760–1850* (Oxford, 1991), p. 90.

competition, reflected in the rule that contracts in restraint of trade are void, unless proved to be reasonable.[40] The result of the two cases shows that this policy, though very influential at the time, was by no means absolute, and had to be weighed both against Lumley's legitimate interests and also against the public interest in the stability of opera management for the efficient presentation of operas, and in the due observance of contracts. This last consideration played an important part in both cases. Lord St Leonards' comments linking specific performance with national good faith are striking, and were echoed by commentary in the contemporary press.[41] In the Queen's Bench, Crompton J said that 'it would seem unjust, and contrary to the general principles of law' if Gye were not (on the facts assumed) to be liable. Erle and Wightman JJ were also plainly influenced by very general considerations of justice and policy.[42]

Unjust enrichment is not a phrase that occurs in either of the two cases and neither could be classified as 'an unjust enrichment case', but the concept was nevertheless influential: the whole gist and tenor of the judgments in both courts was that Gye ought not to profit at Lumley's expense, the competition between the theatres being such that Lumley's loss was Gye's gain. The concepts of wrongdoing and unjust enrichment were distinct, but also interrelated. The question whether Gye was unjustly enriched and the question whether he was a wrongdoer were not resolved independently: it was the very fact that Gye's enrichment from the transaction was perceived to be unjust that led the court to the conclusion that his conduct was wrongful, and vice versa, just as the same considerations taken together tended to support the conclusions that Lumley had something analogous to a proprietary interest,[43] that it should be protected by injunction – against Gye as well as against Wagner – and that the result conformed to public

---

[40] M. J. Trebilcock, *The Common Law of Restraint of Trade: A Legal and Economic Analysis* (Toronto, 1986).

[41] *The Times*, 3 May 1852, 5f ('Spectator'), 11 May 1852, 5b–c (leading article).

[42] See Erle J, note 33 above, and Wightman J at 238 ('general principle').

[43] The tort of inducing breach of contract has sometimes been defended on the ground that it protects a property interest, e.g. F. S. McChesney, 'Tortious Interference with Contract Versus "Efficient" Breach: Theory and Empirical Evidence' (1999) 28 *Journal of Legal Studies* 131. As with the question of profits derived from breach, this line of argument does not support treating the breach of every contract as tortious, because not every contractual interest is for all purposes proprietary in nature. Similar principles have affected film and sports celebrities in later periods. See *Warner Bros Pictures Inc. v. Nelson* [1937] 1 KB 209; *Flood v. Kuhn*, 407 US 258 (1972). Proprietary language, and its converse, appears in this context also (players may be 'traded' unless 'free agents').

policy, considered from the point of view both of restraint of trade and observance of contracts.

The courts' conclusions were not derived from strict inferential logic, and no computer, even with all previous decisions in its database, could have predicted them.[44] The result was determined, in both courts, partly by what may be called overall judgment, an idea that cannot be reduced to any other single concept. This is not to say that considerations of contract, wrongdoing, unjust enrichment, property, and public policy were irrelevant, but it is to suggest that none of them, standing alone, would have been sufficient. Taken separately, each strand in the reasoning was open to the objection of circularity, but cumulatively the various concepts tended to support each other, and formed a persuasive reason for the result.

The point about interrelationship of concepts may be taken a step further. The tendency to make too sharp a separation of legal concepts from each other may lead, and in the case of *Lumley* v. *Gye* has led, to the formulation of legal rules far wider than necessary to explain the result in the particular cases, with consequent enlargement of liability in subsequent cases where the circumstances have differed in crucial respects. The proposition in *Lumley* v. *Wagner* that 'English law enforces, where it can, a literal performance of the contract'[45] is certainly not an accurate statement of the Anglo-American law of specific performance before or since 1852.[46] If this passage were relied on in argument in a modern case on specific performance, the court would probably say that Lord St Leonards' words had to be read in their context, where the circumstances of the particular case showed that there were good reasons for granting the injunction.[47] The reason for caution in extending the case is that against the plaintiff's interest must be set the defendant's interest in freedom to break her contract on payment

---

[44] Samuel and Rinkes, *Law of Obligations and Legal Remedies*, p. 14, G. Samuel, 'Classification of Obligations and the Impact of Constructivist Epistemologies' (1997) 17 *Legal Studies* 448 at 451.

[45] 21 LJ Ch 902. The passage at 1 De G. M. & G. 619 differs somewhat, but is to similar effect. In *The Times*, 27 May 1852, 6f, the passage reads, 'This Court had always enforced performance of agreements both to the spirit and the letter.'

[46] See S. M. Waddams, 'The Choice of Remedy for Breach of Contract', in J. Beatson and D. Friedmann (eds.), *Good Faith and Fault in Contract Law* (Oxford, 1995), S. M. Waddams, 'Breach of Contract and the Concept of Wrongdoing' (2000) 12 *Supreme Court Law Review (2d)* 1.

[47] This is partly what is meant by the saying that equitable remedies are 'discretionary'. A recent example of refusal of a decree of specific performance is *Cooperative Insurance Society* v. *Argyll Stores (Holdings) Ltd* [1998] AC 1, HL.

of money compensation for the loss (if any) caused by the breach.[48] This right has not been absolute, but it has been an important aspect of personal freedom, and overridden only for sufficient reason. The considerations that have tended to justify an injunction include the following (all present in *Lumley* v. *Wagner*): the restraint on the defendant's freedom of action was comparatively slight; the plaintiff had something analogous to a proprietary interest; a money remedy would have been ineffective; and the defendant was likely (unless restrained by injunction) to confer an unjust benefit on the plaintiff's competitor. It is these considerations that have lain behind the rules, adopted in many common law jurisdictions, to the effect that an injunction will not be issued unless the defendant's services are unique, and that the plaintiff must have an interest in restraining the defendant's conduct that is independent of the interest in inducing performance of the positive side of the contract.[49] As we shall see, a similar criterion has been suggested for determining when there should be an accounting of profits made in breach of contract: an accounting would be appropriate, it has been suggested, where the plaintiff has a legitimate interest in preventing the defendant's profit-making activity.[50]

Thus *Lumley* v. *Wagner* has been, in many jurisdictions, rather narrowly confined, but the same cannot be said of *Lumley* v. *Gye*, which has been extended to circumstances very far removed from those of the original case. Why, one may ask, should this be?[51] The wide proposition that deliberate inducement of a breach of a contract always amounts to a tort has caused much difficulty. The hypothetical case of a father advising his daughter to break an engagement of marriage is one where there is a strong public and private interest in freedom of action on the part of both. No injunction has in any such case been issued against the daughter or against the father, nor has

---

[48] See Waddams, 'Breach of Contract and the Concept of Wrongdoing', note 46 above, and chapter 8 below.

[49] See *Whitwood Chemical Co.* v. *Hardman* [1891] 2 Ch 416, CA; *Macdonald* v. *Casein Ltd* [1917] 35 DLR 443; *Detroit Football Co.* v. *Dublinski* (1956) 4 DLR (2d) 688, reversed on other grounds 7 DLR (2d) 9; A. L. Corbin on *Contracts* (St Paul, 1964), s. 1206; I. C. F. Spry, *The Principles of Equitable Remedies* (Sydney, 1980), p. 537; R. J. Sharpe, *Injunctions and Specific Performance* (2nd edn, Toronto, 1992), para. 9.300; E. A. Farnsworth, *Contracts* (Boston, 1982), p. 825; Trebilcock, *Common Law of Restraint of Trade*, pp. 156–8.

[50] *Attorney General* v. *Blake (Jonathan Cape Ltd, Third Party)* [2001] 1 AC 268, HL, at 285. See chapter 6 below.

[51] Tony Weir has pointed out the inconsistency of favouring 'efficient breach', while treating as tortious an inducement to break a contract: A. J. Weir, *Economic Torts* (Oxford, 1997), p. 4.

an action in tort succeeded against the father. Again, generally speaking, an ordinary employee has been free in modern times to change employment, even without giving proper notice to a former employer, subject to the obligation to pay damages. It has been perceived as an undue restriction on that freedom either to restrain the employee by injunction, or to hold the second employer, even with knowledge of the inadequate notice, liable in tort. In the light of an appreciation of the background facts, *Lumley v. Gye* can be distinguished from such a case just because it was not a case of an ordinary employee. Johanna Wagner was a 'hot property', and it was precisely for this reason that the injunction was granted. The case therefore was a very special one, and hardly need stand for the general proposition that inducement of all breaches of contract is always tortious. It could equally be explained by postulating a much narrower rule, for example that inducing breach of contract is wrongful where it infringes something analogous to a proprietary interest, where it causes an unjust enrichment, and where the public policy favouring freedom of action is outweighed by strong countervailing considerations. In practice, as we shall see,[52] the courts have not always attached all the usual consequences of torts to inducing breach of contract.

We must now turn to the ultimate disposition of the litigation in *Lumley v. Gye*. The overruling of the demurrer was not, as has often been supposed, the end of the case. Relying on a provision in the then recent Common Law Procedure Act of 1852, Gye had obtained the court's permission to demur and plead, that is, to argue the demurrer while reserving his right to dispute the facts later, something that the old procedure would not have allowed.[53] This new procedure rested on the assumption, reflecting the 'scientific' spirit of the time, that the law could be satisfactorily declared in isolation from particular facts, an assumption that the ultimate result in *Lumley v. Gye* calls into question. Undoubtedly the drafter of Lumley's declaration thought that it stated facts sufficient to include Gye's conduct: 'maliciously' would include 'knowingly', and it would be easy to show that Gye knew of Wagner's arrangements with Lumley. What the drafter failed to foresee, and what the Queen's Bench judges also probably failed to foresee, was that Gye would be able convincingly to assert that he honestly (though

[52] P. 154 below.
[53] A question arising out of the new provisions was litigated: 22 LJ Ex. 9, 1 WR 39, 20 LT 71, and 103. Gye was required to make an affidavit that he believed he had a meritorious defence.

mistakenly and perhaps unreasonably) believed that Wagner was legally entitled to terminate her contract with Lumley on the ground that Lumley had not made the advance payment on 15 March, as promised.

The case was tried before Lord Campbell and a special jury, which answered specific questions. By another recent change in the law the parties were competent witnesses:[54] Gye gave evidence, but Lumley did not, an omission of which much was made by Gye's counsel at the trial.[55] Wagner herself was not available as a witness, though an unsuccessful attempt had been made to take her evidence by commission.[56] Lumley lost the case, because on the crucial question of Gye's state of mind, the judge directed the jury that 'if the defendant *bona fide* believed that the agreement with the plaintiff had ceased to be binding upon Miss Wagner the *scienter* [necessary element of knowledge] was not proved, and the defendant would be entitled to the verdict', and on this point the jury found for the defendant.[57] A motion for a new trial was dismissed by the full Queen's Bench, Lord Campbell pointing out that the court had indicated in overruling the demurrer in the previous year that bad faith was an essential part of the tort. On this point Gye had given evidence that he honestly thought on 5 April that Wagner was free from her obligation to Lumley. Lord Campbell commented, in supporting the dismissal of the motion for a new trial, that 'the jury had believed Mr Gye and he [Lord Campbell] was not prepared to say they were wrong'.[58]

The fact that Lumley eventually lost his case has been largely overlooked, and often misstated. There is some excuse for the error: the verdict is not very conspicuously reported in the law reports;[59] it was misleadingly described by Lumley in his memoirs,[60] and the result was misstated in both

---

[54] 14 & 15 Vic. c. 99.

[55] Lumley's counsel said that the reason for Lumley's absence from the witness box was that he did not wish to reveal his weak financial position, but this was not convincing as Her Majesty's Theatre had closed by the time of the trial. More probably his advisers feared that he would have difficulty in supporting the strict accuracy of some of the Chancery affidavits.

[56] The court gave leave for a new commission to be issued, on payment by Gye of Lumley's costs of the abortive first commission, 3 El & Bl 114, 22 LT 220, 18 Jur 466, *The Times*, 23 Feb. 1854, 12b, but Gye did not pursue the matter because his counsel were afraid that if it was favourable to Gye, Lumley would object successfully to its admissibility, Gye's diary, 17 Jan. 1854, Royal Opera House Archives.

[57] *The Times* 23 Feb. 1854, 12c. Gye thought that 'the judge summed up very much against me', Diary, 22 Feb. 1854.

[58] *The Times*, 6 June 1854, 10b.

[59] 18 Jur 468n., 23 LT 66, 157, 23 LJQB 116n.   [60] Lumley, *Reminiscences*, p. 333.

relevant articles in the *Dictionary of National Biography*,[61] and elsewhere.[62] The result, however, is important to a full understanding of the case. The requirement that the plaintiff prove actual dishonesty on the defendant's part made the action substantially less attractive to plaintiffs than it might at first have appeared. Lumley's failure goes a considerable way to explain why no similar case was litigated for nearly thirty years: a defendant, in order to escape liability, had only to say (convincingly) that he honestly believed that the contract-breaker had some excuse, for which purpose a mistake, even an unreasonable mistake, on a point of law would suffice. Gye knew that Lumley would dispute the matter, he expected to be asked by Wagner for an indemnity, and willingly gave it.[63] It might fairly be said that he was reckless as to Lumley's interest, and later cases have held that recklessness is a sufficient mental element to support the imposition of liability for intentional torts.[64] The general tone of the Queen's Bench judgments strongly suggests that all the judges expected that the court's decision would lead to Gye's being held liable. Had the facts been determined first, it seems very probable that the legal principle would have been formulated in such a way as to include 'recklessness' or 'turning a blind eye'.[65]

Attention to the background of these cases in the light of the historical evidence is not of merely antiquarian or anecdotal interest; it assists in understanding the perceptions of the judges, and therefore of their reasons, including those reasons that were not expressed or recorded in the law reports. The evidence tends to show that the conclusions were not reached in either Chancery or the Queen's Bench by allocating the facts to pre-existing categories, or by reference to anything like a pre-existing map or scheme, but by the operation of several concurrent and cumulative considerations, a method which, as we shall see in the course of the following pages, has operated also in respect of many other legal issues. This is not to say that legal concepts and categories were unimportant, or that reason played no part. On the contrary, the evidence shows that concepts were influential, that categorization was crucial, and that judicial reasoning was conscientious to

---

[61] *Dictionary of National Biography*, s.nn. Frederick Gye and Benjamin Lumley.

[62] H. Rosenthal, *Two Centuries of Opera at Covent Garden* (London, 1958), p. 97.

[63] *The Times*, 22 Feb. 1854, 11b.

[64] A recent example is *Three Rivers District Council* v. *Governor and Company of the Bank of England (No. 3)* [2000] 2 WLR 1220, HL (misfeasance in public office).

[65] These expressions have been used in modern cases, e.g. *Emerald Construction Co.* v. *Lowthian* [1966] 1 WLR 691, CA, *Daily Mirror* v. *Gardner* [1968] 2 QB 762, CA.

the point of being, at times, laborious.[66] What the evidence does suggest, however, is that the relation between the concepts was complex, as was the relation of the facts to the law, that categorization was itself dependent on these complexities, and that the reasoning in neither court was governed by precise logic.

---

[66] See, for example, Waddams, 'Johanna Wagner', note, p. 23 above, at 444–5.

3

Liability for economic harms

In a complex society the activities of some necessarily damage the economic interests of others, but often no legal obligation to pay compensation
has been recognized even though the damage is foreseeable, foreseen, and
intended.[1] Such cases are 'of daily occurrence'[2] and include competition
in trade and business, invention and promotion of new products, services,
and techniques, activities of labour unions, political contests, consumer
boycotts, campaigns against activities thought to be immoral or unhealthy,
defamatory statements that are true or privileged, use of land, advice to a
person adverse in interest to the plaintiff, contractual negotiation with the
plaintiff,[3] and advice to a donor not to proceed with an intended gift. 'It is
essential to an action in tort', the Privy Council said in 1860, 'that the act
complained of should . . . be legally wrongful as regards the party complaining, that is, it must prejudicially affect him in some legal right; merely that
it will harm him in his interests is not enough'.[4] A distinction between physical injury and economic harm has therefore on this view been necessary:
intentional injury to person or tangible property always affects the person
injured 'in some legal right', damage to economic interests only sometimes.[5]
But, as to precisely when, as John Fleming has said, 'no consensus . . . has
emerged after [long] judicial grappling with the problem'.[6]

Whether the defendant's conduct is 'legally wrongful' and whether the
plaintiff is affected 'in some legal right' are not questions that can be independently resolved: each is an aspect of the other, and both have often been

[1] *Allen* v. *Flood* [1898] AC 1, HL.
[2] *Rogers* v. *Rajendro Dutt* (1860) 13 Moo PC 209 at 241.
[3] *Gran Gelato Ltd* v. *Richcliff Group Ltd* [1992] Ch 650, *Martel Building Ltd* v. *Canada* [2000] 2
SCR 860, 193 DLR (4th) 1.
[4] Note 2 above.
[5] A. J. Weir, *Economic Torts* (Oxford, 1997), p. 9, Lord Oliver in *Murphy* v. *Brentwood District
Council* [1991] 1 AC 398 at 487, *Bow Valley Husky (Bermuda) Ltd* v. *St John Shipbuilding Ltd*
[1997] 3 SCR 1210, 153 DLR (4th) 385.
[6] J. Fleming, *The Law of Torts* (9th edn, Sydney, 1998), p. 194.

influenced by considerations of property, unjust enrichment, and public policy.[7] It is for this reason that attempts to explain liability for economic harm solely in terms of the defendant's fault have led to an intellectual impasse: wrongdoing in the sense of blameworthy conduct has been neither necessary nor sufficient for imposition of liability;[8] some reference to the idea of the plaintiff's entitlement is also needed.[9]

The interconnexion of concepts is revealed most clearly by cases where the court, faced with a novel question, has resolved it in the plaintiff's favour. In many such cases the court has not determined as a *prior* question whether the plaintiff had a legal right: it has been the very determination that the defendant's conduct was wrongful that has made it possible *thenceforth* to say that the plaintiff had a legal right, a proposition that we have seen illustrated by the cases of *Lumley* v. *Wagner* and *Lumley* v. *Gye* (1852–3) discussed in the last chapter. An earlier illustration is the eighteenth-century case of *Keeble* v. *Hickeringill*[10] (1705) where the defendant fired guns in order to frighten ducks away from his neighbour's decoy (a complicated duck-trap). The plaintiff had no property in the ducks, but the holding of the court in the plaintiff's favour made it possible to say that the court recognized, to a limited degree, a legally protected interest in the enterprise of operating the decoy.[11] Brian Simpson's study of this case has shown (what is apt to escape

---

[7] In *Rogers* v. *Rajendro Dutt*, note 2 above, the defendant, the government officer in charge of marine services at Calcutta, in order to punish the plaintiff for profiteering in a wartime situation (the Indian 'Mutiny'), instructed river pilots, whose services were a practical necessity, not, for a period of about a month, to pilot any ships towed by the plaintiff's tug. The plaintiff's claim succeeded in the Supreme Court of Calcutta, but failed in the Privy Council, which was plainly influenced by the fact that the defendant had acted in what he perceived to be the public interest, and stressed the absence of 'any indirect motive, or . . . direct malice' (at 240). Compare *Gershman* v. *Manitoba Vegetable Producers Marketing Board* (1976) 69 DLR (3d) 114, where the defendant was held liable for destroying the plaintiff's business without sufficient reason.

[8] A further example is the tort of passing off (palming off), where a person who represents his goods as those of another may be liable without proof of fault. Considerations of property and unjust enrichment have been influential.

[9] P. Benson, 'The Basis for Excluding Liability for Economic Loss in Tort Law', in D. G. Owen (ed.), *Philosophical Foundations of Tort Law* (Oxford, 1995), p. 431.

[10] (1705) 11 East 574n. See A. W. B. Simpson, *Leading Cases in the Common Law* (Oxford, 1995), ch. 3.

[11] The plaintiff might be said to have something akin to a limited easement. Cases denying liability in comparable situations include *Bradford Corporation* v. *Pickles* [1895] AC 587, HL (diversion of percolating water, discussed at pp. 212–15 below), and *Hunter* v. *Canary Wharf Ltd* [1997] AC 655, HL (interference with television signals). Had they been decided in the opposite sense, it would have been said that the law recognized, perhaps to a limited degree, legally protected interests in receiving (respectively) percolating water and television signals.

the modern reader) that the establishment and maintenance of a decoy required a very elaborate and expensive investment of time, land, money, staff, animals, and machinery.[12] In the light of this knowledge it can be seen that the court was influenced by general considerations of justice, including particularly the substantial investment made by the plaintiff, the absence of legitimate reason for the defendant's conduct, and by considerations of public policy:

> And when we know that of long time in the kingdom these artificial con-trivencies of decoy ponds and decoy ducks have been used for enticing into these ponds wildfowl, in order to be taken for the profit of the owner of the pond, who is at the expense of servants, engines and other management, whereby the markets of the nation may be furnished; there is great reason to give encouragement thereto; that the people who are so instrumental by their skill and industry so to furnish the markets should reap the benefits and have their action.[13]

A twentieth-century illustration is supplied by the well-known American case of *International News Service* v. *Associated Press*[14] (1918) where the defendant copied published news derived from the plaintiff's news service, and sold it to other newspapers, taking advantage of the telegraph and of the time difference between the American east and west coasts to pass the news as current. There had been no prior legal recognition of the interest claimed by the plaintiff, for most commentators would have said that published news was in the public domain. It is precisely the decision of the United States Supreme Court in this case that made it possible to say that the plaintiff had been 'prejudicially affected in some legal right'. This case illustrates also the influence, common in cases of economic harm, of the concepts of unjust enrichment (in the general sense) and of public policy. A reason adduced in favour of the result in *International News Service* v. *Associated Press* was that the defendant was 'endeavouring to reap where it has not sown' and 'appropriating to itself the harvest of those who have sown',[15] and to be weighed on the other side were forceful policy arguments that may be summarized as freedom of action, all the stronger in this case because it involved prior restraint by injunction of free speech on matters of public interest.[16]

---

[12] Simpson, *Leading Cases*, ch. 3.   [13] 11 East 577–8 per Holt CJ.
[14] 248 US 215 (1918).   [15] *Ibid.*, at 239–40.
[16] See opinions of Justices McKenna and Brandeis, dissenting.

In a number of cases obligations have been imposed that are closely related to contracts, but which cannot be categorized as themselves contractual. Thus, liability has in some cases been imposed on a person who, though not a contracting party, acts so as to defeat the plaintiff's expectations arising from a contract with another person. One such instance is the tort of inducing breach of contract (later extended to 'interference with contractual relations') discussed in the last chapter. Another example is use of property in a manner that the user knows to be contrary to restrictions agreed by a previous owner. The courts have, regularly in the case of land,[17] and occasionally in the case of chattels,[18] protected the plaintiff's interests. The obligations so imposed on the defendant cannot be classified as contractual, for the defendant had made no contract. But contract was far from irrelevant, and considerations of property, trust,[19] wrongdoing, unjust enrichment, and public policy were also crucial, and interconnected. The source of the plaintiff's expectation was a contract, and if the plaintiff had a legitimate interest[20] in restricting subsequent users of the property, the defendant acted wrongfully in defeating that interest, and would have been unjustly enriched if, having bought property at a reduced price (reflecting the anticipated restricted use), she could then ignore the restriction.

The element of unjust enrichment appeared very clearly in *Tulk* v. *Moxhay*[21] (1848), a case of a covenant to maintain a garden square in London for the benefit of local residents. Lord Cottenham, in enforcing the obligation against a subsequent owner, said:

> Of course the price would be affected by the contract, and nothing could be more inequitable than that the original purchaser should be able to sell the property the next day for a greater price, in consideration of the assignee being allowed to escape from the liability which he had himself undertaken.[22]

The link with the concept of property is also apparent here. The covenantee's interest may be described, and has been described, as a property right.

---

[17] *Tulk* v. *Moxhay* (1848) 2 Ph 774 .

[18] *DeMattos* v. *Gibson* (1858) 4 D & J 276, *Lord Strathcona SS Co.* v. *Dominion Coal Co.* [1926] AC 108, PC, *Trudel* v. *Clairol Inc. of Canada* [1975] 2 SCR 236 (Quebec law). But against this is *Taddy* v. *Sterious* [1904] 1 Ch 354.

[19] S. Worthington, *Proprietary Interests in Commercial Transactions* (Oxford, 1996), pp. 108–15.

[20] Hence the restrictions in the land cases that the plaintiff had to have an interest in neighbouring land, and could only enforce negative covenants.

[21] (1848) 2 Ph 774.   [22] *Ibid.*, at 778.

The authors of a leading English textbook commented on *Tulk* v. *Moxhay*: 'Thus was invented a new interest in land', describing it also as 'a new kind of property right created by equity'.[23] This was not a position reached by use of a pre-existing map. This slide from personal to proprietary right shows that the concepts do not exist in isolation from each other as though separate continents on a map, or separate genera or species in a taxonomic diagram. It is the decision itself in this case that enables a commentator to say that the covenantee has a property right.

The cases considered so far are cases where the plaintiff has the benefit of an obligation as against one person, and another interferes with it. We turn now to the converse situation, where the defendant is bound by an obligation, contractual or tortious, but the loss is suffered by some one other than the person to whom the obligation is primarily owed. These cases raise the prospect of the defendant's avoiding the normal consequences of wrongdoing on account of a transaction between potential claimants that is, from the defendant's point of view, wholly fortuitous. The courts have in a wide variety of circumstances resisted this conclusion. 'It is absurd to suggest', the House of Lords said in one case, 'that the claim to damages would disappear . . . into some legal black hole so that the wrongdoer escaped scot-free.'[24] The same metaphor ('black hole') was expressly accepted by the House of Lords in two subsequent cases as a persuasive reason for imposing liability.[25]

The image of a legal 'black hole' indicates that liability cannot be derived from any known head of obligation. As a matter of strict logic, this does not seem in itself a persuasive reason for imposing liability. On the contrary, if obligations were logically derived from a pre-existing scheme, the absence of any relevant head would be a powerful reason against liability. But the gist of the argument was to exactly the contrary effect: the defendant had caused loss to one or both of the potential claimants; that he should avoid liability entirely because of a fortuitous transaction between the claimants was perceived as absurd and unjust. An underlying reason was that if such an argument had succeeded, the defendant would have been (in a general sense) unjustly enriched at the expense of the potential claimants jointly: if

---

[23] R. Megarry and H. Wade, *The Law of Real Property* (2nd edn, London, 1959), pp. 726, 135.

[24] *GUS Property Management Ltd* v. *Littlewoods Mail Order Stores Ltd* [1982] SC 157, 177, HL (Sc).

[25] *Linden Gardens Trust Ltd* v. *Lenesta Sludge Disposals Ltd* [1994] 1 AC 85 at 109, *Alfred McAlpine Construction Ltd* v. *Panatown Ltd* [2001] 1 AC 518 at 534, 568, 574, and 575.

liability (to one or the other) was in the normal course of events justified and expected, it would be anomalous if the defendant fortuitously avoided liability to both.

Some cases of this sort have involved the shipping of goods where the property in the goods is transferred after the contract for carriage is made. A carrier who fails to deliver the goods might argue that it cannot be liable to the consignor (with whom the contract was made) because the consignor suffers no loss, nor can it be liable to the consignee, because there was no contract with the consignee. The consequences of this apparent logic have never been accepted by the courts. In a case of 1771, where the consignor brought the action, Lord Mansfield said 'there was neither law nor conscience in the [defendant's] objection. The vesting of property may differ according to the circumstances of cases, but it does not enter into the present question.'[26]

Somewhat analogous is the case of non-performance of a building contract, where the person employing the builder is not, at the time the loss occurs, the owner of the land on which the deficient building stands. The argument that the employer had suffered no loss and therefore could recover no damages was described by the House of Lords in 1993 as 'formidable, if unmeritorious', and as 'apparently soundly based in principle and... supported by authority'.[27] Nevertheless the argument was rejected. It is evident that the court's conclusion was based not on strict logic or any resort to a scheme of classification, but on very general considerations of justice. Lord Browne-Wilkinson said, adapting words of Lord Diplock in an earlier case, that 'it is truly a case in which the rule [i.e., of liability] provides a remedy where no other would be available to a person sustaining loss which under a rational legal system *ought to be compensated* by the person who has caused it'.[28] Another way of supporting the conclusion would be to say that the defendant would be unjustly enriched if it could evade liability for the normal and direct consequences of its wrong by virtue of a fortuitous

---

[26] *Davis* v. *James* (1771) 5 Burr 2680–81.

[27] *Linden Gardens* v. *Lenesta*, note 25 above, at 111. Professor Coote has argued that non-performance might itself cause loss to the promisee equal to the full value of the performance, but this idea has not been accepted by the courts. See B. Coote, 'Contract Damages, Ruxley, and the Performance Interest' [1997] *Cambridge Law Journal* 537, B. Coote, 'The Performance Interest, *Panatown*, and the Problem of Loss' (2001) 117 *Law Quarterly Review* 81.

[28] *Linden Gardens*, note 25 above, at 115, citing *The Albazero* [1977] AC 774, 846–7 [emphasis added].

relationship between the potential claimants that was not expected to have any such effect.

Analogous problems and analogous solutions are to be found in several other contexts. An agent can recover damages, even though the actual loss is suffered by the principal. A bailee can recover full compensation for damage to goods, even though the loss is partly, or mainly, suffered by the bailor.[29] The owner of property wrongfully damaged can recover in full from the wrongdoer, even though the property was insured, and the loss actually felt by the insurer. A person wrongfully injured can recover the cost of care gratuitously supplied, even though the cost is borne by the provider of the care.[30]

If, as I have suggested, one of the underlying reasons for imposing the obligation in these cases is avoidance of unjust enrichment at the expense of the potential claimants jointly, some legal device is necessary that in effect joins the claimants in the litigation, in order to ensure that the defendant's obligation is not *enlarged* by the transaction between the claimants, and to ensure a proper accounting among them. These objects have been secured in the case of insurance by the device of subrogation: the insurer is subrogated to the insured's claim against the wrongdoer, and the proceeds of the claim go to indemnify the insurer. Similarly, an agent must account to the principal, and a bailee to the bailor. In the case of the gratuitous provider of care it has again been widely, though not universally, held that the injured person holds the compensation in trust for the provider.[31] In the building contract cases, some similar liability to account is required, by trust, subrogation, implied assignment, or joinder of parties, in order to avoid, as Lord Browne-Wilkinson put it, 'another piece of legal nonsense',[32] by which he meant the prospect of a party who had suffered no loss receiving compensation, leaving the party who had really suffered the loss empty-handed.[33]

---

[29] *The Winkfield* [1902] P 42, CA.

[30] The parallel is made by J. Cartwright, 'Damages, Third Parties and Common Sense' (1996) 10 *Journal of Contract Law* 244 at 257–8.

[31] *Cunningham* v. *Harrison* [1973] QB 942, CA, *Thornton* v. *Prince George School Board* [1978] 2 SCR 267, *Hunt* v. *Severs* [1994] 2 AC 350, HL.

[32] *Alfred McAlpine* v. *Panatown*, note 25 above, at 578.

[33] Similar considerations lie behind *Morrison Steamship Co.* v. *Greystoke Castle* [1947] AC 265, HL. The problem addressed in *Murphy* v. *Brentwood District Council* [1991] 1 AC 398, HL, of defective performance of a building contract and subsequent sale of the land, might similarly be resolved by an action in the name of the original owner, with a requirement of due accounting to subsequent owners.

The net effect of these cases has been, indirectly, to impose an obligation to compensate for economic harm. But this obligation has not been derived by the courts from any classification system, nor could these cases have been located on any map or diagram in actual use.

Direct liability for causing economic loss by negligence might seem to offer a solution to these problems that would be logical, principled, and elegant. For a short time between about 1970 and 1980 it appeared that English and Scottish law might take this route,[34] but a series of decisions of the House of Lords dealing with defective buildings put a stop to this development in those jurisdictions.[35] The law on this point in other jurisdictions is less clear.[36] In the case of defective performance of a building contract, the apparent simplicity of the concept of a direct action in negligence has proved illusory. The difficulties, to be discussed more fully in a later chapter,[37] are that the standard of performance due from the builder depends on the building contract (to which the subsequent owner is not a party), and the extent of the loss suffered by the subsequent owner depends on the price paid and the expectations engendered by the sale contract (to which the builder is not a party). The direct action in negligence has proved unsatisfactory because it could not offer a framework that took these matters into account or that could adjust the rights of all three parties.

'Relational' economic loss is the name sometimes given to loss suffered by one person as the result of physical injury to the person or property of another. Damage to a bridge, for example, may cause loss to those who had expected to use it. This kind of loss has, in most jurisdictions, been said to be irrecoverable,[38] but there are exceptions. The exceptional cases where recovery has been permitted are closely analogous to those discussed in the preceding paragraphs. Thus, it was held in *Morrison Steamship Co. v. Greystoke Castle*[39] that a cargo owner who contributed to general average expenses (in that case fees incurred at a port of refuge) after a collision at sea

---

[34] *Dutton v. Bognor Regis Urban District Council* [1972] 1 QB 373, CA, *Anns v. Merton London Borough Council* [1978] AC 728, HL, *Junior Books Ltd v. Veitchi Co.* [1981] 1 AC 520, HL (Sc).

[35] *D. & F. Estates Ltd v. Church Commissioners for England* [1989] 1 AC 177, HL, *Murphy v. Brentwood District Council* [1991] 1 AC 398, HL.

[36] B. Feldthusen, *Economic Negligence* (4th edn, Toronto, 2000), ch. 4.

[37] See pp. 156–62 below.

[38] *Cattle v. Stockton Waterworks Co.* (1875) LR 10 QB 453; *Robins Dry Dock & Repair Co. v. Flint* 272 US 303 (1927), *Bow Valley Husky (Bermuda) Ltd v. St John Shipbuilding Ltd*, note 5 above.

[39] [1947] AC 265 (HL).

might make a claim against the ship responsible for the collision.[40] If such a claim were not permitted the wrongdoing ship would benefit unjustly by a fortuitous arrangement, namely the scheme for sharing the loss among the innocent ship- and cargo owners. If the wrongdoer could benefit in this way, the plaintiff would be compelled to contribute not (as intended by the law of general average[41]) in relief of its fellow adventurers but in relief of the wrongdoer, who would thereby be unjustly enriched. Other exceptional cases where relational loss can be recovered are cases of joint ownership (analogous to the bailment cases), cases of 'transferred loss' (where part of the loss suffered by a property owner is transferred to the plaintiff) and cases of joint venture (where it is fortuitous which of several affiliated entities is the owner and which the profit-earner). All these are cases where the defendant would be (in a general sense) unjustly enriched if relieved by a purely fortuitous arrangement from the natural consequences of damage to property. In all of them also some mechanism has been needed, as with the cases described earlier, for protecting the defendant from overlapping claims, and for settling disputes among the potential claimants.[42] One such possibility, used in some of the instances mentioned above, has been a requirement that the action be brought in the name of the property owner, with the proceeds to be held on trust for others as their interests appeared. The very need for such a device shows that obligations are not derived from simple and separate sources, for if the claimant were personally entitled to the award there would be no justification for requiring the proceeds to be held on trust for another person.

The thrust of these comments is not to argue either in favour of or against this particular procedure, but to point out the instability of the methods of classifying obligations: the cases in all the groups just mentioned could readily be reclassified as property damage cases. For example, the general average cases have been doubted because they appear as a puzzling anomaly in the law of liability for economic loss,[43] but a procedural reform (whereby the action had to be brought in the name of the ship-owner and the

---

[40] *The Sucarseco* 294 US 394 (1935), *Morrison* v. *Greystoke Castle*, note 33 above.

[41] See pp. 83–4 below.

[42] If the wrongdoer had to pay both the cargo owner directly and the innocent ship-owner indirectly for the loss of the cargo, the latter would be unjustly enriched. In the *Sucarseco*, for example, the court said that 'we have the anomalous situation that it is the *Toluma* [damaged ship] that is opposing the cargo-owner's claim, while the *Toluma* has collected from the cargo-owner its share of the general average expense', 51 Ll LR 241 (Hughes CJ).

[43] Lord Keith in *Murphy* v. *Brentwood* [1991] 1 AC 398, at 468.

proceeds held in trust for the cargo owners) would remove the cases altogether from the category of 'pure' economic loss and put them into the entirely non-controversial category of property damage, for there is nothing in the nature of the loss itself to exclude recovery. If, in *Morrison Steamship Co. v. Greystoke Castle*, the ship-owner had also owned the cargo, its claim for the full amount of the fees incurred at the port of refuge after the collision would have been entirely non-controversial. The effect of general average was merely to distribute a loss for which the wrongdoer was undoubtedly responsible.[44] An insurer, as was suggested above, is enabled in effect to recover economic losses caused by negligent damage to insured property, but so effective and uncontroversial has been the notion of subrogation (where the insurer claims in the name of the insured) that it is rarely suggested that there is any conflict here with the general rule that pure economic loss is irrecoverable. As Fleming observed, 'the general rule serves less to exclude than to channel claims so as to spare the defendant from more than one suit'.[45]

The issues just discussed have obvious affinities with those associated with third party beneficiaries to contracts, and here we can see demonstrated the consequences of over-stringent classification. Quite commonly an elderly person has sought to provide for a relative by conveying property to another person in return for that person's promise to benefit the relative after the promisee's death. Such promises were regularly enforced both at law and in equity until the mid-nineteenth century,[46] when doubt was thrown on enforcement because the circumstances did not conform strictly to the nineteenth-century pattern of contractual obligation, no agreement having been made with nor consideration supplied by the beneficiary.

Looked at solely from the perspective of contract, and accepting nineteenth-century ideas about consideration and agreement, this appears as a logically necessary conclusion, and here English law, contrary to its usual habits of thought, and unlike American law,[47] accepted for nearly 150 years the logic of a stringent classification of concepts. But the consequence

---

[44] See *The Sucarseco* at 51 Ll LR 421: 'The Jason [general average] Clause merely distributed a loss for which the *Sucarseco* [wrongdoing ship] was responsible.'

[45] J. Fleming, *The Law of Torts* (5th edn, Sydney, 1977), p. 172. Feldthusen also makes the comparison with subrogation and joinder of actions, *Economic Negligence*, pp. 239, 265.

[46] *Dutton* v. *Poole* (1678) 8 T Raym 302, *Tweddle* v. *Atkinson* (1861) 1 B & S 393. See Lord Denning in *Beswick* v. *Beswick* [1966] Ch 538, CA at 552–6. See also the discussion of secret trusts at pp. 63–4 below.

[47] *Lawrence* v. *Fox* 29 NY 268 (1859) and see A. L. Corbin, *Contracts* (12 vols., St Paul, 1951), vol. IV, pp. 1–75.

was, in the circumstances just described, as few have denied, gross injustice: the beneficiary could not sue because she was not a party to the contract; the promisee's estate could sue, but could recover no substantial damages because it had suffered no loss.

The courts of equity had enforced the promise in these cases by declaring the promisee to be a trustee of the promise for the beneficiary. In an Ontario Chancery case of 1872 where the facts were in outline as envisaged in the last paragraphs, the judge said, after noting the then quite recent English common law case of *Tweddle* v. *Atkinson,*

> This, however, in my opinion only goes to show the applicability to a case like the present of a remedy in this Court [i.e., Chancery] . . . There can be no doubt, as I have already said, that this $400 [the money to be paid to the beneficiary], if recovered in an action at law by a personal representative of John Mulholland [the promisee], would not be assets in his hands to be distributed by him according to the Statute of Distributions [as on an intestacy] but would be imposed with a trust in equity in favour of the plaintiff. This *must* be so [emphasis in original], for the only other alternative is that it was in the power of the defendant entirely to defeat any or all of the gifts which the settlor made to his children [the beneficiaries] by compelling the personal representative to bring an action, the fruits of which would be free from any trust and liable to be distributed amongst the next of kin, which would, of course, be absurd. Then if the money, when recovered by the administrator, would be affected by a trust it must also be that the right of action which the personal representative has is also bound by a like trust.[48]

This line of reasoning, though approved by the House of Lords in 1919,[49] and supported by Professor Corbin,[50] was subsequently rejected by the English courts on the ground that a trust required proof of a distinct intention in the mind of one or both of the contracting parties that a trust should be created.[51] Of course there has rarely in such cases been evidence of conscious animadversion to the legal concept of trust, and where this has been strictly required the plaintiff's argument has failed. Such compartmentalized thinking resulted in the defeat of liability, for it appeared that

---

[48] *Mulholland* v. *Merriam* (1872) 19 Gr 288.
[49] *Les Affreteurs etc.* v. *Walford* [1919] AC 801, HL.
[50] A. L. Corbin, 'Contracts for the Benefit of Third Persons' (1930) 46 *Law Quarterly Review* 12.
[51] *Green* v. *Russell* [1959] 2 QB 226, CA, *Re Schebsman* [1944] Ch 83, CA.

the claim satisfied neither the requirements of contract (considered alone) nor those of trust (considered alone).

Trust is a proprietary concept, and a judicial declaration that the promise is held in trust for the beneficiary amounts to an assertion that the promise is (in effect) something that belongs to the beneficiary. Considerations of unjust enrichment (in its general sense) are also involved, for it would, as has been said, be 'grossly unjust'[52] if the promisor could take the property conveyed to him by the promisee and then fail to make the agreed payments to the beneficiary. The concepts are intertwined: the promisor's enrichment is to be avoided just because he is seeking to keep for himself something that justly belongs to the beneficiary. A rule that third party beneficiaries can never enforce contracts is apt, as experience has shown, to cause unjust enrichment, but not every particular case involves enrichment. Avoidance of unjust enrichment has not been the *sole* reason for permitting third party beneficiaries to enforce contracts, but neither has it been irrelevant. The concepts of contract, property, and unjust enrichment, considered separately, have each proved insufficient to support liability, but cumulatively they were, even eventually in England, persuasive.

In Canada the strict privity rule was relaxed by judicial decision.[53] In England the law was eventually altered by statute.[54] But since it is not appropriate to enforce every contract that would benefit a third party, it did not prove easy to draft in statutory form the limits to enforceability. One difficulty is the definition of the class of persons entitled to enforce such contracts, for there are many persons who would benefit by performance of a contract between others ('incidental' beneficiaries) to whom it would not be appropriate to give a contractual remedy.[55] The second main difficulty is the case where the contract is rescinded or modified by subsequent agreement between the contracting parties.[56] If the beneficiary is thought to merit something like a proprietary interest, the modification of her rights must be ineffective; on the other hand, if the case is likened to that of an incomplete gift, where the donor has changed his mind, it will not be appropriate to treat

---

[52] For example by Lord Reid in *Beswick* v. *Beswick* [1968] AC 58 at 73.

[53] *London Drugs Ltd* v. *Kuehne & Nagel International Ltd* [1992] 3 SCR 299.

[54] The Contracts (Rights of Third Parties) Act 1999. See N. H. Andrews, 'Strangers to Justice No Longer: The Reversal of the Privity Rule under the Contracts (Rights of Third Parties) Act 1999' [2001] *Cambridge Law Journal* 353.

[55] S. 1 of the English Act dealing with this question contains seven subsections.

[56] This is s. 2 of the English statute, with seven subsections and eight subparagraphs.

the beneficiary as having a vested right. Third party beneficiary contracts may be of either kind. An additional point is that if the beneficiary has changed her position in reliance on the promise it will often be appropriate to give a remedy, but one that may fall short of full enforcement of the promise.[57] Another problem is the interaction of a general statute with the many specific statutes that have modified the rules of privity in various specialized contexts.[58]

The trust approach has had the merit of sufficient flexibility to take into account concepts of property and unjust enrichment so as to exclude incidental beneficiaries and prospective donees. As with the other kinds of case considered above, a mechanism is needed for protecting the promisor from double claims by promisee and beneficiary,[59] and for resolving disputes, if any, between the potential claimants. An additional merit of the trust approach is that the claim is made in the name of the promisee, who can be joined by the beneficiary as a defendant if necessary, thereby enabling the promisor to raise any legitimate defence that he might have against the promisee,[60] and enabling the court to resolve any dispute between promisee and beneficiary. The trust approach has supplied an effective framework for the just resolution of some kinds of contractual claims by third parties, and may continue to do so in the future in jurisdictions where there is no general statute, or where such a statute does not apply.[61]

Another somewhat analogous set of circumstances that has created conceptual difficulties arises where an intended disposition of property after death fails on account of bad advice. The typical case is the lawyer by whose negligence a will is invalidly executed or attested. In 1861 it was thought so clear that such a claim must fail that the instance was used as an absurdity in order to discredit an argument concerning an *inter vivos* transfer where the intending transferor became bankrupt. 'If this were law' Lord Campbell said of the argument in question,

---

[57] Mere 'communication of assent', or reliance in any degree, is sufficient in the English statute to give full enforcement; this may produce extravagant results.
[58] This is s. 6 of the English statute.
[59] S. 5 of the English statute.   [60] S. 3 of the English statute.
[61] Existing exceptions to the privity rule were preserved by the English statute, s. 7(1). See A. Burrows, 'The Contracts (Rights of Third Parties) Act 1999 and its Implications for Commercial Contracts' [2000] *Lloyd's Maritime and Commercial Law Quarterly*, 540 at 549–50.

a disappointed legatee might sue the solicitor employed by a testator to make a will in favour of a stranger, whom the solicitor never knew or before heard of, if the will were void for not being properly signed and attested. I am clearly of the opinion that this is not the law of Scotland or of England and it can hardly be the law of any country where jurisprudence has been cultivated as a science.[62]

'Scientific' jurisprudence then appeared to demand clear and distinct classification, and on these facts it appeared that no action arose in contract (for there was no contract between pursuer and defender), nor did it fall into any category of wrongdoing then recognized.

It was not until 1995 that the House of Lords was required to face this question directly. In *White* v. *Jones*[63] a solicitor had delayed unduly in implementing the testator's instructions, with the consequence that the latter died before an intended new will could be executed. The House of Lords, by a majority of three to two, held that the solicitor was liable to the intended beneficiaries. In reaching this conclusion it is plain that the law lords who formed the majority did not proceed by deduction from any pre-existing classification. Lord Goff, who gave the principal speech for the majority, acknowledged that there were serious conceptual difficulties in the plaintiff's way. Lord Goff conceded that the 'strict lawyer may well react by saying that the present claim can lie only in contract',[64] but against this he set the need for 'practical justice', a phrase he used several times,[65] implicitly contrasting it with the 'science' of the former century and the 'strict' law of his own.

The case has some affinities with the transferred loss (or 'black hole') cases discussed above, in that the person who could sue for breach of contract (the estate) had suffered no loss, whereas the person who had suffered loss (the intended beneficiary) could not sue. Lord Goff put this point 'in the forefront' and said that it was of 'cardinal importance'[66] to fill this 'lacuna' in the law. He recognized that strictly speaking *White* v. *Jones* was

---

[62] *Robertson* v. *Fleming* (1861) 4 Macq 167, 177 (Lord Campbell was dissenting, but Lord Cranworth agreed with this point, at 234).

[63] [1995] 2 AC 207, HL. To similar effect, with a variety of reasons among the majority judges, is *Hill* v. *Van Erp* (1997) 188 CLR 159.

[64] *White* v. *Jones*, note 63 above, at 261.

[65] *Ibid.*, at 258, 260, 263, 264, 265, 268, 269.   [66] *Ibid.*, at 260.

not a case of transferred loss, but he said that 'even so, the analogy is very close'.[67]

The case also has affinities with that of a third party beneficiary, but again it is not precisely analogous, and would not fall within the English statute of 1999,[68] because the beneficiary was never intended to have contractual rights against the solicitor. Lord Campbell made a similar point in the Scottish case of 1861, where he said, in answer to the argument that in Scotland third party rights were recognized, 'The Scottish authorities, under the head of *jus quaesitum tertio* have no application, for these contemplate a vested right absolutely acquired by a consummated transaction.'[69]

The case has affinities also with reliance on negligent misrepresentation,[70] but the solicitor in *White* v. *Jones* could not be said intentionally to have assumed any responsibility directly to the beneficiary, nor did the latter rely on the solicitor. Yet reliance *by the client* is a crucial feature as can be seen by considering a case where the lawyer advises erroneously that no new will is needed at all. The loss to the intended beneficiary would be the same as in *White* v. *Jones* and would clearly be caused not by the lawyer's assuming any responsibility to the beneficiary but by the client's reliance on the lawyer's advice. The element of reliance also tends to rebut the argument that the plaintiff, if successful, receives compensation for mere failure to complete a gift: the counter-argument is that the plaintiff is entitled to be put in the position he or she would have occupied if the lawyer had declined altogether to act, for in that case the testator would probably have secured competent advice.[71]

Lord Goff's other reasons were the injustice to the plaintiffs of denying a remedy, the fact that the solicitors' profession could hardly complain of being liable in the circumstances, and the fact that solicitors performed a quasi-public service.[72] Taken together these points suggest that the solicitors' profession and its insurers would be improperly advantaged if they could enjoy a monopoly on testamentary business (with power to

---

[67] *Ibid.*, at 265. *White* v. *Jones* is not a case of transferred loss, because the loss could never have fallen on the original contracting party.
[68] Note 54 above.   [69] *Robertson* v. *Fleming* (1861) 4 Macq 167, at 177.
[70] See chapter 4 below.
[71] See *Gorham* v. *BT* [2000] 1 WLR 2129, CA (no compensation for loss occurring because of client's failure to act after being correctly advised), J. Stapleton, 'The Normal Expectancies Measure in Tort Damages' (1997) 113 *Law Quarterly Review* 257.
[72] Also Lord Browne-Wilkinson at [1995] 2 AC 276.

exact monopoly prices) without bearing the consequences of negligently caused losses.[73] He asserted that the court 'will have to fashion an effective remedy....'[74] Having considered and rejected various possible contractual remedies, he concluded that it was possible 'to fashion a remedy to fill a lacuna in the law and so prevent the injustice which would otherwise occur'.[75] He rested his conclusion not on a general principle of negligence, but on the theory that the solicitor's assumption of responsibility to his client 'should be held in law to extend to the intended beneficiary', a reason which may be described as a mixture of contractual and tortious ideas.

The merits of the conclusion in *White* v. *Jones* may be debated: the problem is resistant to classification, and has been resolved in various ways in other jurisdictions. Two law lords dissented, and a differently constituted panel might well have reached the opposite conclusion, or might have rested the conclusion on contractual grounds, or on a general principle of negligence. The point made here is that Lord Goff's conclusion was not reached by logical deduction from a pre-existing map or diagram of legal concepts. On the contrary, he thought that neither contractual principles, considered alone, nor 'an ordinary action in tortious negligence' could support liability. Nor could unjust enrichment or public policy, standing alone, support the result. But the breach of contract and the negligence when combined with considerations of unjust enrichment, public policy, and general considerations of justice amounted cumulatively (in the eyes of the majority of the court) to a sufficiently persuasive case.

Sir Guenter Treitel has said that 'the disappointed beneficiary cases... are best regarded as *sui generis*'.[76] It is certainly true that the issue raised in these cases cannot readily be allocated to any one of contract, tort, unjust enrichment, or property, and this is, no doubt, what Treitel's comment was intended to indicate. But the phrase 'sui generis' might be taken to signify a separate and additional genus. This would be pressing a metaphor too far, for the reasoning in *White* v. *Jones* does not *exclude* considerations of contract, tort, unjust enrichment, and property, but rather combines them, together with considerations of public policy. It is therefore impossible to define a distinct 'genus' to which *White* v. *Jones* belongs, and, pending

---

[73] But in *Gorham* v. *BT*, note 71 above, liability was imposed on an insurance salesman, where the corresponding arguments are weaker.

[74] [1995] 2 AC 260.   [75] *Ibid.*, at 268.

[76] G. H. Treitel, *The Law of Contract* (10th edn, London, 1999), p. 569.

judicial determination, uncertainty necessarily remains as to the kinds of defendants,[77] and the kinds of transactions[78] in respect of which liability will be imposed.

The cases considered in this chapter have mostly been classed as tort, but they cannot be explained exclusively in terms of wrongdoing without giving attention also to the idea of entitlement. The two ideas are interrelated. The defendant's conduct has been called wrongful when it interferes with an entitlement of the plaintiff's; but the plaintiff has been seen to have an entitlement when the defendant's conduct is adjudged to be wrongful. The idea of entitlement has proprietary connotations but these are not cases of property rights in the strict sense. Many of them have been closely associated with contracts either, as in *Lumley* v. *Gye*, discussed in chapter 2, because the defendant interferes with the plaintiff's expectations pursuant to a contract with another person, or, as in the third party beneficiary cases, because the defendant's conduct constitutes a breach of contract with another person than the plaintiff, but in which the plaintiff is adjudged to have a sufficient interest. Many, but not all, of the cases have been influenced by considerations of unjust enrichment. They cannot be allocated exclusively to the law of property, or to any single subdivision of the law of obligations.

---

[77] See *Gorham* v. *BT*, note 71 above.

[78] See D. Baker, 'Solicitors' Liability for Failure of an Inter Vivos Gift' (2000) 22 *Adelaide Law Review* 51.

4

Reliance

Reliance on the promises and assertions of others, express or implied, is very common in human affairs, and its protection has been a prominent feature of Anglo-American law. Effective protection has often been afforded by contract law, but in a number of circumstances reliance occurs in the absence of an enforceable contract, and here other legal concepts have been deployed. But it has not proved possible to explain the protection of reliance in terms of any other single legal concept.

Very frequently one person makes an assertion on which another relies. In a wide variety of circumstances the courts have held that the person making the assertion is precluded from later contradicting it. The clearest examples relate to statements of fact. If a deadline for enrolment in a university programme is imminent, and a prospective student is informed by the university, before the deadline and while spaces remain in the programme, that she is duly enrolled, the university is estopped (i.e., precluded), after the deadline has passed, from denying the truth of the information, even if the student in fact was not duly enrolled, and even in the face of a mandatory rule in the most stringent language imaginable to the effect that no student shall in any circumstances be enrolled after the deadline. It will be seen from this example that the principle of estoppel is capable of having far-reaching effects on other legal rules, and it has often been the source of obligations that are not assignable to any of the usual divisions shown on diagrams or maps.[1] Lord Goff has said (2001) that 'in the end I am inclined to think that the many circumstances capable of giving rise to an estoppel cannot be accommodated within a single formula, and that it is unconscionability which provides the link between them'.[2] By this he meant that the underlying reason for estoppel is that it would be unfair for a person, having made an

---

[1] D. Jackson, 'Estoppel as a Sword' (1965) 81 *Law Quarterly Review* 84, M. Halliwell, 'Estoppel: Unconscionability as a Cause of Action' (1994) 14 *Legal Studies* 15.
[2] *Johnson* v. *Gore Wood & Co.* [2002] 2 AC 1 at 41, HL.

assertion that induces another to act to her detriment, to go back on the assertion.

The effect of estoppel is to protect the plaintiff from harm, and to that extent there is an affinity with tort, but there is no need for proof of wrongdoing: the assertion may be due to an honest and perfectly reasonable mistake (due to computer malfunction, for example). The Privy Council put it in this way (1892):

> The law of this country gives no countenance to the doctrine that in order to create estoppel the person whose acts or declarations induced another to act in a particular way must have been under no mistake himself, or must have intended to mislead or deceive ... [T]he principle on which the law ... rest[s] is, that it would be most inequitable and unjust to him that if another, by a representation made, or by conduct amounting to a representation, has induced him to act as he would not otherwise have done, the person who made the representation should be allowed to deny or repudiate the effect of his former statement, to the loss and injury of the person who acted on it.[3]

Estoppel clearly has a close relation to contract: the words or conduct of one person that induce expectations in another give rise to a legal obligation. Yet the obligation is not purely contractual. Neither promise nor bargain have been required, nor has the remedy been always equivalent to the plaintiff's expectation. Moreover, if the concept of estoppel were applicable to a promise standing alone, it would largely have subsumed contract law. In a number of instances estoppel has indeed been a means of enforcing promises. An important example is the Australian case of *Waltons Stores (Interstate) Ltd v. Maher*[4] (1987), where an owner of land demolished a building and commenced construction of a new one to the specifications of a prospective tenant. No binding lease was ever effected, but the prospective tenant was held to be estopped (in the view of the majority of the court) from retreating from an implied promise to complete the contract.

One of the simplest imaginable examples of reliance arises when a landowner promises to give the land to another person (for example, a relative) and the other person, relying on the promise, builds on the land. The promisor (or, as it has more usually been, his or her estate) then seeks to revoke the promise. These facts have presented a problem for

---

[3] *Sarat Chunder Dey v. Gopal Chunder Laha* (1892) LR 19 Ind App 203, PC, at 215–16.
[4] (1987) 164 CLR 387.

Anglo-American law because the transaction, being gratuitous, is not enforceable as a contract. Property has not been legally transferred; neither is the promisor guilty of any tort. Nevertheless the courts of equity gave a remedy to the promisee.[5] These cases could not be reconciled with orthodox contract doctrine and have therefore been ignored or marginalized by many writers on contract law. They have usually been described as cases of proprietary estoppel, but this phrase is scarcely explanatory. In some of the cases avoidance of unjust enrichment was evidently a crucial factor: in the leading case of *Dillwyn* v. *Llewelyn*[6] for example (1862), the plaintiff had expended the very large sum of £20,000 in improving land that was originally worth only £1,500. One of the considerations in the mind of a court faced with such facts has been the enrichment that would enure to the defendant if no measure of enforcement were available, and one of the reasons for favouring proprietary estoppel as a rule is that unjust enrichment is *very apt* to occur in such circumstances, and so the rule tends to prevent unjust enrichment. But unjust enrichment has not been present in every particular case,[7] and the remedy has not normally been measured by enrichment. As Peter Birks wrote (1985), 'the doctrine has a *dimension* to it which has nothing to do with restitution/unjust enrichment'.[8] This is true, but it does not follow that considerations of unjust enrichment have been irrelevant. Many of the cases have had the effect of protecting reliance, but the measure of recovery is not, where the plaintiff becomes effectively the owner of the land, restricted to out-of-pocket loss. Non-contractual reliance has sometimes been protected by concepts of wrongdoing, but in these cases there is no wrongdoing in the ordinary sense. Though the phrase 'equitable fraud' has sometimes been employed, no actual proof of wrongdoing has been required: the defendant acts fraudulently, in the eyes of equity, by failing to do what is just. As expressed in *Wilmott* v. *Barber* (1880), 'the plaintiff must prove that he [the defendant] has acted fraudulently, *or* that there has

---

[5] *Dillwyn* v. *Llewelyn* (1862) 4 D F & J 517, 6 LT 878, *Ramsden* v. *Dyson* (1866) LR 1 HL 129, *Wilmott* v. *Barber* (1880) 15 Ch D 96, *Plimmer* v. *Wellington* (1884) 9 App Cas 699, PC, *Inwards* v. *Baker* [1965] 2 QB 29, CA, *Crabb* v. *Arun DC* [1976] Ch 179, CA, *Greasley* v. *Cooke* [1980] 1 WLR 1306, CA, *Stiles* v. *Tod Mountain Devt Ltd* (1992) 64 BCLR (2d) 366, SC.

[6] (1862) 6 LT 878 at 879.

[7] See J. Beatson, *Anson's Law of Contract* (27th edn, Oxford, 1998), p. 119.

[8] P. Birks, *Introduction to the Law of Restitution* (Oxford, 1985), p. 290 (emphasis added). R. Goff and G. Jones, *The Law of Restitution* (London, 1966), and P. Maddaugh and J. McCamus, *The Law of Restitution* (Toronto, 1990), included discussion of these cases in their books, but A. Burrows, *The Law of Restitution* (London, 1993), wrote flatly at p. 404 that these cases 'have not been restitutionary'.

been such an acquiescence on his part as would make it fraudulent for him *now* to assert his legal rights'.[9] The word 'fraudulent' in the last clause of this passage means 'unjust', and cannot be explained except in terms of concepts other than wrong-doing. The defendant must, by action or inaction, induce the plaintiff's reliance, but no proof of intention to mislead or deceive is required.[10] The only 'fraud' required to be proved is an unwillingness to do what equity considers just. A similar comment may be made in relation to the concept of unconscionability, earlier mentioned.[11] If equity protects the plaintiff's reliance, it will be, by that very fact, against conscience for the defendant to defeat it. 'Inequitable', 'fraudulent', 'unconscionable', and 'unconscientious' have been, in this context, four ways of saying the same thing.[12]

Reasons have been mentioned why the cases considered here cannot readily be assimilated into contract law, namely, that there is no bargain, no consideration, and, in the ordinary common and legal use of the word, no contract. But there is another reason, and that is that no promise has been required: it has been sufficient that the defendant acquiesced in the plaintiff's reliance in circumstances where, having done so, it was unreasonable to leave the reliance unprotected.[13] Definitions of contract law based on the concept of promise have not therefore been able to accommodate these cases.

In one of the leading cases on this question, *Ramsden* v. *Dyson*[14] (1866), the House of Lords spoke not in terms of promise but of 'expectation created or encouraged' and reliance occurring 'with the knowledge of the [defendant] and without objection by him'.[15] In the passage earlier quoted from *Willmott* v. *Barber* it was said to be sufficient for the plaintiff to prove 'such an *acquiescence* on his [the defendant's] part as would make it fraudulent for him now to assert his legal rights'.[16] In the twentieth-century

---

[9] *Wilmott* v. *Barber*, note 5 above, at 106 (emphasis added), *Gerrard* v. *O'Reilly* (1843) 3 D & War 414 (Ir Ch).

[10] *Wilmott* v. *Barber*, note 5 above, at 105 (Fry J). This is a common usage in equity. See L. Sheridan, *Fraud in Equity* (London, 1956).

[11] P. 57 above. See M. Spence, *Protecting Reliance: the Emergent Doctrine of Equitable Estoppel* (Oxford, 1999), pp. 55–66, *Giumelli* v. *Giumelli* (1999) 161 ALR 473, Aust. HC.

[12] See A. Robertson, 'Reasonable Reliance in Estoppel by Conduct' (2000) 23 *University of New South Wales Law Review* 87, at 96–7.

[13] *Spiro* v. *Lintern* [1973] 1 WLR 1002, CA; *Waltons Stores* v. *Maher*, note 4 above (implied promise to complete).

[14] (1866) LR 1 HL 129.

[15] *Ibid.*, at 170 (Lord Kingsdown, dissenting, but this statement was accepted by the other lords).

[16] *Wilmott* v. *Barber*, note 5 above, at 106 (emphasis added).

case of *Crabb* v. *Arun District Council*[17] (1976) the plaintiff divided his land on the strength of an expectation that an essential right of way would be granted by the defendant. There had been inconclusive discussions on this question, and the trial judge found that, though there had been 'agreement in principle', the defendant had given 'no definite assurance' and made 'no firm commitment'. But the defendant put up gates at the point where the right of way was contemplated, leading the plaintiff to believe that a right of way would be given. The Court of Appeal held that this was sufficient:

> The defendants knew that the plaintiff *intended* to sell the two portions separately and that he would need an access at [the point where the gates were erected]. Seeing that they knew of his intention – and they did nothing to disabuse him but rather confirmed it by erecting gates . . . – it was their conduct which led him to act as he did: and this raises an equity in his favour against him.[18]

A further reason why cases of this sort cannot be readily assimilated to contract law is the extent of the remedy, which is not necessarily equivalent to enforcement of the plaintiff's full expectation. In the *Crabb* case the court said on this point, 'Here equity is displayed at its most flexible',[19] contemplating that the court might require payment by the plaintiff of a reasonable price for the right of way, though on the facts of the case this was not done because the plaintiff had lost the use of the land pending resolution of the dispute.

In these cases, as in the others considered in earlier chapters, it can be seen that several legal concepts have operated simultaneously and cumulatively. The plaintiff could state no case for recovery in contract, for there was no contract. Nor (without the help of estoppel, or until the court would 'raise an equity') could the plaintiff claim the land as his or her property, because title was vested in the defendant. Nor was the defendant guilty of wrongdoing (in the ordinary sense of the word), for he or she had no legal obligation to perform the promise. Nor has there been in every case an unjust enrichment. Yet the cumulative impact of these concepts has been sufficiently persuasive. In a recent case (2001) the English Court of Appeal emphasized the interrelationship of concepts on this question. The trial judge had dismissed the claim primarily because he found that there was no irrevocable promise or 'mutual understanding' between the parties.

---

[17] [1976] Ch 179, CA.   [18] *Ibid.*, at 189.   [19] *Ibid.*

The Court of Appeal reversed the decision on the ground that the various relevant considerations, though each in itself insufficient, might have a cumulative effect:

> the quality of the relevant assurances may influence the issue of reliance, . . . reliance and detriment are often intertwined, and . . . whether there is a distinct need for a 'mutual understanding' may depend on how the other elements are formulated and understood. Moreover the fundamental principle that equity is concerned to prevent unconscionable conduct permeates all the elements of the doctrine. In the end the court must look at the matter in the round. . . . [T]he cumulative effect of the judge's findings and of the undisputed evidence is that . . . Mr Gillett had an exceptionally strong claim on Mr Holt's conscience.[20]

Similar questions have arisen, and similar solutions have been adopted, in respect of unenforceable contracts. The Statute of Frauds,[21] enacted in 1677 in order to prevent the fraudulent assertion of contractual obligations, provided that certain contracts, notably contracts for the sale of interests in land, were unenforceable unless evidenced by a signed writing. Where a purchaser under an oral contract took possession of the land and built on it, and the landowner subsequently repudiated the contract, considerations arose similar to those discussed in the preceding paragraphs. The purchaser's reliance and the vendor's enrichment were considerations tending strongly in favour of the purchaser; against these had to be set the express statutory provision that the contract was unenforceable. But this point was in turn weakened because the very acts constituting the reliance and causing the enrichment – taking possession and building – tended themselves to show that the contract had probably been made and therefore might be said to satisfy the underlying purpose for which the Statute of Frauds had been enacted, though not, of course, the actual requirements of the statute itself. In such circumstances, by what was misleadingly called the doctrine of part performance, the courts of equity enforced the contract. Neither reliance alone, nor enrichment alone, nor proof of the contract alone (except by a signed writing) could support this result. Frederick Pollock (1876) said that the plaintiff's right rested 'not on a contract but on a principle akin to estoppel', though adding that 'the practical result is that the agreement is enforced'.[22] A century later the difficulty

---

[20] *Gillett v. Holt* [2001] 1 Ch 210, CA, at 225, 234.   [21] 29 Car II, c. 3.
[22] F. Pollock, *Principles of Contract at Law and in Equity* (London, 1876), pp. 558–9.

of classification was again noted and described as 'an uneasy oscillation between regarding the doctrine [of part performance] as a principle vindicating conscientious dealing and as a rule of evidence'.[23] These comments show that the cases cannot be allocated to a single category, or explained by a single concept, but that, cumulatively, various reasons have been effective.[24]

Closely related to these cases are those of informal instructions for disposition of property after death, called, by 'a not altogether felicitous expression',[25] secret trusts. The typical case has been of a testator leaving property to a person by will, having privately instructed the person to give the property, in whole or in part, to some other person. Enforcement of such a gift appears on the face of it to contravene the Wills Act, which requires a will to be executed according to certain formalities, and, in cases involving oral instructions relating to land, to contravene also the Statute of Frauds. Nevertheless the courts of equity have enforced the intended gifts in these cases by requiring the person named in the will to hold the property on trust for the intended donee.

The justice of this result has rarely been doubted, but the precise reason is difficult to explain in terms of legal concepts. The question, as Lord Buckmaster said in 1929, 'is one which in various forms has for over 200 years been the subject of vexed controversy'.[26] It cannot be explained in terms of property because the intended gift has not been completed according to the necessary legal formalities: 'it is because there is no one to whom the law can give relief...that relief, if any, must be sought in equity'.[27] Reference has been made in many of the cases to prevention of fraud, but, as elsewhere in equity, this does not mean actual wrongdoing: the fraud is the refusal to recognize the trust that equity imposes:

> It was contended...that the fraud for the avoidance of which the trust is enforced, must be the personal fraud of the legatee, but I think the answer is that, if it would be a fraud on the part of the legatees to refuse to carry out the trust, the residuary legatees cannot take advantage of and thus make themselves parties to such fraud.[28]

---

[23] Lord Simon in *Steadman v. Steadman* [1976] AC 536, HL, at 560.
[24] See B. Smith, 'Cumulative Reasons and Legal Method' 27 *Texas Law Review* 454 (1949).
[25] A. W. Scott, *The Law of Trusts* (Boston, 1939), s. 55.
[26] *Blackwell v. Blackwell* [1929] AC 318, HL, at 325.
[27] *Ibid.*, at 334 (Lord Sumner).   [28] *Ibid.*, at 342 (Lord Warrington).

Considerations of unjust enrichment have been prominent in these cases,[29] as the words 'take advantage of', just quoted, indicate, but it is not obvious, without assuming the result, that the enrichment is at the expense of the intended beneficiary rather than of the estate.[30] Restitution *to the estate* would, of course, be a most unattractive prospect, for it would completely defeat the testator's intention. Thus, considerations of intention and agreement are also relevant, and, as Peter Jaffey has pointed out,[31] there is a very close affinity between these cases and those of promises in favour of third party beneficiaries discussed in the last chapter.[32]

From the example earlier given of the university official who assures a student that she is enrolled it will be seen that the line between statement of fact and promise is indistinct. The official who makes the assertion might say 'your name is already on the list', or she might say 'I will enter your name on the list today (before the deadline)', or she might say 'I will accept your application tomorrow (after the deadline)'; the first of these utterances is a statement of fact; the last two are promises, but they all have the same practical effect of inducing the student to let the deadline pass. Lord St Leonards made this point in 1854 in a case where a bondholder promised not to enforce the bond, and the obligor changed his position in reliance. The majority held that there was no estoppel because this was a promise and not a statement of fact, but Lord St Leonards pointed out in dissent that there is scarcely a practical distinction between saying 'I have cancelled the bond, or have destroyed it or burnt it' and 'I have got the bond, but you may safely rely on it that I never intend to use it'.[33]

Protection was given to reliance on such promises in a number of nineteenth-century English and American cases.[34] In a New York case (1920) Justice Cardozo gave the hypothetical example of a land sale contract under which the seller agrees to change the wallpaper of a room, but, the buyer subsequently indicating that new wallpaper is not required, the seller accordingly leaves the old wallpaper in place. The buyer would not

---

[29] Scott, *Trusts*, s. 55.1; P. Birks, *An Introduction to the Law of Restitution* (Oxford, 1985), pp. 64–5, 135–6.

[30] L. Smith, 'Three-Party Restitution: A Critique of Birks's Theory of Interceptive Subtraction' (1991) 11 *Oxford Journal of Legal Studies* 481 at 513–14.

[31] P. Jaffey, *The Nature and Scope of Restitution* (Oxford, 2000), pp. 112, 265.

[32] See pp. 49–52, above.

[33] Lord St Leonards in *Jorden* v. *Money* (1854) 5 HLC 185; K. C. T. Sutton, *Consideration Reconsidered* (St Lucia, Queensland, 1974), p. 46.

[34] *Hughes* v. *Metropolitan Railway Co.* (1877) 2 App Cas 439, HL; *Birmingham & District Land Co.* v. *North West Railway Co.* (1888) 40 Ch D 268.

be permitted on the day of closing (completion) to reinstate his original contractual rights without notice so as to put the seller in default. Justice Cardozo added that (on reasonable notice) 'the buyer may change his mind again and revert to his agreement. He may not summarily rescind because of the breach which he has encouraged.'[35] This comment shows that Cardozo derived his principle not from any map or scheme, but from very general considerations of justice. He plainly did not consider that the buyer's indication amounted to a binding contract: on the contrary, he said that the 'buyer may change his mind'.

The relation of estoppel with other grounds of obligations presents difficult conceptual problems. Estoppel standing alone does not state a complete reason for imposing an obligation.[36] Conceptually speaking, it is more akin to a rule of evidence than to a substantive ground of obligation. The effect of estoppel has been, as we have seen, to protect reliance in various circumstances, but if every instance of reliance raised an estoppel, it would subsume much of contract law. In order to avert this consequence, various limits have been suggested, but none of them has been found entirely satisfactory. It has been suggested that estoppel applies only to statements of fact and not to promises,[37] but the distinction is hard to put into practice,[38] hard to justify in principle, and does not correspond with many of the actual decisions.[39] It has been suggested that estoppel can only operate as a defence or part of a cause of action, not as a cause of action in itself, and it has been linked, through the common law concept of waiver, with the idea of relinquishment of rights.[40] It is true that estoppel is an 'auxiliary' concept in the sense that it does not in itself seem to state a complete cause of action, but it is often a matter of chance which party is plaintiff and which defendant in litigation, and in practice, as we have seen in the examples discussed, estoppel often has had the practical effect of creating an obligation in favour of plaintiffs.[41]

---

[35] *Imperator Realty Co. Inc.* v. *Tull* 127 NE 263, at 267 (NYCA, 1920).
[36] 'Estoppel is not, as a contract is, a source of legal obligation', Goff J in *Amalgamated Investment & Property Co.* v. *Texas Commerce International Bank* [1982] QB 84, at 105.
[37] *Jordan* v. *Money* (1854) 5 HLC 185, *Citizens Bank of Louisiana* v. *First National Bank of New Orleans* (1873) LR 6 HL 352, 360, *Maddison* v. *Alderson* (1883) 8 App Cas 467, HL, at 473, *Chadwick* v. *Manning* [1896] AC 231, HL, at 238, *George Whitchurch Ltd* v. *Cavanagh* [1902] AC 117, HL, at 130, Sutton, *Consideration Reconsidered*, p. 45.
[38] See p. 64 above.   [39] E.g., *Waltons Stores* v. *Maher*, note 4 above.
[40] *Charles Rickards Ltd* v. *Oppenheim* [1950] 1 KB 616, CA.
[41] 'Its effect may be to enable a party to enforce a cause of action which, without the estoppel, would not exist', Goff J in *Amalgamated Investment & Property Co.* v. *Texas Commerce International Bank* [1982] QB 84 at 105.

In American jurisdictions the concept of promissory estoppel was widely used in a variety of contexts, particularly in order to enforce charitable subscriptions. In the first *Restatement of Contracts* (1932) a section (s. 90) was included as follows:

> A promise which the promisor should reasonably expect to induce action or forbearance of a definite and substantial character on the part of the promisee and which does induce such action or forbearance is binding if injustice can be avoided only by enforcement of the promise.

An important practical and theoretical question relates to the proper remedy. If reliance is the reason for enforcing the promise, there is a strong argument for restricting the remedy to the extent of the reliance. The point may be illustrated by considering a gratuitous promise to give valuable land on which the promisee then erects a small building; the effect of enforcing the promise in full would be to go much further than protection of reliance, substantially to enforce an incomplete gift, and to give the promisee the benefit of a bargain that had not been made.[42] Section 90 of the first *Restatement* said that the promise 'is binding'. In its context this meant fully binding, like other contractual obligations, and this reflected Williston's view.[43] Corbin, on the other hand, took the more flexible view that the remedy might be adjusted according to the extent of the promisee's reliance.[44] The question of classification was crucial here. Williston would no doubt have said that a limited remedy for reliance might be appropriate somewhere in the law, but not in a restatement of *contracts*. Corbin's view prevailed, however, in the *Second Restatement*, where the significant words were added at the end of the section: 'The remedy granted for breach may be limited as justice requires.'

The question whether the principle thus stated is truly 'part' of the law of contracts has not been answered, just because the question assumes a definitional precision that has been absent from the history of Anglo-American law. A complicating factor is that in jurisdictions where reliance has not been recognized as a ground of liability, other concepts have been enlarged: many cases that fall in American jurisdictions under section 90 of the *Restatement* have been categorized in English law, with some stretching

---

[42] See *Giumelli* v. *Giumelli*, note 11 above (money remedy only for promise to convey land on which plaintiff relied).

[43] S. Williston, *Selections from Williston's Treatise on the Law of Contracts* (rev. edn, New York, 1938), p. 202.

[44] A. L. Corbin, *Contracts* (12 vols., St Paul, 1964), vol. IA, s. 205.

of the concept of bargain, as unilateral contracts. If contract is defined strictly as bargain, the reliance principle is not properly part of contract law, for there is often no bargain; if contract is defined as consisting of promises fully enforceable as a matter of right, the principle (as qualified in the *Second Restatement*) must similarly be excluded, for the promisee's right is only to protection of reliance; if contracts are restricted to obligations voluntarily assumed by persons of full capacity, estoppel must be excluded, for, as Pollock pointed out, persons lacking contractual capacity (such as minors, or, in the days of Pollock's first edition, married women) may be estopped;[45] if contracts are taken to include all promises enforceable in whole or in part, then the principle is included, but it could plausibly be argued that the principle should then be stated in wider terms than 'promises', since it applies also to protect reliance on representations of fact, and on conduct amounting to silent acquiescence. But there is no other obvious location on any map of the law of obligations so far devised to which the principle could be readily allocated, for it requires neither wrongdoing nor unjust enrichment; as the principle is certainly of vital interest to every student of contract law, it has retained its closest associations there, but for pragmatic rather than theoretical reasons.

In 1970 Professor Grant Gilmore gave a series of lectures in Ohio, subsequently published as *The Death of Contract*, in which he suggested that section 90 of the *Restatement* could absorb the whole of contract law, which could disappear as an independent concept:

> What is happening is that 'contract' is being reabsorbed into the mainstream of 'tort' ... By passing through the magic gate of s. 90, it seems, we can rid ourselves of all the technical limitations of contract theory.[46]

The consequence of this approach would be to enforce only promises on which there had been actual reliance, and to give a right of enforcement only to the extent of that reliance. Shortly afterwards, in England, Patrick Atiyah was advancing the similar thesis that there was no justification for enforcement of promises except to the extent of actual proved reliance.[47]

---

[45] F. Pollock, *Principles of Contract at Law and in Equity* (London, 1876), p. 561. For an analysis of recent cases, see R. Hillman, 'Questioning the "New Consensus" on Promissory Estoppel: An Empirical and Theoretical Study' (1998) 98 *Columbia Law Review* 580.

[46] G. Gilmore, *The Death of Contract* (Columbus, Ohio, 1972), pp. 87, 90.

[47] P. S. Atiyah, 'Contracts, Promises and the Law of Obligations' (1978) 94 *Law Quarterly Review* 193, P. S. Atiyah, *Promises, Morals, and the Law* (Oxford, 1981), P. S. Atiyah, *The Rise and Fall of Freedom of Contract* (Oxford, 1979).

These suggestions aroused considerable academic interest, but had little impact on judicial decisions. Their effect would have been to reduce the remedy for breach of contract to the measure of the promisee's reliance, and to remove altogether the enforcement of purely executory contracts. It is true to say that protection of reliance has been an important effect of contract law, but it is a considerable step from that proposition to the conclusion that protection of reliance must be the *sole* purpose and effect of contract law. The proposals are of interest from the point of view of the present study, in that they suggest a simplification of legal concepts by abolishing the concept of 'contract'. But simplification of concepts, standing alone, is a very weak reason for making substantial legal changes, and for discarding legal rules found, over several centuries, to have answered the needs of justice. Convenience and elegance of concepts are not the primary ends to be attained by the legal system.

If, indeed, it could be convincingly claimed that the proposed changes were insubstantial in practice and merely restated in more convenient or elegant form the actual past practice of the courts, there would be a stronger case for the proposed simplification, but historical evidence does not support that claim. The principle suggested by Gilmore and Atiyah would cast doubt on many features of Anglo-American contract law as it has been administered in the past, notably the availability of specific enforcement, the enforceability of formal contracts, the ability of parties to treat their transactions as final, and the contractual allocation of risks;[48] it would be likely to reduce very substantially the degree to which contractual parties could, in practice, plan their actions with firm confidence that the counter-performance promised, or its equivalent, would be forthcoming.[49]

Where one party withdraws from contractual negotiations before formation of a binding contract, a remedy has sometimes been given to the other party for expenses incurred in anticipation of the contract. These cases are difficult to classify, as Ewan McKendrick has pointed out, mentioning, as possible bases of liability, 'breach of contract, unjust enrichment, tort, equitable or promissory estoppel, unjust sacrifice, *culpa in contrahendo* [fault in contracting], and breach of a duty of good faith and fair dealing'.[50] Where

---

[48] S. Waddams, 'The Modern Role of Contract Law' (1983) 8 *Canadian Business Law Journal* 2.
[49] L. Fuller and W. Perdue, 'The Reliance Interest in Contract Damages' (1936) 46 *Yale Law Journal* 52.
[50] E. McKendrick, 'Work Done in Anticipation of a Contract which does not Materialise', in W. R. Cornish and others (eds.), *Restitution, Past, Present, and Future* (Oxford, 1998), p. 163 at p. 167.

there is no corresponding benefit to the defendant it is difficult to explain liability as depending on unjust enrichment.[51] The fact that a contract was contemplated is important, but contractual principles alone do not explain the result, for, by hypothesis, the primary contract contemplated is not binding, and the implication of a secondary contract to pay a reasonable compensation is open to the observation that it is fictitious.[52] The idea of fault is present in the suggestion in some of the cases of the relevance of the defendant's unreasonable conduct in breaking off negotiations, with the implication that if the plaintiff had broken off negotiations there would be no liability;[53] yet it is not in itself a wrong to withdraw from incomplete negotiations, even for selfish reasons.[54] Goff and Jones concluded that 'it is not easy to glean any clear principles from this body of case law'.[55] As Jack Beatson has said, 'even within the law of restitution it is not possible to explain everything by reference to the principle of unjust enrichment, and . . . a further principle based on the need to protect injurious reliance is the basis for some restitutionary claims'.[56]

Estoppel, though it can, as we have seen, have far-reaching effects, does not itself describe any ground of obligation; it prevents a party from making certain assertions. For this reason estoppel can only operate in the framework of an otherwise recognized cause of action. The claimant must assert a cause of action that *if not contradicted* would be sufficient to support the result sought; the defendant may then be precluded from adducing the contradictory evidence. Estoppel has been effective where the parties are in some sort of near-contractual relationship, or where they have had dealings in respect of identifiable property, but it falls short of a rule that reliance will always be protected.

Statements of fact made with intent to deceive were, since early times, actionable as the tort of deceit, but liability did not, until the twentieth century, extend to statements that were merely careless. In 1914 the House

---

[51] For this reason *Estok* v. *Heguy* (1963) 40 DLR (2d) 88, where money spent on land was of no actual benefit to the landowner, is criticized by R. Goff and G. Jones, *The Law of Restitution* (3rd edn, London, 1986), p. 383. See also R. Dietrich, *Restitution: A New Perspective* (Sydney, 1998), p. 66.

[52] See Birks' comments (*Introduction*, p. 372) on *Way* v. *Latilla* [1937] 3 All ER 759, HL.

[53] *Brewer Street Investments Ltd* v. *Barclays Woollen Co. Ltd* [1954] 1 QB 428, *Sabemo* v. *North Sydney Municipal Council* [1977] 2 NSWLR 880.

[54] *Walford* v. *Miles* [1992] 2 AC 128, HL.

[55] Goff and Jones, *Restitution* (3rd edn), p. 510.

[56] J. Beatson, *The Use and Abuse of Unjust Enrichment* (Oxford, 1991), p. v. See also p. 21.

of Lords held that a solicitor was liable for carelessly inducing a person, to whom he owed a fiduciary duty, to take an improvident step,[57] and in the New York case of *Glanzer* v. *Shepherd*[58] (1922) a public weigher was held liable for overstating the weight of beans purchased. In 1963 the House of Lords held in *Hedley Byrne & Co Ltd* v. *Heller & Partners, Ltd*[59] that a bank might be liable to a lender for giving a negligent credit reference. In that case Lord Devlin, who gave the principal speech, stressed the close relationship of the principle he proposed with contract law, speaking of 'circumstances in which, but for the absence of consideration, there would be a contract', and limiting himself to the proposition that 'wherever there is a relationship equivalent to contract, there is a duty of care'.[60] It is difficult to say, however, just what relations that are not actually contractual are 'equivalent to contract', and subsequent cases have not insisted on this limitation.[61]

The conceptual basis of the obligation contemplated in *Hedley Byrne* v. *Heller* is wrongdoing, and, unlike liability for breach of contract, it requires proof of negligence. It might be thought to follow also that proof of negligence, combined with foreseeability of harm, would be sufficient to justify liability, as in negligence law generally, but liability for negligent misrepresentation has in certain respects resisted assimilation into the general law of negligence. Thus, it has been held that negligent advice, although it causes loss by inducing the plaintiff to enter into a losing transaction, only leads to liability in respect of the kind of loss in respect of which it was the defendant's duty to advise.[62] It has been held also that the managing director of a franchisor corporation who makes a negligent statement that induces the plaintiff to enter into a losing franchise contract is not personally liable in the absence of an 'assumption of personal responsibility'.[63] Here the logic of tort law seemed to point to liability, for the reliance on the statement was clearly proved, and loss to the franchisee was obviously foreseeable as highly probable if the statement should prove false. But the counterargument was that the imposition of a personal obligation would subvert

---

[57] *Nocton* v. *Ashburton* [1914] AC 932, HL.   [58] 233 NY 236 (1922).
[59] [1964] AC 465, HL.   [60] *Ibid.*, at 529–30.
[61] *Smith* v. *Eric S. Bush* [1990] 1 AC 831, HL, *Queen* v. *Cognos Inc.* [1993] 1 SCR 87, 110.
[62] *Banque Bruxelles Lambert SA* v. *Eagle Star Insurance Co. Ltd* [1997] AC 191, HL (Lord Hoffmann at 211, 212).
[63] See *Williams* v. *Natural Life Health Foods Ltd* [1998] 1 WLR 830, HL.

the general understanding of both parties that the plaintiff was dealing with the corporation only, and should look to the corporation, and not to its individual officers, for compensation for losses arising out of the transaction. This general consideration prevailed over strict logic. Lord Steyn (who spoke for the House of Lords) expressly recognized that the requirement of assumption of responsibility might be, from a purely conceptual point of view, illogical and even (he suggested) incoherent, but he said, rejecting academic comment on this point,

> In my view the general [academic] criticism is overstated. Coherence must sometimes yield to practical justice... [W]hile the present structure of English contract law remains intact the law of tort, as the general law, has to fulfil an essential gap-filling role. In these circumstances there was, and is, no better rationalisation for the relevant head of tort liability than assumption of responsibility.[64]

The Supreme Court of Canada has in somewhat similar manner declined to impose liability on a party to contractual negotiation for loss negligently caused to the opposite party. Although the requirements of negligence liability as stated in former cases (duty of care, breach, proximity) were apparently satisfied, the court found that there were 'compelling policy reasons to conclude that one commercial party should not have to be mindful of another commercial party's legitimate interests in an arm's length negotiation'.[65]

Fraudulent and negligent misrepresentations may be analysed in terms of wrongs, but innocent misrepresentation is not in itself a wrong, nor is it a breach of contract. Here considerations of unjust enrichment have been prominent. In the leading case on rescission of contracts for misrepresentation a transaction induced by a false statement was set aside, even though the statement was not made fraudulently or negligently. The court did not use the words 'unjust enrichment', but the concept was plainly influential:

> A man is not to be allowed to get a benefit from a statement which he now admits to be false... Even assuming moral fraud must be shewn in order to set aside a contract, you have it where a man, having obtained a beneficial contract by a statement which he now admits to be false, insists upon keeping

---

[64] *Ibid.*, at 837.
[65] *Martel Building Ltd* v. *Canada* [2000] 2 SCR 860 at 882, 193 DLR (4th) 1 at 17.

that contract. To do so is a moral delinquency: no man ought to seek to take advantage of his own false statements.[66]

The concepts of benefit obtained and kept, and of advantage taken, are founded on unjust enrichment (in the general sense of that phrase). The 'moral delinquency' is not wrongdoing in the ordinary sense, but, as in the cases of proprietary estoppel discussed earlier, and of unconscionability, a species of equitable fraud: what is wrongful is not the making of the false statement but the attempt to take what equity considers to be an unfair advantage. But enrichment, standing alone, would not justify setting aside a valid contract, even when combined with some degree of mistake. An enrichment caused by mistake may be called an unjust enrichment, but to set aside a contract for mistake it must be shown that the mistake was so radical as to overcome the reasons in favour of enforcing an otherwise valid contract,[67] whereas relief for misrepresentation has been available on proof simply that the misrepresentation was 'material' (i.e. that it induced the transaction).[68] Mistake alone would not have supported relief, but mistake combined with the factor that it was induced by reliance on the very words or conduct (albeit innocent) of the party seeking enforcement, was found sufficient.

Most important contracts in modern times are not entered into by the parties personally, but by means of agents on one or both sides. Commonly an agent, anxious to conclude a transaction, exceeds his authority. If contractual obligation depended on subjective intention or will, the principal would not in such a case be responsible. But the most prominent rule of agency law is that a principal may be liable for acts of the agent that have not been authorized. The effect is to protect a third party who deals with the agent in reliance on the supposition that the agent has the principal's authority. The obligation thereby imposed on the principal does not depend on actual consent, and cannot be assimilated entirely even to the objective principle of contractual liability.[69] Explanations have been offered in terms of wrongdoing,[70] estoppel, unjust enrichment, risk allocation, enterprise

---

[66] *Redgrave* v. *Hurd* (1881) 20 Ch D 1 at 12–13.
[67] See chapter 8 below.   [68] *Redgrave* v. *Hurd* (1881) 20 Ch D 1.
[69] The doctrine of undisclosed principal 'is certainly difficult to accommodate within standard theories of contract', F. Reynolds, *Bowstead and Reynolds on Agency* (16th edn, London, 1996), p. 409. Ratification also presents difficulties, *ibid.*, p. 62.
[70] G. McMeel, 'Philosophical Foundations of the Law of Agency' (2000) 116 *Law Quarterly Review* 387 at 410 points to analogies with vicarious liability in tort.

liability, and public policy, for it is the principal who usually sets the train of events in motion, and whose enterprise is expected to benefit from the agent's activities.[71] None of these concepts has been sufficient in itself to explain or justify the law of agency, but cumulatively they have been effective. As Gerard McMeel has said, 'each illuminates different facets of a complex structure'.[72]

Trust, confidence, and reliance are closely related concepts, and where common law courts have failed to protect reliance the law has often been supplemented by the equitable concept of fiduciary duty. An example previously mentioned is *Nocton* v. *Ashburton*[73] (1914) where a solicitor was held liable for negligent misrepresentation fifty years before a general duty in such circumstances was recognized in English law. The concept of fiduciary duty, though of pervasive and fundamental importance in Anglo-American private law, has usually, with notable exceptions,[74] been omitted from conceptual maps and diagrams. Fiduciary relations cannot be allocated to the law of property to the exclusion of obligations, or vice versa; nor can they be subordinated to contracts, wrongdoing, or unjust enrichment; nor can they be visualized as parallel to but separate from these concepts, for they have close affinities with all of them. As with other equitable concepts,[75] their very function has been, in a sense, to subvert the categories established by the common law. The concepts of wrongdoing, contracts, unjust enrichment, property, and public policy have operated with cumulative effect. Breach of fiduciary duty, though not a common law tort, is a wrong. But it depends not on a duty 'towards persons generally'[76] but on a fiduciary relationship between claimant and defendant, which usually, though not always,[77] springs from a contract between them.

Benefits derived from breach of fiduciary duty must be restored. This aspect of fiduciary duties has been treated by many writers as part of the law of unjust enrichment.[78] Other writers have objected, however, that restitution

---

[71] W. Seavey, 'The Rationale of Agency' (1920) 29 *Yale Law Journal* 859.

[72] G. McMeel, 'Philosophical Foundations' note 70 above.   [73] [1914] AC 932, HL.

[74] E. Weinrib, 'The Juridical Classification of Obligations', in P. Birks (ed.), *The Classification of Obligations* (Oxford, 1997), p. 37.

[75] See chapter 9 below.

[76] P. H. Winfield, *The Province of the Law of Tort* (Cambridge, 1931), p. 32.

[77] An adult, for example, may be a fiduciary for a young child.

[78] R. Goff and G. Jones, *The Law of Restitution* (5th edn, London, 1998), p. 718, P. Maddaugh and J. McCamus, *The Law of Restitution* (Toronto, 1990), pp. 33, 52–3, G. Palmer, *The Law of Restitution* (4 vols., Boston, 1978), vol. I, p. 141, A. Burrows, *The Law of Restitution* (London, 1993).

of profits depends on proof of wrongdoing and therefore belongs to the law of wrongs.[79] From a historical perspective both views are correct: unjust enrichment is an important reason for requiring profits to be restored; but it is true also that the result cannot be attributed to unjust enrichment considered in isolation from other legal concepts. An important feature of fiduciary duties is that the claimant can often assert, in addition to a personal obligation, a property interest in such benefits and in their proceeds. This has crucial consequences where the recipient is insolvent,[80] and has caused a sharp division of opinion among courts and commentators.[81]

Considerations of public policy have played a prominent role in the establishment of fiduciary relationships and in the extension of the consequences of breach of them. Justice Cardozo called the fiduciary concept 'part of a pervasive policy of the law to protect the integrity of commercial organizations'.[82] Paul Finn has said that 'it originates, self-evidently, in public policy'.[83] In *Norberg v. Wynrib*,[84] a physician who had taken advantage of a patient's dependence on drugs for his own sexual gratification was held by two members of the Supreme Court to be a fiduciary, and to be liable for aggravated and punitive damages. The judgments have strong moral and public policy overtones. Again, in *Hodgkinson v. Simms*,[85] an accountant on whom an investor had relied for advice was held to be a fiduciary, and to be liable for loss caused by a general decline in market values, in addition to an obligation to restore profit derived from the transaction. La Forest J said that 'the remedy of disgorgement... is simply insufficient to guard against the type of abusive behaviour engaged in... in this case. The law of fiduciary duties has always contained within it an element of deterrence.'[86]

The fluidity of the concept of fiduciary duty, its proprietary implications, its interaction with concepts of contract, wrongdoing, and unjust enrichment, and its response to changing views of public policy all militate against the easy inclusion of fiduciary duties on any map or diagrammatic scheme of private law.

---

[79] P. Birks and C. Mitchell in *English Private Law* (Oxford, 2000), 15.04–08, 15.180n, and other writings of Birks; see chapter 6 below.

[80] *Chase Manhattan Bank v. British Israel Bank (London) Ltd* [1981] Ch 105.

[81] See chapter 9 below.

[82] *Beatty v. Guggenheim Exploration Co.* 122 NE 378, 380 (NYCA, 1919).

[83] P. Finn, 'Contract and the Fiduciary Principle' (1989) 12 *University of New South Wales Law Review* 76.

[84] [1992] 2 SCR 226, 92 DLR (4th) 449.   [85] [1994] 3 SCR 377, 117 DLR (4th) 161.

[86] *Ibid.*, at 208–9.

Cases involving the misuse of confidential information, often described as 'sui generis',[87] have also been said to be 'distinct' from but 'intertwined' with the law of fiduciary duty.[88] Francis Gurry has written that 'attempts to confine it exclusively within one conventional jurisdictional category should be resisted'.[89] In the notorious case of *Prince Albert* v. *Strange* (1849), a bookseller and publisher, William Strange, had come into possession of copies of private etchings and engravings made personally by Queen Victoria and Prince Albert, the copies having been obtained surreptitiously by another person. Strange was restrained not only from publishing copies of the engravings themselves,[90] but from publishing a descriptive catalogue of them. Strange's conduct was, no doubt, perceived at the time as a disgraceful invasion of royal privacy, but it was not obvious that it fell into any known category of legal wrong. The Queen and the Prince had no property in the catalogue, and Strange was in breach of no personal obligation, and had committed no wrong previously recognized by the common law.[91] Counsel for the defendant, though expressly disavowing any 'sympathy with the defendant privately',[92] opposed the injunction precisely on this ground:

> A confusion seems to be created by mixing up the several distinct matters which compose the whole. First there is a right of property in the canvas of a painting; and, secondly, there is a right of property in the form of the idea which adorns the canvas...And, further, if a party is bound by any contract, he may be restrained from using the knowledge he has obtained respecting the painting...But the possessor, independently of contract, has no right or property in the idea which is acquired by another party from a knowledge of that particular chattel...[93]

Counsel argued that 'in all cases the jurisdiction is founded on property or upon breach of contract or of confidence'.[94] But the Lord Chancellor (Cottenham) rejected the dichotomy, and put his decision on both grounds:

---

[87] G. Jones, 'Restitution of Benefits Obtained in Breach of Another's Confidence' (1970) 86 *Law Quarterly Review* 463 at 464; F. Gurry, *Breach of Confidence* (Oxford, 1984), pp. 26, 58–61 (chapter title 'A Sui Generis Action'), *Cadbury Schweppes Inc.* v. *FBI Foods Ltd* [1999] 1 SCR 142 at 158, 162.

[88] La Forest J in *LAC Minerals Ltd* v. *International Corona Ltd* [1989] 2 SCR 579 at 657.

[89] Gurry, *Breach of Confidence*, p. 26.

[90] This was conceded by the time the case was argued before the Lord Chancellor, 12 LT 441.

[91] 12 LT 441.   [92] *Ibid.*   [93] 1 H & Tw 9, at 10.   [94] 12 LT 441.

It was argued by one of the defendant's counsel that the case for injunction must rest on *one either* of two grounds – of property in the plaintiff, or breach of contract or of trust by the defendant. It is my opinion that *both* these grounds exist in this case[95] ... Upon the first question, ... that of property, I am clearly of opinion, that, the exclusive right and interest of the plaintiff in the composition and works in question being established ... the plaintiff is entitled to the injunction ... But this case by no means depends solely on the question of property; for a breach of trust, confidence, or contract itself would entitle the plaintiff to the injunction ... The possession of the defendant ... must have originated in a breach of trust, confidence, or contract in Brown, or some person in his employ, taking more impressions than were ordered ... I am bound to assume that the possession of the etchings or engravings, on the part of the defendant ... has its foundation in a breach of trust, confidence or contract.[96]

This takes the concept of property beyond anything recognized at common law;[97] considerations of wrongdoing,[98] breach of contract, and breach of fiduciary obligation were also in play, and all interrelated with each other and with the concept of property. The concept of unjust enrichment,[99] though not by that name, also had appeared strongly in the court below:

That the object of printing and publishing the catalogue was money, was gain, no man, of course, can doubt: and that it would be very saleable ... is highly probable. What, however, can be the defendant's right, or that of any person but the owners of the plates, to this benefit? It is for them to use, or bestow or withhold, nor can a stranger be allowed to say that they do not want it. They alone are entitled to decide whether, and when, and how, and for whose advantage, their property shall be made use of.[100]

Considerations of public policy were also plainly influential. The Vice-Chancellor who heard the case at first instance described the defendant's conduct as

---

[95] 12 LT 442 (emphasis added).   [96] 1 H & Tw 9 at 24.
[97] As Gurry points out, *Breach of Confidence*, p. 50, the case goes beyond statutory or common law copyright in recognizing 'a proprietary right in the substance of the information'.
[98] See P. M. North, 'Breach of Confidence: Is There a New Tort?' (1973) 12 *Journal of the Society of Public Teachers of Law* 149.
[99] But Birks and Mitchell, in *English Private Law*, 15.04, treat abuse of confidence as belonging 'wholly to the law of wrongs, not the law of unjust enrichment'.
[100] 2 De G & Sm 652 at 698 (Knight Bruce V-C).

An intrusion not only in breach of conventional rules, but offensive to that inbred sense of propriety natural to every man – if intrusion, indeed, fitly describes a sordid spying into the privacy of domestic life – into the home (a word hitherto sacred among us), the home of a family whose life and conduct form an acknowledged title ... to the most marked respect in this country.[101]

Two years later, in *Morison v. Moat* (1851), a case involving a secret medical formula, another Vice-Chancellor also stressed the interrelation of concepts:

Different grounds have indeed been assigned for the exercise of that jurisdiction. In some cases it has been referred to property, in others to contract, and in others, again, it has been treated as founded upon trust or confidence, meaning, as I conceive, that the Court fastens the obligation on the conscience of the party, and enforces it against him in the same manner as it enforces against a party to whom a benefit is given the obligation of performing a promise on the faith of which the benefit has been conferred: but upon whatever grounds the jurisdiction is founded, the authorities leave no doubt as to the exercise of it.[102]

Later cases have stressed considerations of public policy. In *Argyll v. Argyll* (1967) the Duke of Argyll was restrained at the suit of his former wife from publishing confidential details about their marriage. The court said of confidential communications between husband and wife that 'preservation of those communications inviolate is an objective of public policy', referring later to the policy of the law as 'the basis of the court's jurisdiction'.[103] The possibility of countervailing public policy interests has also been recognized. In *Norwich Pharmacal Co. v. Customs and Excise Commissioners*,[104] Lord Denning said:

The cases show that the public interest has two sides to it. On the one hand it is usually in the public interest that when information is received in confidence ... it should not be used for other purposes ... On the other hand, confidences will sometimes be overcome by a higher public interest, such as the interest of justice itself, the prevention of wrongdoing, or the security of the State ... So in every case it is a question of weighing the public interest. The courts must consider the relationship and rule upon it as and when it comes before them.

[101] *Ibid.*, at 697–8.   [102] 9 Hare 241 at 255 (Turner V-C).
[103] *Argyll v. Argyll* [1967] 1 Ch 302 at 324, 332. See Gurry, *Breach of Confidence*, p. 26.
[104] [1974] AC 133, CA, at 140–1.

In the modern Canadian case of *LAC Minerals Ltd* v. *International Corona Resources Ltd*[105] (1989) the plaintiff revealed valuable information in anticipation of a joint venture with the defendant. No joint venture resulted, but the defendant took advantage of the information to acquire land for its own benefit. Three of the five judges in the Supreme Court of Canada held the defendant liable for breach of confidence, and two for breach of fiduciary duty. A differently constituted majority held that the plaintiff was entitled to a proprietary interest in the land acquired by the defendant. Considerations of reliance, unjust enrichment, property, contract, wrongdoing, and public policy were all clearly influential. As Sopinka J said, 'the foundation of [the] action for breach of confidence does not rest solely on one of the traditional jurisdictional bases for action of contract, equity, or property. The action is *sui generis* relying on all three to enforce the policy of the law that confidences be respected.'[106]

Very similar (though not involving a misuse of confidential information in the usual sense) is the situation where the defendant acquires property on the understanding that it will be shared with the plaintiff, and the plaintiff in reliance on the understanding refrains from attempting to acquire the property independently. In these cases the understanding is too uncertain or too preliminary to constitute a contract. The defendant's conduct is not, in the ordinary sense, wrongful. The usual requirements of unjust enrichment are not satisfied, for the plaintiff may not have suffered any loss corresponding to the defendant's gain. Nor does the plaintiff lose any pre-existing property interest. But considerations of contract, enrichment,[107] wrongdoing, and property, together with the concept of fiduciary relationship and general considerations of public policy have combined to support the imposition in these circumstances of a constructive trust:[108]

> Equity will intervene by way of constructive trust, not only to compel a defendant to restore the plaintiff's property to him, but also to require a defendant to disgorge property which should have been acquired, if at all, for the plaintiff. In the latter category of case, the defendant's wrong lies not in the acquisition of the property, which may or may not have been lawful, but in his subsequent denial of the plaintiff's beneficial interest . . .

---

[105] [1989] 2 SCR 574, 61 DLR (4th) 14.   [106] *Ibid.*, at 615 (SCR), 74 (DLR).

[107] Maddaugh and McCamus include these cases in *The Law of Restitution*, p. 649.

[108] *Chattock* v. *Muller* (1878) 8 Ch D 177; *Pallant* v. *Morgan* [1953] Ch 43, *Banner Homes Group Plc.* v. *Luff Developments Ltd* [2000] Ch 372, CA.

[The defendant's] possession of the property is coloured from the start by the trust and confidence by means of which he obtained it, and his subsequent appropriation of the property to his own use is a breach of that trust.[109]

A map or diagram that supposes a separation between property and obligations, and the whole field of obligations occupied by contract, wrongs, and unjust enrichment, cannot accommodate the cases discussed in this chapter. They cannot be assimilated with contracts because there is no requirement of bargain, consideration, or promise, and because the remedy does not always correspond to the plaintiff's expectation; nor can contracts be subordinated to reliance, or vice versa. The cases cannot be assimilated with wrongdoing, because the obligation arises without any wrongful conduct; although it is possible to say that the defendant acts wrongly, once having induced the plaintiff's reliance, in failing to protect it, this 'wrong' is the failure to satisfy the obligation that the law *has imposed* (to protect the reliance), and cannot itself constitute the reason for the obligation. Failure to acknowledge an obligation cannot be the reason for imposing it. Nor can the cases be assimilated with unjust enrichment because in many of them the defendant is not enriched, and the amount awarded has not usually been measured by enrichment. The concepts of obligation and property cannot be disentangled: in the proprietary estoppel cases, for example, as in other kinds of equitable case, the consequence of the court's judgment has undoubtedly been to create property interests, but the primary reason for the intervention of equity has not been in any real sense to vindicate prior property rights, but rather to afford a protection to reliance that the ordinary law of obligations had failed to give. The establishment of a fourth category of obligations, or consignment of the reliance cases to a separate 'miscellaneous' category, would scarcely resolve the difficulties, because reliance has not been so much *separate* from the concepts of property, contract, tort, and unjust enrichment, as intimately linked with all of them.

---

[109] [2000] Ch 372 at 397.

5

Liability for physical harms

It follows from the idea of correction of wrongs that compensation is due for injury wrongfully caused to person or property, but the converse proposition, namely that in the absence of wrongdoing there is no liability, cannot be asserted of Anglo-American law without many explanations, qualifications, and exceptions. Frederick Pollock said (1923), with some acerbity, of what he called 'the dogma of "no liability without fault"', and which he thought to be 'more or less prevalent in certain American law schools', that 'as an English lawyer I can only say that we never heard of it here. Stated as a general proposition, it is contrary to the whole law of trespass, to much of the law of nuisance, to the whole law of defamation, and to the responsibility of principals for their agents.'[1] Lord Wright made a similar comment fifteen years later on the same maxim (no liability without fault): 'That may be regarded as a statement of an ideal of what the law should be, or of the existing law. In the latter sense it is demonstrably inaccurate, whether we look at the old or the modern common law.'[2] In many kinds of case liability has been imposed for harm to person or property without proof of wrongdoing in the ordinary sense of blameworthy conduct. Since some of these cases have been classed as legal wrongs and some have not, and since writers address themselves to different questions, some historical and some not, and since writers define their own terms, discussion of these matters is laden with terminological, rhetorical, historical, and linguistic difficulties. The purpose of the present enquiry is to examine instances in past Anglo-American law of liability for physical harms that have been influenced by more than one concept, and that cannot readily be allocated to a single category.

[1] F. Pollock, 'A Plea for Historical Interpretation' (1923) 39 *Law Quarterly Review* 162 at 167.
[2] Lecture at Harvard Law School (1938), reprinted in Lord Wright of Durley, *Legal Essays and Addresses* (Cambridge, 1939), p. 124.

Legal categories have not always corresponded with the concepts they suggest. Thus, suppliers of defective goods have been held liable for personal injury and property damage on the basis of breach of implied warranty that the goods are reasonably fit for their purpose. Formally the basis of liability has been contractual, but the practical effect of the objective principle of contract formation combined with liability for consequential damages has been to impose on a business supplier an obligation that can be explained neither in purely contractual terms, nor purely in terms of wrongdoing.[3]

A somewhat less obvious illustration arises from the objective test of negligence. A defendant whose conduct falls short of what is objectively reasonable has not been excused from liability even though her conduct was due to inexperience or inherent incapacity for which she was not to blame, or to a momentary and pardonable lapse of judgment.[4] Holmes (1881) considered this a 'dilemma', a term which he later elaborated by saying 'that at the bottom of liability there is a notion of blameworthiness but yet that the defendant's blameworthiness is not material'.[5] Tony Honoré has said: 'the objective standard of competence, though purporting to be based wholly on fault, really imposes a form of strict liability'.[6] John Fleming wrote, for this reason, that 'moral blameworthiness and legal default do not invariably coincide' and that 'considerations of moral fault are out of place especially in relation to traffic accidents where personal liability has been largely displaced by insurance'.[7] It was in the context of a traffic accident that Lord Denning said, in 1971, of an inexperienced driver, that

> The learner-driver may be doing his best, but his incompetent best is not good enough... Thus we are, in this branch of the law, moving away from the concept 'no liability without fault'. We are beginning to apply the test, 'On whom should the risk fall?' Morally the learner-driver is not at fault; but legally she is liable to be because she is insured and the risk should fall on her.[8]

---

[3] See pp. 97–9 below.
[4] *Vaughan* v. *Menlove* (1837) 3 Bing NC 468, *Commonwealth* v. *Pierce* (1884) 138 Mass 165.
[5] O. W. Holmes, *The Common Law*, ed. M. Howe (Boston, 1963 [1881]), p. 86 (marginal note in Holmes' copy of *The Common Law*).
[6] T. Honoré, 'Responsibility and Luck' (1988) 104 *Law Quarterly Review* 530. See also P. Birks, 'The Concept of a Civil Wrong', in D. G. Owen (ed.), *Philosophical Foundations of Tort Law* (Oxford, 1995) p. 45, A. A. Ehrenzweig, 'Negligence Without Fault' 54 *Columbia Law Review* 1422 (1966).
[7] J. Fleming, *The Law of Torts* (5th edn, Sydney, 1977), pp. 108, 113.
[8] *Nettleship* v. *Weston* [1971] 3 All ER 581, CA, 586, *Roberts* v. *Ramsbottom* [1980] 1 WLR 823.

In several other kinds of case the law has imposed liability to make compensation for harm even though the person causing the harm has committed no fault. These cases include general average, expropriation, nuisance, flooding of land, harm caused by unusual and hazardous enterprises, vicarious liability, products liability, liability for animals, and cases where there is a defence of necessity. They cannot be fully explained in terms of wrongdoing (in the ordinary sense of the word), but neither can they readily be explained in terms of any other single concept. The examination of the cases shows that concepts of contract, unjust enrichment, property, and public policy, as well as the concept of wrongdoing, have been influential. 'As a matter of history', Pollock wrote in 1887, 'such cases cannot easily be referred to any definite principle.'[9] Twenty years later he wrote that 'the classification of actionable wrongs is perplexing, not because it is difficult to find a scheme of division, but because it is easier to find many than to adhere to any one of them': whichever of the plaintiff's loss or the defendant's conduct is taken as 'the primary line of distinction, the results can seldom be worked out without calling in the other'.[10]

Maritime emergencies sometimes require the jettison of goods. Where this occurs all the other owners of cargo and the ship itself have, from early times,[11] been treated as participants in a common adventure and required to make a proportionate contribution to the loss.[12] The master, in ordering the jettison, deliberately destroys the claimant's goods, but he commits no wrong; still less do the owners of goods not jettisoned commit any wrong, yet they are all bound to contribute. The law of general average contribution incorporates several legal concepts. Contractual considerations have been influential but, considered alone, cannot satisfactorily explain these cases.[13]

---

[9] F. Pollock, *The Law of Torts* (London, 1887), p. 393.

[10] *Encyclopaedia Britannica* (11th edn, 29 vols., Cambridge, 1910–11), vol. xxvii, p. 64.

[11] The principle was part of the very ancient Rhodian Sea Law, and recognized by Roman law: V. Heutger, 'Lex Rhodia and Unjust Enrichment' in E. J. H. Schrage (ed.), *Unjust Enrichment and the Law of Contract* (The Hague, 2001), p. 217.

[12] M. Mustill and J. Gilman (eds.), *Arnould's Law of Marine Insurance and Average* (16th edn, London, 1981), c. 26, R. Colinvaux (ed.), *Carver's Carriage by Sea* (13th edn, London, 1982), c. 14, D. Wilson and J. Cooke (eds.), *Lowndes and Rudolph, General Average and the York–Antwerp Rules* (11th edn, London, 1990), 00.09–00.30.

[13] *Burton v. English* (1883) 12 QBD 218 at 220–21 (Brett MR), *Milburn v. Jamaica Fruit Importing Co.* [1900] 2 QB 540 at 546, 550, Carver, *Carriage of Goods by Sea* (6th edn, London, 1918), para. 364.

Principles of unjust enrichment have been of primary importance,[14] but not all cases of general average are cases of unjust enrichment,[15] for payment of average may be required even though the facts show that no benefit was derived from the sacrifice.[16] Francis Rose, while leaving open the question of whether general average is strictly a part of the law of unjust enrichment, has emphasized its close affinity: 'it is clear that many of the principles which govern the law of restitution [unjust enrichment] also operate within… general average'.[17] Public policy is also relevant to this branch of maritime law, for it is in the public interest that owners of goods should sacrifice them in order to save life and the property of others. General average is sometimes treated as analogous to cases of compulsory contribution to another person's legal obligation.[18] There is certainly some force in this analogy, but the jettison of goods from a ship resembles much more closely an *expropriation* by the master in the interests of the common adventure.[19]

The expropriation or taking of land for public use is an everyday occurrence and, in most jurisdictions, legislation provides for payment of reasonable compensation. The fact that legislation is often operative and effective does not, however, mean that the subject is unrelated to judicial reasoning. The existence of the legislation, and in the United States of an express constitutional provision,[20] show that it is consistent with public policy that, if an individual is called upon to sacrifice his or her property for the public welfare, the public should pay a fair price. Otherwise the community at large would be enriched at the expense of the individual property owner. Legislation is never comprehensive, and from time to time issues of expropriation arise outside a statutory framework. Expropriation

---

[14] The subject was included by R. Goff and G. Jones in *The Law of Restitution* (London, 1966), but has been omitted from other books on the subject.

[15] See J. Dietrich, *Restitution: A New Perspective* (Sydney, 1998), p. 157.

[16] Because it proves to be unnecessary or futile. Colinvaux, *Carver's Carriage by Sea*, p. 976, para. 1361, Mustill and Gilman, *Arnould*, para 919. It has been held to be otherwise if, because of a mistake of fact, there is no peril at all: *Joseph Watson and Sons Ltd* v. *Firemen's Fund Ins. Co. of San Francisco* [1922] 2 KB 355.

[17] F. D. Rose, 'Restitution and Maritime Law' in Schrage (ed.), *Unjust Enrichment*, p. 367 at p. 380.

[18] Goff and Jones, *The Law of Restitution*, p. 174 (though saying that it is 'sui generis'), and subsequent editions.

[19] G. Virgo, *Principles of the Law of Restitution* (Oxford, 1999), p. 322, considers the doctrine of general average to fall within the law of restitution for unjust enrichment, but places it under 'necessity'. J. Dietrich, *Restitution: A New Perspective* (Sydney, 1998), p. 157, rejects unjust enrichment as the basis of general average.

[20] Fifth Amendment (1791).

(usually in wartime) may occur by prerogative power, and in such cases the property owner has been held to be entitled to compensation,[21] one of the principal reasons being that 'it was equitable that burdens borne for the good of the nation should be distributed over the whole nation and should not be allowed to fall on particular individuals'.[22] Where there is a statutory power but no express provision for compensation, an obligation to pay compensation has been implied.[23] Considerations of unjust enrichment are evidently very prominent here, but, as with general average, it would be difficult to explain the law exclusively on that basis, because compensation has been payable even though no benefit has in fact been derived by the government: for example, where an oil refinery is destroyed to prevent its falling into the hands of an enemy, the facts may show that the destruction was unnecessary, the enemy advance being later halted short of the refinery, or the enemy having, as it turns out, no use for the refinery.

Property may be destroyed or damaged by governmental authorities in peacetime in order to prevent the spread of fire, or in order to impede the activities of criminals. Livestock may be destroyed to prevent the spread of disease. The land of one person may be deliberately flooded in order to protect other landowners, or to benefit the public at large. Property may be injuriously affected by countless other kinds of government action.[24] In such cases the authorities do no wrong, but, as the severity of the damage increases – especially as it approaches destruction of the property – so does the force of the argument for payment of compensation, for otherwise those benefited would be (in a general sense) unjustly enriched. Tony Jolowicz has said in this context that 'it is difficult to think of a stronger case for compensation out of public funds'.[25] John Fleming wrote that 'if property

---

[21] *Burmah Oil* v. *Lord Advocate* [1965] AC 75, HL. The speeches of the majority make it clear that the value of the property to the claimant must be discounted by the probability of its falling into enemy hands if not expropriated. A similar discounting may be appropriate in respect of general average, if the property might have been lost in any event: Colinvaux, *Carver's Carriage by Sea*, para. 1361. But in *United States* v. *Caltex (Philippines) Inc.* (1952) 344 US 149, on similar facts, the US Supreme Court held that there was no right to compensation under the Fifth Amendment to the US Constitution.

[22] *Attorney General* v. *De Keyser's Royal Hotel* [1920] AC 508, HL, at 553 (Lord Moulton).

[23] *Attorney General* v. *De Keyser's Royal Hotel*, note 22 above, *BC Power Corp Ltd* v. *A-G BC* (1962) 34 DLR (2d) 25 at 44, *Manitoba Fisheries Ltd* v. *R* [1979] 1 SCR 101, 88 DLR (3d) 462, *R* v. *Tener* [1985] 1 SCR 533, 17 DLR (4th) 1, *Cream Silver Mines Ltd* v. *British Columbia* (1991) 85 DLR (4th) 269 at 282–3.

[24] *City of Toronto* v. *J. F. Brown Co.* (1917) 55 SCR 153.

[25] J. A. Jolowicz, 'Public Interest and Private Damage' [1985] *Cambridge Law Journal* 370 at 371.

is sacrificed in the public interest by a public agent, democratic values might well suggest that the cost be borne by the community. This principle is widely recognized in the statutory, if not constitutional, obligation to provide fair compensation for property taken for public purposes under powers of eminent domain.' But, as Fleming also pointed out, Anglo-American law has not been consistent on this question.[26] Often in such cases the statute that authorizes the damage or destruction has provided for compensation,[27] or compensation has been made by administrative practice.[28] Obligations to compensate have also sometimes been imposed on the basis of nuisance.[29]

Flooding commonly gives rise to situations where a person can preserve his own property only by damaging a neighbour's. In *Whalley v. Lancashire and Yorkshire Railway Co.*[30] the defendant's railway embankment was threatened by accumulated flood water, and in order to prevent its collapse the defendant cut trenches in it, flooding the plaintiff's land. The jury found that the cutting of the trenches was reasonably necessary for the protection of the defendant's property, and that it was not done negligently. They awarded £130, the amount of the additional damage to the plaintiff over and above what would have occurred in any event. The court upheld the verdict, though not altogether without trouble, finding that the case 'raises points of some difficulty and nicety':[31]

> But now comes this question, the danger has not been brought by a person on his own land, but it has come there – an extraordinary danger – which, if left standing there, will injure his property, but not that of his neighbour. Can he then, in order to get rid of and cure the misfortune which has so happened to himself, do something which will transfer the misfortune to his neighbour? That seems to be contrary to the well known maxim that you must not, when you have the choice, elect to use your own property so as to cause injury to your neighbour ... The defendants did something for the preservation of their own property which transferred the misfortune from their land to that

---

[26] J. Fleming, *The Law of Torts* (9th edn, Sydney, 1998), p. 104, referring to *Rigby* v. *Chief Constable* [1985] 1 WLR 1242, and *Lapierre* v. *A-G* [1985] 1 SCR 241.

[27] Water Resources Act 1991 s. 177 sch. 21 para. 5(1), Land Drainage Act 1991 s. 14(5).

[28] Police authorities often, as a matter of policy, pay for repair of damage caused by police to the property of innocent persons.

[29] *Tock* v. *St John's Metropolitan Area Board* [1989] 2 SCR 1181, *Rideau Falls Generating Partnership* v. *City of Ottawa* (1999) 174 DLR 4th 160, Ont. CA, and see pp. 88–91 below.

[30] (1884) 13 QBD 131, CA.   [31] Lindley LJ at 139.

of the plaintiff, and therefore it seems to me that they are liable . . . [I]n order to get rid of the misfortune which had happened to them, and which, rebus sic stantibus [with things as they were], would not have injured the plaintiff, they did something which brought an injury upon the plaintiff. Under those circumstances it seems to me the defendants are liable.[32]

This is the language not so much of wrongdoing as of unjust enrichment. Though the court was not called upon to determine the point it is probable that it would have refused an injunction, had one been sought in time, to prevent the trenches being cut.[33] The defendant was expressly found to have acted reasonably, and it may be assumed that the collapse of the railway line, which was established by statutory authority, would have caused a loss to the defendant and to the public far exceeding £130. The defendant's conduct was therefore, in a real sense, justified, and for this reason punitive damages, like an injunction, or interference by self-help, would have been inappropriate. Nevertheless compensation was due, in order to prevent the railway from profiting at the plaintiff's expense.

Necessity may justify action in many circumstances other than flooding. In the well-known Minnesota case of *Vincent* v. *Lake Erie Transportation Co.*[34] (1910) the defendant secured its ship to the plaintiff's wharf in order to escape a storm. The ship was saved but the wharf was damaged, and the ship owner was required to pay compensation. An obligation to recompense the wharf owner could not be explained solely on the basis of wrongdoing, but was nevertheless imposed, partly in order to avoid an unjust enrichment.[35] The court expressly made the analogy with expropriation:

> Theologians hold that a starving man may, without moral guilt, take what is necessary to sustain life; but it could hardly be said that the obligation would not be upon such person to pay the value of the property so taken when he became able to do so. And so public necessity, in times of war or peace, may require the taking of private property for public purposes; but under our system of jurisprudence, compensation must be made.[36]

[32] 13 QBD 137–8 (Brett MR).
[33] *Shelfer* v. *City of London Electric Lighting Co.* [1895] 1 Ch 287.   [34] 124 NW 221 (1910).
[35] See *Restatement of Restitution* s. 122, 'Benefits Derived from the Exercise of Incomplete Privilege', R. A. Epstein, 'A Theory of Strict Liability' 2 *Journal of Legal Studies* 151 at 158–9, and 'Defences and Subsequent Pleas in a System of Strict Liability' (1973–4) 3 *Journal of Legal Studies* 165 at 213.
[36] *Ibid.*, at 222, per O'Brien J.

Writers on unjust enrichment and on tort have each sought to displace this case into the other's subject. George Palmer excluded this case from restitution because the remedy was not measured (nor, he thought, should be measured) by the defendant's enrichment:

> The decision is satisfactory but the unjust enrichment explanation is not. Instead the case should be accepted as one instance of tort liability without fault, in the sense that the defendant's conduct was not blameworthy. It is fair to impose liability for harm consciously inflicted on another for the purpose of saving oneself from loss, but the liability should be imposed without regard to whether or not the action was successful in that purpose.[37]

On the other hand Ernest Weinrib explained the case in exactly opposite terms:

> Given the impossibility of construing the defendant's conduct as wrongful, we should not seek to explain the case on tort principles. Instead we should look to principles that specifically allow for liability in the absence of wrongdoing. These principles are restitutionary.[38]

These are not cumulative arguments in the mind of either writer, but two such contrary opinions may lead the reader to doubt that the issue can be assigned exclusively to either category. From a historical perspective each writer is correct in what he includes: tort (as Palmer says) and unjust enrichment (as Weinrib says) have both been influential in necessity cases. The inclusion of this subject in both the *Restatement of Restitution* and in the *Second Restatement of Torts*[39] also tends to show that the case has not been understood exclusively in terms of either, but has had dimensions of both.

Similar considerations would apply to a case where an aircraft in distress dumped fuel, thereby saving the aircraft and its passengers but damaging the plaintiff's property. The *Second Restatement of Torts*[40] and statutory provisions in many jurisdictions[41] provide for strict liability in such a case.

---

[37] G. Palmer, *The Law of Restitution* (Boston, 1978), para. 2.10.
[38] E. Weinrib, *The Idea of Private Law* (Cambridge, Mass., 1995), p. 196.
[39] Ss. 197(2), 263. See also R. Keeton, 'Conditional Fault in the Law of Torts' (1959) 72 *Harvard Law Review* 401 at 410–18.
[40] S. 520A.
[41] Air Navigation Act 1920 10 & 11 Geo 5 c. 80, s. 9, referred to by Lord Wright in this context, *Legal Essays and Addresses*, p. 125, replaced by Civil Aviation Act 1982, s. 76(2). See Fleming, *The Law of Torts* (9th edn), p. 372.

But it cannot be said that the law has been consistent. In *Romney Marsh* v. *Trinity House*[42] no liability was imposed for damage caused to a sea wall by leaving a vessel there while valuable property was removed, and in *Esso Petroleum Co. Ltd* v. *Southport Corp.*[43] no liability was imposed for pollution damage caused by emergency discharge of oil from a ship. In the circumstances of this last case a form of strict liability has been adopted by international convention.[44]

Nuisance cases often raise similar issues. Ice may be broken up on a river in order to prevent flooding with the consequence, however, of causing damage to a landowner downstream.[45] The actions of the defendant have been fully justifiable in many nuisance cases – often they have been expressly authorized by statute and very certainly in the public interest – but nevertheless compensation has often been required for harms.[46]

In *Bamford* v. *Turnley*,[47] (1860) where a nuisance was caused by brick burning, the defendant sought to avoid liability on the grounds that his activity was useful and in the public interest, and that all feasible precautions had been taken to minimize the nuisance. Baron Bramwell rejected these arguments:

> But it is said that . . . it is lawful because it is for the public benefit. Now, in the first place, that law to my mind is a bad one which, for the public benefit, inflicts loss on an individual without compensation. But further, with great respect, I think this consideration misapplied in this and in many other cases. The public consists of all the individuals of it, and a thing is only for the public benefit when it is productive of good to those individuals on the balance of loss and gain to all. So that if all the loss and all the gain were borne and received by one individual, he on the whole would be a gainer. But whenever this is the case – whenever a thing is for the public benefit, properly understood – the loss to the individuals of the public who lose will bear compensation out of the gains of those who gain. It is for the public benefit that there should be railways, but it would not be unless the gain of having the railway was sufficient to compensate the loss occasioned by the use of the land required for its site; and accordingly no one thinks it would

---

[42] (1870) LR 5 Ex 204.   [43] [1956] AC 218, HL.
[44] International Convention on Civil Liability for Oil Pollution, Merchant Shipping Act (UK) 1995 c. 21, s. 153(1)(a). See C. J. S. Hill, *Maritime Law* (5th edn, London, 1998), p. 420.
[45] *Rideau Falls Generating Partnership* v. *City of Ottawa* (1999) 174 DLR 4th 160, Ont. CA.
[46] *Tock* v. *St John's Metropolitan Area Board*, note 29 above, *Marcic* v. *Thames Water Utilities Ltd* [2002] 2 WLR 932, CA.
[47] (1860) 3 B & S 66.

be right to take an individual's land without compensation to make a railway. It is for the public benefit that the trains should run, but not unless they pay their expenses. If one of those expenses is the burning down of a wood of such value that the railway owners would not run the train and burn down the wood if it were their own, neither is it for the public benefit they should if the wood is not their own. If, though the wood were their own, they still would find it compensated them to run the trains at the cost of burning the wood, then they obviously ought to compensate the owner of such wood, not being themselves, if they burn it down in making their gain. So in like way in this case a money value cannot be easily put on the plaintiff's loss, but it is equal to some number of pounds or pence, £10, £50 or what not: unless the defendant's profits are enough to compensate this, I deny that it is for the public benefit he should do what he has done; if they are, he ought to compensate.[48]

The underlying consideration here, as in a number of Bramwell's other judgments,[49] was not so much that the defendant had committed a wrong (in the sense of blameworthy conduct) as that he would be unjustly enriched if he could make a profit at his neighbour's expense.[50] It follows also from this line of thinking that the conduct, though a legal wrong for some purposes, was not a wrong in the fullest legal sense, for the appropriate remedy in such cases must (on Bramwell's line of thinking) be compensatory damages, and not an injunction, abatement by self-help,[51] or punitive damages. The tendency to suppose that injunctions are automatically available for nuisances has not necessarily been beneficial to plaintiffs, because it may well have led, in the case of socially desirable activities, to the courts' refusal to find the activity a nuisance in the first place, thus leaving the plaintiff with no remedy at all.[52]

Similar views to Baron Bramwell's were expressed in the political forum. Air pollution was a question of lively public debate in England in the 1860s, on account not only of brick burning but also of chemical (especially alkali)

---

[48] *Ibid.*, at 84.
[49] See pp. 93–7 below. He favoured liability in *Fletcher* v. *Rylands* (1865) 3 H & C 774 at 788.
[50] Brian Simpson also has attributed to Bramwell the view that 'an enterprise which did not pay for the harm it did was being unjustly enriched'. *Leading Cases in the Common Law* (Oxford, 1995), p. 175.
[51] Bramwell himself made these points (pp. 85–86) while conceding that 'the present law may be defective' [i.e. in permitting injunction or abatement].
[52] S. Tromans, 'Nuisance – Prevention or Payment?' [1982] *Cambridge Law Journal* 87 at 105, R. Sharpe, *Injunctions and Specific Performance* (2nd edn, Toronto, 1992), para. 4.420.

works and copper smelting.[53] In a proposed addition to the report of a parliamentary committee in 1862, Lord Grey wrote:

> It is not just that any individual should be allowed, for his own profit, to inflict damage upon his neighbours, and even when a town or district derives so much benefit from the extension of some of those manufactures which have formed the subject of this inquiry, as to be willing to submit to the evils that arise from them, it is not just that particular persons whose property is damaged should be denied, as they practically are, the means of obtaining compensation for their loss.[54]

William Keates, a copper smelter and former director of chemical works, giving evidence to a Royal Commission in 1878, considered that compensation should be paid for damage caused by pollution, even if the polluter was not at fault, and even if statutory standards were met:

> Now the farmers, who are very much against me individually, got a notion that Lord Derby's Act,[55] as we call it, had given chemical manufacturers a sort of licence; that is to say, that it was useless to attack them, because they could produce certificates of their having condensed so much, and that consequently the law would not take cognizance of what they had done. That of course was a popular prejudice. [Question: A misapprehension?] A misapprehension. But although chemical works may condense all that the Act of Parliament requires, it does not prevent damage ... I was a director of large chemical works ... and although they were well conducted, and although we had certificates of the inspectors, who did their duty in every way, still I believe that we committed considerable damage, and we paid for it.[56]

In *St Helen's Smelting Company* v. *Tipping*[57] this view (that actual damage ought to be paid for) had been accepted by the House of Lords in its judicial capacity to the extent of upholding a jury verdict for a plaintiff whose land had been damaged by copper-smelting works. It was strenuously argued for the defendant that there should be no liability for damage caused by

---

[53] Simpson, 'Victorian Judges and the Problem of Social Cost: *Tipping* v. *St Helen's Smelting Company* (1865)' in *Leading Cases*, p. 163.

[54] Select Committee of House of Lords on Injury from Noxious Vapours, PP 1862 xiv, xvi–xvii.

[55] 26 & 27 Vic c. 124, requiring 95 per cent of muriatic acid produced by alkali works to be condensed. See Simpson, *Leading Cases*, p. 178.

[56] Royal Commission on Noxious Vapours PP 1878 xliv, qq 3214–5 (evidence of William Keates). See Simpson, *Leading Cases*, p. 186.

[57] (1865) 11 HLC 642.

operation of an industry beneficial to the public, carried on in an industrial district, and managed with all possible care, but this argument was rejected by all the judges (summoned to advise the House) and by the law lords themselves without even calling on the plaintiff's counsel. Liability still depended in each case on the particular facts and on the jury: Brian Simpson has summarized the effect of *St Helen's* v. *Tipping* by saying that 'A properly conducted business in an appropriate location was not, as a matter of law, immune from nuisance liability.'[58] Where the pollution rendered neighbouring land more or less unusable, disputed cases were sometimes settled on terms that the defendant purchased the land,[59] showing the close analogy of these cases with expropriation.[60]

Where a landowner engages in an unusual activity known to expose neighbours to risk, liability has been imposed even though there is no fault in the way in which the activity is conducted. In *Rylands* v. *Fletcher* (1868), a case involving the underground escape of water from a reservoir into a mine on nearby land, Blackburn J, in language later approved by the House of Lords, drew together several kinds of case, including the nuisance cases:

> the person who for his own purposes brings on his land and collects and keeps there anything likely to do mischief if it escapes, must keep it in at his peril, and, if he does not do so, is prima facie answerable for all the damage which is the natural consequence of its escape . . . The general rule, as above stated, seems on principle just. The person whose grass or corn is eaten down by the escaping cattle of his neighbour, or whose mine is flooded by the water from his neighbour's reservoir, or whose cellar is invaded by the filth of his neighbour's privy, or whose habitation is made unhealthy by the fumes and noisome vapours of his neighbour's alkali works, is damnified without any fault of his own; and it seems but reasonable and just that the neighbour, who has brought something on his own property which was not naturally there, harmless to others so long as it is confined to his own property, but which he knows to be mischievous if it gets on to his neighbour's, should be obliged to make good the damage which ensues if he does not succeed in confining it to his own property.[61]

---

[58] Simpson, *Leading Cases*, p. 189.   [59] E.g. *Houghton* v. *Bankart* (1861) 3 De G F & J 16.

[60] Ernest Weinrib has also linked *Vincent* v. *Lake Erie* with the nuisance cases, finding the results (though not all of the terminology and reasoning) in both kinds of case to be consistent with his concept of corrective justice, and adducing proprietary concepts by reference to 'the interaction of one property owner with another'. Weinrib, *The Idea of Private Law*, p. 196; see also p. 203.

[61] (1866) LR 1 Ex. 265, at 279–80; (1868) LR 3 HL 330, at 339–40.

Simpson has shown that the decision in *Rylands* v. *Fletcher* was influenced by then recent flood disasters.[62] Also influential was the existence and operation of private Acts of Parliament for acquisition of land rights.[63] It might be in the public interest for land to be acquired and flooded as a reservoir, but in that case the owner of the land so acquired ought to be compensated. If the operator of a reservoir should construct a reservoir that necessarily flooded his neighbour's land, compensation would similarly be payable, just as in the case where floodwater was diverted onto the neighbour's land.[64] If these principles applied where damage was certain, they must also apply where a very high degree of risk was known to be present. This line of thinking cannot, as a matter of history,[65] be subordinated to concepts of fault: the plaintiff's complaint is not that the defendant has been careless; on the contrary, the more carefully and accurately the defendant has calculated that he can make a profit by exposing the plaintiff to the risk, the stronger the case for compensation if the risk materializes. As with the other instances considered in this chapter, it can be said that the landowner would be (in the general sense of the words) unjustly enriched if his or her neighbours were compelled to bear part of the cost of the enterprise.[66]

One of the difficulties in formulating a general principle of strict liability is to distinguish an identifiable enterprise (to which it is judged to be feasible and desirable to allocate costs of the damage it causes) from the ordinary activities of daily life.[67] In *Rylands* v. *Fletcher* the suggestion was made that strict liability would apply only to 'non-natural' uses of land, and this was evidently an attempt to formulate such a distinction, but no simple rule has evolved because the distinction includes an implicit judgment as to which activities ought (if the defendant chooses to pursue them at all) to bear these costs. The lack of a simple determining concept has led to doubts about the

---

[62] Plaintiff's counsel opened by saying, 'A large collection of water is a thing pregnant with dangers, and it behoves anyone who makes a collection for his profit, to beware how he may prejudice his neighbours by mismanaging it', (1865) 11 Jur (NS) 714, Simpson, *Leading Cases*, p. 213.

[63] Simpson, *Leading Cases*, pp. 220–21.

[64] See pp. 85–6 above. Simpson points out that the Waterworks Clauses Act of 1847 contained a clause preserving any common law rights to compensation for flooding, *Leading Cases*, p. 220.

[65] Pollock, *Law of Torts*, p. 393.

[66] Fuller calls the rule of liability a kind of tax, L. Fuller, *The Morality of Law* (New Haven, 1964), p. 75. See also R. Keeton, 'Conditional Fault', note 39 above, linking this question with *Vincent* v. *Lake Erie*.

[67] See G. Fletcher, 'Fairness and Utility in Tort Theory' (1972) 85 *Harvard Law Review* 537. Ernest Weinrib, while accepting the results in these cases, has characterized them as an extension rather than as a denial of the fault principle. Weinrib, *The Idea of Private Law*, p. 190.

scope of the principle, which in some accounts of tort law has appeared as an anomalous exception to a general principle of fault.[68] But such accounts are not supported by historical evidence. John Fleming, the leading Anglo-American torts scholar of the twentieth century, in commenting on the rejection of *Rylands* v. *Fletcher* by the Australian High Court,[69] wrote that 'it would ... be a historical misinterpretation to suggest that negligence had at last overtaken a rule redolent of archaism'.[70]

Where an enterprise has been perceived to be in the public interest it has often been specifically authorized by statute. Much confusion has surrounded the question of what effect this has on the legal rights of persons injured by the inevitable consequences of the enterprise. Statutory authorization necessarily excludes certain remedies: the court cannot, in the face of a valid statutory authorization of an enterprise, issue an injunction requiring it to cease; nor would a criminal prosecution for public nuisance succeed;[71] nor would an award of punitive damages be appropriate; similarly the injured person would not be entitled to take measures to interfere with the defendant's activity by self-help. All these would be inconsistent with the statute. But it is by no means inconsistent with the statute that the enterprise should pay money compensation for damage. It might well be in the public interest both that the enterprise should operate and that it should pay reasonable compensation for the losses inevitably caused to individuals. On the line of reasoning discussed above in *Rylands* v. *Fletcher* and *Bamford* v. *Turnley* it would be quite consistent (in the absence of clear language actually removing the plaintiff's prior rights) to construe the statute to allow the enterprise to operate, but to preserve the rights of persons injured by it to compensation to which they were otherwise entitled by law. As Baron Bramwell said in the case of a traction engine (authorized to be on the road by the Locomotive Acts), 'the statutes do not make it lawful to damage property without paying for the injury'.[72] In the important case of *Hammersmith Railway* v. *Brand*[73] (1869) the issue came to the House of Lords for

---

[68] Rejected in Australia: *Burnie Port Authority* v. *General Jones Pty Ltd* (1994) 179 CLR 520. Restricted in *Cambridge Water Co.* v. *Eastern Counties Leather Plc* [1994] 2 AC 264, HL. But see Fleming's defence of strict liability, *The Law of Torts* (Sydney, 1957) pp. 306–9, maintained in subsequent editions (9th edn, 1998, pp. 367–71), and J. A. Jolowicz, 'Liability for Accidents' [1968] *Cambridge Law Journal* 50.

[69] *Burnie Port Authority* v. *General Jones Pty Ltd*, note 68 above.

[70] J. Fleming, 'The Fall of a Crippled Giant' (1995) 3 *Tort Law Review* 56 at 61.

[71] See *R* v. *Pease* (1832) 4 B & Ad 30.   [72] *Powell* v. *Fall* (1880) 5 QBD 597.

[73] (1869) LR 4 HL 171.

resolution in respect of railways. The judges were summoned, and five out of the six who attended thought that compensation was payable for damage caused by nuisance, despite statutory authorization, Baron Bramwell again expressing a forceful opinion to this effect:

> One reason only for [denying compensation] is given. It is said that the railway and the working of it are for the public benefit, and therefore the damage must be done, *and be not compensated*. Admitting that the damage must be done for the public benefit, that is no reason why it should be uncompensated. It is to be remembered that that compensation comes from the public which gets the benefit. It comes directly from those who do the damage, but ultimately from the public in the fares they pay. If the fares will not pay for this damage, and a fair profit on the company's capital, the speculation is a losing one and all the gain does not pay all the loss and leave a fair profit. Either, therefore, the railway ought not to be made, or the damage may well be paid for.[74]

This argument was rejected by a three to two majority in the House of Lords, but the fact that it found favour with seven of the eleven judges who considered the case shows that the concept was not alien to English judicial thinking. Some courts have favoured compensation,[75] though many others, following *Hammersmith Railway* v. *Brand* and other nineteenth-century English railway cases,[76] have held that statutory authority necessarily excludes compensation.[77]

Where the defendant is a public agency there is the added consideration that the courts ought not to interfere with the autonomy of government action. Curiously enough, strict liability is easier to reconcile with a policy of judicial respect for government autonomy than is liability for negligence. Where liability is strict the court is not called upon to make any kind of review of government action; in performing its judicial function of determining that compensation is due for the plaintiff's loss, the court does not undertake to criticize in any way the actions of the government, for wrongdoing is not in issue. How a municipal authority should exercise its powers may be 'non-justiciable';[78] whether it should pay a sum of money compensation is not. But where liability is based on negligence the court can only

---

[74] *Ibid.*, at 191 (emphasis in original).

[75] *Jones* v. *Festiniog Railway* (1868) LR 3 QB 733, *Allen* v. *Gulf Oil Refining Ltd* [1980] QB 156, *Powell* v. *Fall*, note 72 above. See *Tock* v. *St John*, note 29 above.

[76] *Vaughan* v. *Taff Vale Ry* (1860) 5 H & N 679.

[77] *Dunne* v. *Northwest Gas Board* [1964] 2 QB 806.

[78] *Barrett* v. *Enfield London Borough Council* [2001] 2 AC 550, HL.

award compensation through a finding of fault, and in this context it has been said that 'Policy decisions of government must be immune from the application of private law standards of tort liability,'[79] and distinctions have been drawn between 'policy' and 'operational' decisions that have proved very difficult to put into practice.[80]

The point may be illustrated by comparing some Canadian decisions on injuries caused by objects falling on highways. In two Supreme Court of Canada cases decided in 1997 involving falling rocks and ice,[81] liability was imposed on the highway authority for the negligence of an independent contractor although the highway authority was not itself at fault. There was no suggestion that this conclusion interfered in any way with government autonomy. But in *Swinamer* v. *Nova Scotia*[82] (1994), where an overhanging tree fell on a highway due, the trial judge found, to government negligence, it was held by the Supreme Court of Canada that a decision in the plaintiff's favour implied an improper judicial review of government policy; the consequence was that the plaintiff, who had, like the persons struck by rocks and ice, equally been injured during normal use of a highway by a dangerous condition against which he could not possibly have guarded, and who had suffered terrible injuries,[83] was left to bear the entire financial burden of them himself.

The cases on liability for animals may be similarly analysed. Cattle trespass was mentioned by Blackburn J in the passage quoted above from *Rylands* v. *Fletcher*. One of the costs of keeping cattle is the damage they do to neighbouring land, and strict liability has been imposed for such damage from early times.[84] A related instance also mentioned by Blackburn J in *Rylands* v. *Fletcher* was the strict liability of the owner of an animal known to be dangerous:[85] 'the law is perfectly clear that in actions for damage occasioned by animals that have not been kept in by their owners, it is quite immaterial whether the escape is by negligence or not.'[86]

---

[79] *Swinamer* v. *Nova Scotia* [1994] 1 SCR 445 at 465–66, 112 DLR (4th) 18 at 31 (Cory J).

[80] *Just* v. *BC* [1989] 2 SCR 1228, *Brown* v. *BC* [1994] 1 SCR 420.

[81] *Lewis* v. *British Columbia* [1997] 3 SCR 1145, *British Columbia* v. *Mochinski* [1997] 3 SCR 1176.

[82] [1994] 1 SCR 445, 112 DLR (4th) 18.   [83] *Ibid.*, at 451 (SCR), 21 (DLR).

[84] 'Well established in the fourteenth century, if not before', Fleming, *The Law of Torts*, p. 336, G. Williams, *Liability for Animals* (Cambridge, 1939), pp. 127–35.

[85] LR 1 Ex 265, 280. This is the so-called *scienter* action; Williams, *Animals*, pp. 265–364, though not himself favouring strict liability; see p. 363.

[86] Blackburn J in *Fletcher* v. *Rylands* LR 1 Ex 265 at 282, referring to Williams J in *Cox* v. *Burbidge* (1863) 13 CBNS 430, at 478.

There are close analogies also with nuisance.[87] The argument for compensation succeeded in a case of 1885 where the defendant bred pheasants on his land close to his neighbour's grain crop. Here the element of unjust enrichment was prominent, because the feeding of the pheasants on the grain must have been foreseen as inevitable, and would plainly not only do damage to the crop, but would confer a direct benefit on the defendant by reducing the cost of supplying his own feed. The defendant was held liable to pay compensation, but not primarily on the ground of wrong-doing. Pollock B said that the applicable principle was 'Not so much negligence as ... an infraction of the rule "sic utere tuo ut alienum non laedas" [so use what is yours that you do not harm another's].'[88] The analogies with expropriation, with nuisance, and with the other instances considered in this chapter are strong: if compensation were not made the plaintiff would be compelled to contribute to the cost of the defendant's enterprise. Some means were needed here of identifying enterprises to which costs might feasibly be attributed, and, just as in *Rylands* v. *Fletcher*, reference was made to the defendant's 'extraordinary and non-natural use of the land'.[89]

Principles of strict liability were applied in the nineteenth century to steam-driven traction engines on highways.[90] In *Watkins* v. *Reddin* (1861), where a horse was frightened by a traction engine and caused personal injury, Erle CJ instructed the jury that

> The plaintiff is entitled to your verdict, if the engine was calculated by its noise and appearance to frighten horses, so as to make the use of the highway dangerous to persons riding or driving horses. For the defendant has clearly no right to make a profit at the expense of the security of the public.[91]

The emphasis on 'profit' at the plaintiff's expense again shows the influence of the concept of unjust enrichment, and this was, by Baron Bramwell, combined with the economic arguments that he adduced in the nuisance cases. In 1880 he said (in a case of property damage caused by a traction engine):

---

[87] Williams, *Animals*, pp. 235–62.
[88] Per Pollock B in *Farrer* v. *Nelson* (1885) 15 QBD 258 at 260.   [89] *Ibid.*
[90] J. R. Spencer, 'Motor-Cars and the Rule in *Rylands* v. *Fletcher*' [1983] *Cambridge Law Journal* 65 at 69–93.
[91] (1861) 2 F & F 629 at 634.

It is just and reasonable that if a person uses a dangerous machine, he should pay for the damage which it occasions; if the reward which he gains for the use of the machine will not pay for the damage, it is mischievous to the public and ought to be suppressed, for the loss ought not to be borne by the community or the injured person.[92]

This case was repeatedly followed over the following forty years in relation to traction engines, but was not extended to motor vehicles nor was it directly applied to other products.[93]

Long before the development, in the twentieth century, of a general principle of negligence,[94] business sellers had been held liable to buyers of goods for breach of warranty. The action of warranty, which can be traced back to the fifteenth century,[95] was originally brought in tort for a false statement inducing a sale, and the buyer's damages were the difference between the price paid and the value of the goods received. In the eighteenth century the practice arose of bringing warranty actions in assumpsit,[96] a change of practice that eventually had important consequences, as warranties came to be treated as promises in substance as well as in form. One such consequence was the restriction, in English law, of the buyer's remedy for an express representation on the reasoning that a warranty required contractual intention.[97] On the other hand the application of a contractual measure of damages resulted in an extension of the seller's liability in two respects. One was the allowance of the 'expectation' measure of damages for loss of a good bargain, but far more important from the perspective of products liability was the allowance of consequential damages on the reasoning that the seller, having promised that the goods were sound, was liable for all damage reasonably to be contemplated as liable to result from a defect.[98] A series of nineteenth-century English cases held that such damages included property damage and personal injuries caused to the buyer by defects, and so the result was to extend to the buyer a remedy, without proof of fault, for

---

[92] *Powell* v. *Fall*, note 72 above.

[93] Spencer, 'Motor-Cars and the Rule in *Rylands* v. *Fletcher*', note 90 above at 70n.

[94] *Macpherson* v. *Buick Motor Co.* 217 NY 382, 111 NE 1050, *Donoghue* v. *Stevenson* [1932] AC 562, HL (Sc).

[95] J. Ames, 'History of Assumpsit' (1888) 2 *Harvard Law Review* 1 at 8.

[96] *Stuart* v. *Wilkins* (1778) 1 Doug KB 18, W. Prosser, 'The Assault Upon the Citadel' (1959) 69 *Yale Law Journal* 1099 at 1126.

[97] *Heilbut, Symonds & Co.* v. *Buckleton* [1913] AC 30, HL, criticized by S. Williston, 'Representation and Warranty in Sales' (1913) 27 *Harvard Law Review* 1.

[98] *Hadley* v. *Baxendale* (1854) 9 Exch 341.

damage caused by the use, as well as by the purchase, of defective goods.[99] This consequence extended to the implied warranties codified in the Sale of Goods Act of 1893, resulting in a form of strict liability, a remarkable result, as Fleming pointed out, in that it antedated by many years the development of a general duty of care.[100] The contractual associations of warranty, however, imposed a restriction, since they required proof of a contract between the plaintiff and the defendant. Strict liability as a general principle for products liability developed in the American jurisdictions in the 1960s largely because of the perceived anomaly of holding the retail seller, and only the seller, liable to the buyer, and only to the buyer.[101] The principle of strict liability was incorporated into the *Second Restatement of Torts*, as section 402A, and adopted by most American states. Many other jurisdictions, including Quebec,[102] all countries of the European Union,[103] and Australia,[104] have also adopted strict liability. In Canadian common law jurisdictions an injured plaintiff is (if there is no contractual warranty) required to show negligence, but this burden has been alleviated by something close to a practical presumption of negligence on a showing that the product left the manufacturer's hands in a defective condition and that the plaintiff has been injured in consequence – Cecil Wright called it a 'straddle between "fault" and "strict liability"'.[105] It was the combination of strict liability in warranty (though, as mentioned above, with the perceived anomalies of the contractual restrictions), and something close to strict liability as a matter of practice in negligence that led most of the American jurisdictions, with enthusiastic academic support, to adopt a general principle of strict products liability in the 1960s.[106] Contractual concepts were in play here (the supplier gave

---

[99] *Brown v. Edgington* (1841) 2 Man & G 279, *Randall v. Raper* (1858) El Bl & El 84, *Smith v. Green* (1875) 1 CPD 92, *Randall v. Newson* (1877) 2 QBD 102 (CA).

[100] Fleming, *The Law of Torts* (9th edn), p. 531.

[101] See W. Prosser, 'The Fall of the Citadel (Strict Liability to the Consumer)' (1966) 50 *Minnesota Law Review* 791. Prosser wrote, at 800, 'The "risk distributing" theory – the supplier should be held liable because he is in a position to insure against liability and add the cost to the price of his product – has been an almost universal favorite with the professors; but it has received little mention in the cases, and still appears to play only the part of a makeweight argument.'

[102] Civil Code, 1992, arts. 1468–9.

[103] J. Stapleton, *Product Liability* (London, 1994), pp. 355–9.

[104] Trade Practices Amendment Act, 1992, No. 106.

[105] C. A. Wright, 'The Law of Torts, 1923–1947' (1948) 26 *Canadian Bar Review* 46 at 69. See also S. Waddams, *Products Liability* (4th edn, Toronto, 2002), pp. 70–71.

[106] Prosser, 'Fall of the Citadel,' note 101 above.

an assurance of reasonable quality) as well as considerations of unjust enrichment (the supplier would be unjustly enriched if it did not bear the full cost of the enterprise).

Subsequently there was a partial retrenchment in American jurisdictions, following concern in the 1970s with a products liability insurance crisis, and more recently with the tort liability system more generally.[107] Academic writers suggested that there was no principled basis for strict liability; some writers stressed that strict liability could not be supported on grounds of deterrence; others pointed out that the wealth of the defendant could not in itself justify imposing liability, and that the theory of enterprise liability, standing alone, encountered serious difficulties as an independent source of obligations.[108] In 1998 the American Law Institute published the Products Liability provisions of the *Third Restatement of Torts*.[109] The basic principle of strict liability was maintained but a new provision drew a distinction between manufacturing defects and design defects, providing (though with some ambiguity) that in case of the latter, the plaintiff must prove the availability to the manufacturer of a reasonable alternative design.[110]

The historical links of strict liability with the concept of warranty were now in danger of being forgotten. The developments of the 1960s culminating in section 402A of the *Second Restatement of Torts* had established convincingly that strict liability should not be limited by contractual concepts. This avoided the defects of the former exclusive association of strict liability with contract, but the association of strict liability exclusively with 'tort'[111] has, by a curious irony, led to the opposite defect, with a reintroduction of principles of negligence, and of the very distinction (between tort liability and warranty liability) that the *Second Restatement* had sought to eliminate. The argument for strict liability is that from the warranty point of view a defectively designed product is unmerchantable and unfit for its

---

[107] See J. A. Henderson and T. Eisenberg, 'The Quiet Revolution in Products Liability: An Empirical Study of Legal Change' (1990) 37 *University of California at Los Angeles Law Review* 479.

[108] See Symposium, 'Products Liability: Economic Analysis and the Law' (1970) 38 *University of Chicago Law Review* 1, D. Dewees and M. Trebilcock, *Exploring the Domain of Accident Law* (New York, 1996), pp. 190–91.

[109] American Law Institute, *Third Restatement of the Law: Torts; Products Liability* (St. Paul, 1998).

[110] See J. A. Henderson, 'The Restatement Process and Major Changes in the Restatement (Third)' (1998) 8 *Kansas Journal of Law and Public Policy* 18.

[111] This association is partly due to the patterns of American litigation and legal practice, where personal injury claims are strongly associated with tort.

ordinary purpose, and the injured user should not have to demonstrate that a reasonable alternative design was available to the manufacturer,[112] who might not be a party to the litigation, and who might well in such a case be unidentified, insolvent, or beyond the jurisdiction.

Public policy has often played a part in these debates, but it is difficult to maintain that public safety has ever been a primary justification for strict products liability. Very effective means of deterrence are at hand in this field, namely, regulation under such statutes as (in Canada) the Hazardous Products Act,[113] the Food and Drugs Act,[114] or the Motor Vehicle Safety Act.[115] This is a much surer method than private law of controlling product quality and of influencing the behaviour of manufacturers. Strict liability is apt for cases where it is not in the interest of the community that the production of a product should cease, but where defects occur occasionally as, for example with beneficial drugs, or with a product like a car tyre, where one in a million may be unavoidably defective. The purpose of imposing liability on the manufacturer in such a case has plainly been not primarily to deter or modify the manufacturer's behaviour, but to require it to compensate the injured plaintiff. Taken together with the failure to prohibit the manufacture of the product under the relevant regulations, the message to the manufacturer is, as with the other instances of strict liability considered in this chapter: you have a licence to produce this product, on condition that you pay compensation to persons who are injured by defects.[116] A distinguished German lawyer put the argument in this way in 1984:

> The Roman praetor allowed the farmer to use his horse to carry fruit and vegetables at the Forum Romanum. This method of transport increased the range of goods on offer to society and, for the farmer, increased the possibility for personal profit, but nevertheless created the risk of damage whenever the horse followed its unpredictable nature. The praetor did not, however, accept

---

[112] This is implicitly recognized in the commentary to s. 3 (inference from circumstantial evidence), and comment (e) to s. 2 (no reasonable alternative design possible). No doubt there is truth in the comment that one of the purposes of the distinction was to control American juries: J. Stapleton, 'Restatement (Third) of Torts: Products Liability, an Anglo-Australian Perspective', (2000) 39 *Washburn Law Journal*, 363, at 389–90. In *Denny v. Ford Motor Co.* 662 NE 2d 730 (1995), the New York Court of Appeals held that warranty liability might be more extensive than strict liability in tort.

[113] RSC 1985 c. H-3.   [114] RSC 1985 c. F-27.   [115] SC 1993 c. 16.

[116] See R. E. Keeton, 'Conditional Fault in the Law of Torts', 72 *Harvard Law Review* 401 (1959), J. Fleming, *The Law of Torts*, p. 308 (9th edn, p. 369).

the farmer's excuse that as the horse had never before gone out of control, the damage caused was unforeseeable. To allow the activity, but to allocate the risk, this 'yes, but...' approach is socially the best solution...[117]

This argument combines elements of wrongdoing, contract, and unjust enrichment. Wrongdoing alone would not support liability, for the defendant has done no wrong, in the ordinary sense. The principle is more like an obligation to make good any loss, analogous to an indemnity bond, such as might be agreed between a rational manufacturer and a representative of the community as a condition reasonably demanded of one seeking a licence to profit in the community's market place. There is thus a close analogy with the other kinds of case considered in this chapter: Baron Bramwell's sentiments about railways ('it is for the public benefit that the trains should run, but not unless they pay their expenses... either the railway ought not to be made or the damage may well be paid for') might be adapted to the manufacture of products, even very useful products such as medicines, and blood for medical transfusion.

In 1997 there was published in Canada the report of a public inquiry into contaminated blood. The report, while not using the language of strict liability, suggested that those injured ought to be compensated without proof of fault,[118] one of the underlying reasons being that those who benefit by the supply of blood, a very useful and necessary medical product, would be unjustly enriched if they did not pay the full cost, including the cost of compensating those innocent persons injured by unavoidable contamination. Where, as in Canada, blood is supplied by a public agency, compensation may be seen as a public obligation, as the 1997 report recommended, and as was eventually to some degree achieved through the political process after strong public pressure.[119] Similar considerations have led to the adoption in several jurisdictions of statutory schemes of compensation for those injured by programmes of vaccination.[120] Where the supplier of the product is the government, the question of compensation has inescapable political dimensions, but the lines of demarcation are not distinct: fairness to individuals has itself been an influential political consideration, and judicial reasoning,

---

[117] H. C. Taschner in C. J. Miller (ed.), *Comparative Product Liability*, United Kingdom Comparative Law Series 6 (London, 1986), p. 8.

[118] *Commission of Inquiry on the Blood System in Canada* (Ottawa, 1997).

[119] *Globe and Mail* [Toronto], 23 Nov. 1998, A5 and 24 Nov. 1998 A4, 28 Jan. 1999 A7.

[120] See R. Goldberg, *Causation and Risk in the Law of Torts: Scientific Evidence and Medicinal Product Liability* (Oxford, 1999), ch. 4.

as we see from the instances discussed in this chapter, has often supported
the imposition of liability without fault. As Baron Bramwell's opinions show
in the nineteenth-century nuisance cases, the beneficial character of an enterprise and the excellence of the defendant's motives and conduct have not
always been found to be sufficient reasons for withholding compensation
from those who suffer injuries; in most Anglo-American jurisdictions, the
idea of charitable immunity has been rejected.[121] Strict products liability in
American jurisdictions is itself one of the examples of judicially developed
liability without fault, but the supply of blood has been an exception to
strict liability there.[122]

Vicarious liability is a form of strict liability, in that employers have
been held liable for tortious acts of employees without proof of any fault
on the employers' part.[123] It has been a feature of Anglo-American law of
huge practical significance. Though seldom seriously doubted,[124] it is not
amenable to explanation by any single principle. Pollock wrote that 'no
reason for the rule, at any rate no satisfying one, is commonly given in our
books'.[125] The various justifications that have been offered include the ideas
that the employee's action is to be identified with the employer's, that the
employer controls the employee, that the employee is doing the employer's
business, that liability will induce an employer to take care in selecting and
in supervising employees, that the employer is liable for *all* risks of the
enterprise, that the employer is the only reliable source of compensation,
and that the rule promotes loss internalization and loss distribution. Most
prominent has been the concept that an employer reaps the profits of the
enterprise and would receive an unjust benefit if not required to bear the
risk of damage caused by the improper conduct of its employees.[126] In

---

[121] See (for Canada) *Bazley* v. *Curry* [1999] 2 SCR 534,174 DLR (4th) 45.

[122] *Perlmutter* v. *Beth David Hospital* 308 NY 100 (1954), American Law Institute, *Restatement*.

[123] P. S. Atiyah, *Accidents, Compensation and the Law* (2nd edn, London, 1975), p. 155, *Bazley* v.
Curry, note 121 above, *Lister* v. *Hesley Hall Ltd* [2002] 1 AC 215 at 243 (Lord Millett), but
against this is Lord Hobhouse, at 239.

[124] An exception is T. Baty, *Vicarious Liability* (London, 1916).

[125] Pollock, *The Law of Torts*, p. 67. Also J. A. Jolowicz and T. E. Lewis, *Winfield on Tort* (7th edn,
London, 1963), p. 734, 'A scientific reason for the rule is hard to find. It seems to be based on
a mixture of ideas.'

[126] P. S. Atiyah, *Vicarious Liability in the Law of Tort* (London, 1967), pp. 22–3. Fleming puts this
first among the 'most important' policy considerations: *The Law of Torts* (9th edn), p. 410, and
it was referred to, directly or indirectly, by all the majority judges in *Limpus* v. *London General
Omnibus Co.* (1862) 1 H & C 526. Gareth Jones, 'A Topography of the Law of Restitution', in
P. D. Finn (ed.), *Essays on Restitution* (Sydney, 1990), p. 1, at p. 2, links 'the notion of unjust

an article entitled 'Cumulative Reasons and Legal Method' (1949) Bryant Smith, having shown the insufficiency of each of these reasons standing alone, went on to say:

> For the most part there is no contradiction between these reasons. They point from various and independent directions to the same man. In some instances all of them will apply in a particular case. In other instances one or more will be lacking, and in still others some of the reasons may work at cross purposes.[127]

Smith concluded by advocating consideration of 'the cumulative effect of many reasons for a rule, or, indeed, [the balancing] of cumulative effects of many reasons for and against'.

In *Bazley v. Curry* (1999) a charitable foundation that operated a children's home was held liable for harm deliberately done to the children by an employee, although no fault was found with the management of the home. The reasons given by the Supreme Court of Canada were that the enterprise (though not itself at fault) rather than the injured child should bear the risk, and that public policy favoured strong incentives to select and supervise staff with extreme care.[128] The court specifically described vicarious liability as 'strict', and justified it on the basis of 'loss internalization'[129] and enterprise liability, arguments previously developed mainly in the context of products liability. The parallel with products liability, and with the other instances mentioned in this chapter is apparent. In *Bazley v. Curry* the court said:

> The employer puts in the community an enterprise which carries with it certain risks. When those risks materialize and cause injury to a member of the public despite the employer's reasonable efforts, it is fair that the person or organization that creates the enterprise and hence the risk should bear the loss. This accords with the notion that it is right and just that the person who creates a risk bear the loss when the risk ripens into harm. While the fairness of this proposition is capable of standing alone, it is buttressed by

enrichment' both with products liability and with vicarious liability. Ernest Weinrib, though generally opposing strict liability, supports vicarious liability on the basis of 'a deeply rooted sentiment that a business enterprise cannot justly disclaim responsibility for accidents that may fairly be said to be characteristic of its activities', Weinrib, *The Idea of Private Law*, p. 187, quoting *Ira S. Bushey & Sons Inc.* v. *United States* 398 F 2d 167, 171 (2d Cir, 1968).

[127] B. Smith, 'Cumulative Reasons and Legal Method' (1949) 27 *Texas Law Review* 454 at 459.
[128] *Bazley v. Curry*, note 121 above, at 553–5 (SCR), 59–61 (DLR).
[129] *Ibid.* at 552 (SCR), 59 (DLR).

the fact that the employer is often in the best position to spread the losses through mechanisms like insurance and higher prices, thus minimizing the dislocative effect of the tort within society. 'Vicarious liability has the broader function of transferring to the enterprise itself the risks created by the activity performed by its agents'...[130]

The decision was followed by the House of Lords in *Lister v. Hesley Hall Ltd*,[131] though not all the law lords approved all the reasons of the Canadian court.

Liability has also been imposed in a wide variety of circumstances on enterprises in respect of the negligence of agents other than employees, such as independent contractors, and agents and employees of those contractors. These cases are closely akin to vicarious liability, in that the enterprise is in effect made liable for another's fault – usually that of the independent contractor, or of its employees. They have often been called cases of 'non-delegable duty', but this term is not entirely apt:[132] they amount rather to a kind of imputed guarantee. Liability was, as we have seen,[133] imposed by the Supreme Court of Canada (1997) on a highway authority for harm caused by an independent contractor in improperly maintaining the highway. There was no wrongdoing on the part of the highway authority; the court referred to the reasonable expectation of highway users, thereby importing a contractual concept and suggesting the link with warranty or guarantee that has been so influential in the context of defective products, the guarantee here being not of perfect safety but of reasonable minimum standards of maintenance. It may also be said that other users of the highway and the taxpayers at large would be (in a general sense) unjustly enriched if they saved money by letting the standards of maintenance fall below those minimum standards reasonably to be expected, while leaving those unlucky enough to be injured to bear the whole loss themselves. These considerations apply whether the highway authority maintains the road by using its own employees, or whether it contracts the responsibility to another. It is probably no accidental coincidence that these cases were decided at a time of widespread 'privatization' of the former responsibilities of government. Similar considerations would apply to

[130] *Ibid.* at 554 (SCR), 60 (DLR).   [131] Note 123 above.
[132] See Prowse JA in *BM* v. *BC* (2001) 197 DLR (4th) 385 at 404, quoting Salmond and Heuston, *The Law of Torts* (21st edn, London, 1996), p. 461.
[133] Note 81 above.

other facilities and services for public use, for example, the erection of a grandstand,[134] or the maintenance of railway track. 'Privatization' of public services may possibly be good public policy if it really saves costs, but a transfer of cost from the travelling public to an injured individual is not a saving.

The expression 'vicarious liability' has usually been associated with employment, but it was immediately clear from *Bazley* v. *Curry* that the principle adopted there could not be so confined. In that case (sexual assault on a child) the offender was, in fact, an employee of the defendant children's home, but the court spoke also of 'agents' and 'volunteers'.[135] It is plain that the court's reasoning as to enterprise liability and the internalization of costs, and as to the desirability of strong incentives to take care in selecting staff would apply with equal force to the selection of independent contractors and with even greater force to volunteers. The British Columbia Court of Appeal, in 2001, held the provincial government liable for sexual assaults committed against a child by a foster parent engaged by (but not in an employment relationship with) the government. The majority of the court, linking the Supreme Court decisions discussed in the preceding paragraphs, considered that there was at least as strong a case for compensating child victims of assault as for compensating injured users of the highway. They agreed also that strict liability extended beyond employers to those engaging independent contractors, though there was some disagreement about the proper scope of the terms 'vicarious liability' and 'non-delegable duty'.[136]

These various examples show that liability to compensate for harm has not always been dependent on proof of wrongdoing in the sense of blameworthy conduct. They might be criticized on several grounds but it could not be credibly suggested that they have been exceptional or marginal in the senses of having been infrequent in fact, or insignificant in effect. A persistent and pervasive concept has been, as Fleming put it, that 'what is rightly done in the general interest may yet confer a claim to compensation so that the burden does not fall on a particular person'.[137] Fleming also appealed to the fairness of the general idea that one whose interests have been advanced

---

[134] *Francis* v. *Cockrell* (1870) 5 QB 501.   [135] Note 121 above at 563–5 (SCR), 67–8 (DLR).

[136] *BM* v. *BC*, note 132 above, *KLB* v. *BC* (2001) 197 DLR (4th) 431, *EDG* v. *Hammer* (2001) 197 DLR (4th) 454, BCCA.

[137] Fleming, *Law of Torts* (5th edn), p. 324n. Similar views are expressed in the 9th edn (the last edited by Fleming) p. 380, n.51.

by an act should bear the expense of it.[138] It might be argued that the cases discussed in this chapter could, after all, be classed as cases of wrongdoing, because it is wrongful to inflict harm on another in advancing one's own interests without offering compensation to the other; but if the only wrong is the failure to recognize an obligation to compensate, the wrong cannot itself be the sole source of the obligation.[139] It would be possible alternatively to argue that the instances discussed in this chapter should, as in some civil law jurisdictions,[140] be classified as falling outside tort law, or that 'tort' is a misnomer,[141] and that a new word or set of words should be found to distinguish between 'wrong' in the sense of blameworthy conduct, and 'wrong' in the sense of conduct in respect of which compensation for harm is due. These arguments would not be wholly novel – general average, expropriation, and cases of necessity, for example, are not usually categorized as torts – and, if a general codification of Anglo-American law were to be undertaken, a reclassification might be entertained as a serious possibility. But, as we have seen,[142] an exact correspondence between name and substance has not been attained in respect of any legal category. As with the other examples considered in this study, several concepts have been in concurrent operation: the concept of wrongdoing has not been sufficient in these cases on its own to support liability, but neither has it been completely irrelevant; it has worked in conjunction with the concepts of property, unjust enrichment, and public policy. The contractual concepts of warranty, guarantee, and insurance have also been influential: Pollock treated the cases of strict liability as 'duties of insuring safety'.[143] Cumulatively the various concepts have, in the instances discussed, supported a persuasive case for compensation. The cases are difficult to accommodate in conceptual schemes, but this, standing alone, is a weak reason for rejecting judicial decisions that have, over several centuries, been found to answer to the needs of justice.

---

[138] Ibid. (9th edn), at pp. 106, 368–9.
[139] See p. 79 above, where a parallel point was made about the relation of reliance to wrongdoing.
[140] J. Davies, 'Tort', in P. Birks (ed.), English Private Law (Oxford, 2000), 14.07n.
[141] J. Smith, 'Tort and Absolute Liability – Suggested Changes in Classification' (1916) 30 Harvard Law Review 241 at 319, 409.
[142] See p. 16 above.   [143] Pollock, The Law of Torts, p. 393 (chapter title).

6

Profits derived from wrongs

Sometimes a benefit is derived from a legal wrong that does not cause – or that does not appear to cause – any corresponding loss. The question whether such benefits must be given up, and if so for what reason, has caused much conceptual agonizing; it is an issue that has been found impossible to classify, cutting across the legal categories of contract, tort, property, and unjust enrichment, and often involving general considerations of public policy. An example is the well-known Kentucky case of *Edwards* v. *Lee's Administrator*[1] (1936), where the defendant profited by admitting tourists to see a spectacular cave that was partly underneath the plaintiff's land, though only accessible from the defendant's. The court held that the plaintiff, though not himself in a position to profit from the cave, was entitled to recover a reasonable portion of the defendant's profits. Similarly, a person might use a corner of his neighbour's land without permission for access to a building site, saving himself substantial construction costs, but doing no damage to the land. Or, to take an older example, the plaintiff keeps horses for hire, and the defendant takes one out without permission, and brings it back unharmed. Can he say, in answer to a claim for money, 'Against what loss do you want to be restored? I restore the horse. There is no loss. The horse is none the worse; it is the better for the exercise'?[2]

---

[1] 265 Ky 418, 96 SW 2d 1028 (1936). The case of *Phillips* v. *Homfray* (1883) 24 Ch D 439 has sometimes been taken to foreclose this result in English law, but the decision does not preclude a substantial money award in such cases, and approved an earlier decision in the same litigation, *Phillips* v. *Homfray* (1871) LR 6 Ch App 770, that made such an award. *Phillips* v. *Homfray* (1883) was relied on by the Kentucky court in support of its conclusion. See R. Sharpe and S. Waddams, 'Damages for Lost Opportunity to Bargain' (1982) 2 *Oxford Journal of Legal Studies* 290 at 294, W. M. C. Gummow, 'Unjust Enrichment, Restitution, and Proprietary Remedies', in P. D. Finn (ed.), *Essays on Restitution* (Sydney, 1990), p. 47 at pp. 60–67, W. Swadling, 'The Myth of *Phillips* v. *Homfray*', in W. Swadling and G. Jones (eds.), *The Search for Principle: Essays in Honour of Lord Goff of Chieveley* (Oxford, 1999), p. 277.
[2] Lord Shaw in *Watson Laidlaw & Co. Ltd* v. *Pott Cassels and Williamson* (1914) 31 RPC 104, HL, at 119–20, quoted in *Attorney General* v. *Blake* [2001] 1 AC 268, HL, at 279 as a 'telling example'.

These examples involve trespass to property, and in such cases there exists a variety of legal techniques for protecting the plaintiff's interest. Among these must be included the possibility of the plaintiff's obtaining an actual injunction. If the defendant is restrained by injunction from committing the wrong in the first place, the effect will be, as many judges and commentators have recognized, not necessarily that the defendant will be for ever deprived of the use of the plaintiff's property, but that the defendant will have to bargain for the right to use it on terms agreeable to the plaintiff. That, indeed, is one of the usual characteristics of property, namely that the owner may sell it at the price he or she chooses, or may decline to sell it at all.

Where the wrong has been committed before the trial, the plaintiff's interest can only be protected by an award of money. Several techniques have been used to justify substantial awards in these cases. They include the award of damages in substitution for an injunction,[3] the award of exemplary damages,[4] waiver of tort,[5] accounting of profits,[6] and a related group of cases, sometimes called the 'wayleave' cases, where the defendant has been required to pay a reasonable licence fee for the use of the plaintiff's rights.[7] To these techniques may be added various concepts that enable the plaintiff to assert a proprietary interest in assets held by the defendant, including detinue, tracing, and constructive trust.

Another dimension of the question is the argument that in many of the cases the plaintiff *has* suffered a real loss, though one that is difficult to quantify, by being deprived of the opportunity to bargain with the wrongdoer for a rent, licence charge, or fee.[8] This consideration might in some cases, though not in all, support an award purely on compensatory principles, but,

---

[3] Under Lord Cairns' Act, Chancery Amendment Act, 21 & 22 Vic c. 27 (1858), or its modern equivalent: *Wrotham Park Estate Co. Ltd* v. *Parkside Homes Ltd* [1974] 1 WLR 798, *Bracewell* v. *Appleby* [1975] Ch 408, *Jaggard* v. *Sawyer* [1995] 1 WLR 269, CA.

[4] *Townsview Properties Ltd* v. *Sun Construction & Equipment Co. Ltd* (1974) 56 DLR (3d) 330, Ont. CA, *Epstein* v. *Cressey Development Corp.* (1992) 89 DLR (4th) 32, BCCA.

[5] See R. Goff and G. Jones, *The Law of Restitution* (London, 1966), pp. 427–38, and subsequent editions.

[6] See, for example, *Reid Newfoundland Co.* v. *Anglo-American Telegraph Co. Ltd* [1912] AC 555, PC, *Peter Pan Manufacturing Corp.* v. *Corsets Silhouette Ltd* [1964] 1 WLR 96. S. Doyle and D. Wright, 'Restitutionary Damages – The Unnecessary Remedy' (2000) 25 *Melbourne University Law Review* 1, suggest that accounting should replace damages in all cases of profit derived from wrongs.

[7] *Phillips* v. *Homfray* (1871) LR 6 Ch 770, *Watson Laidlaw & Co. Ltd* v. *Pott Cassels & Williamson*, note 2 above, *Whitwham* v. *Westminster Brymbo Coal Co.* [1896] 2 Ch 538, CA, *Strand Electric & Engineering Co.* v. *Brisford Entertainments Ltd* [1952] 2 QB 246, CA, *Seager* v. *Copydex Ltd (No 2)* [1969] 1 WLR 809, CA.

[8] Sharpe and Waddams, 'Damages for Lost Opportunity to Bargain', note 1 above.

even where it does not, it has not been wholly irrelevant: even if the court's primary objective is taken to be the elimination of the defendant's profit, it cannot weaken the plaintiff's claim to show that an award will also *simultaneously* perform a compensatory function. To put the point at its very lowest, the idea that the plaintiff has suffered an actual but unquantifiable loss has tended to strengthen the claim to some degree, and it has, together with other considerations, been influential in supporting awards related in some measure to the defendant's profit. There has been occasional judicial recognition that 'the principle [supporting a substantial award] need not be characterized as exclusively compensatory, or exclusively restitutionary; it combines elements of both'.[9]

This question has often been linked with unjust enrichment, but the nature of the link is a matter of acute controversy. The plaintiff has suffered no apparent loss, but a substantial money award has nevertheless been found to be justified. With the revival of unjust enrichment in the twentieth century cases making such awards were taken to be among the clearest examples of restitution that reversed unjust enrichments. They were accordingly included in the *Restatement of the Law of Restitution* (1937) and accepted as an important part of the subject during the following fifty years.[10] But in 1985, Peter Birks, while including a discussion of the cases in *An Introduction to the Law of Restitution*, pointed out that they were distinctive, in that they did not require proof of loss on the plaintiff's side corresponding to the defendant's enrichment.[11] Later, Birks called these cases 'remedial restitution' in contrast to 'substantive restitution',[12] but this usage has not lasted.

Other writers increased the emphasis on the distinction, asserting that '"restitution for wrongs" has nothing to do with the cause of action in unjust enrichment',[13] and, more sweepingly, that 'these awards have nothing to do with unjust enrichment'.[14] Birks then further sharpened the point, at the same time making the premisses explicit:

---

[9] *Inverugie Investments Ltd* v. *Hackett* [1995] 1 WLR 713 at 718 (Lord Lloyd); to similar effect is Lord Denning in *Strand Electric Engineering Co. Ltd* v. *Brisford Entertainments Ltd* [1952] 2 QB 246 at 255.

[10] R. Goff and G. Jones, *The Law of Restitution*, P. Maddaugh and J. McCamus, *The Law of Restitution* (Toronto, 1990), J. Beatson, *The Use and Abuse of Unjust Enrichment* (Oxford, 1991), A. Burrows, *The Law of Restitution* (London, 1993).

[11] P. Birks, *An Introduction to the Law of Restitution* (Oxford, 1985), pp. 22–3, 313–14.

[12] P. Birks, *Restitution – The Future* (Sydney, 1992), pp. 1, 10.

[13] L. Smith 'The Province of the Law of Restitution' (1992) 71 *Canadian Bar Review* 672 at 683.

[14] J. Edelman, 'Unjust Enrichment, Restitution, and Wrongs' (2001) 79 *Texas Law Review* 1869 at 1870. See also P. Birks, 'The Concept of a Civil Wrong', in D. Owen (ed.), *Philosophical Foundations of Tort Law* (Oxford, 1995), p. 37, and other writings, M. McInnes, 'The Canadian

The ... categories are exclusive of one another ... [I]t is no more possible for
the selected causative event to be both an unjust enrichment and a tort than it
is for an animal to be both an insect and a mammal ... Wrongful enrichment
belongs in the law of wrongs. The law of unjust enrichment is concerned solely
with enrichments which are unjust independently of wrongs and contracts.
To assert the contrary is to violate one of the basic principles of rationality,
namely that a classified answer to a question must use categories which are
perfectly distinct one from another.[15]

This is carrying the analogy between law and biology a very long way. The
argument is analytically compelling if the premiss is accepted (namely that
every legal question must be assigned exclusively to a single distinct category,
one of which is unjust enrichment as here defined so as expressly to exclude
wrongs and contracts), but it does not offer historical evidence in support
of the premiss. It is not inconsistent, therefore, with the observation that,
in the past, many courts have been influenced, in ordering disbursement
of profits, by various considerations, including concepts of compensation
for loss, property, wrongdoing, public policy, contract, and (in the general
sense of the phrase) unjust enrichment.

A writer is of course entitled to assert that, whatever the past may have
been, it would be preferable in the future to categorize the issue exclusively
as one of wrongs, but then it should be recognized that such categorization
would not itself offer guidance as to which profits, derived in which ways
from which wrongs, ought to be given up. An unqualified principle of disbursement of profits derived from wrongs would tend to prove too much,
for it would support recovery of all profits made by breach of contract,[16] and
by conduct that, though classified for some purposes as wrongful, is justifiable on payment of compensation for harm caused.[17] In cases of necessity,
for example, where the defendant's valuable property is preserved by in-
flicting a small loss on the plaintiff, as in *Vincent* v. *Lake Erie Transportation
Co.*,[18] discussed in the last chapter, it may be appropriate (as the court there
held) for the defendant to make compensation for the loss, but it would be
another thing altogether to require the defendant to account to the plaintiff
for the full value of the property preserved. Where damages are awarded

Principle of Unjust Enrichment: Comparative Insights into the Law of Restitution' (1999) 37
Alberta Law Review 1, G. Virgo, *The Principles of the Law of Restitution* (Oxford, 1999), p. 10.
[15] P. Birks, 'Unjust Enrichment and Wrongful Enrichment' (2001) 79 *Texas Law Review* 1769 at
1781 and 1794.
[16] See pp. 114–19, below.   [17] See chapter 4, above.   [18] 124 NW 221 (Minn SC, 1910).

in substitution for an injunction, the measure of damages is usually the plaintiff's loss, not the defendant's profit: indeed the very reason for withholding the injunction in such cases is usually to deprive the plaintiff of the bargaining power that an injunction would give to extract the defendant's profits.[19] These examples show that the legal issue cannot, in an account of the past, be allocated *either* exclusively to 'wrongs' *or* exclusively to unjust enrichment, and that, in a design for the future, such allocation could not itself be determinative. Since a distinction would still be required between profits that must be disbursed and profits that a wrongdoer might retain, it is likely that concepts of property, compensation for loss, and unjust enrichment, together with general considerations of public policy, would re-enter the debate at the stage of making the distinction, and the apparent simplification of allocating the issue to a single concept (wrongdoing) would evaporate. Various refinements and sub-refinements of terminology have been proposed in this context, but, since no consensus has emerged,[20] the simplicity and precision they seek remain elusive.

The issue (when must wrongfully acquired gains be disbursed?) falls within the ordinary meaning suggested by the phrase 'unjust enrichment', it has been closely associated since 1937 with restitution for unjust enrichment, and the same questions are bound to arise in measuring the defendant's gain as arise in unjust enrichment.[21] Whether or not the issue

---

[19] As in the cases of interference with the right to light. See *Isenberg* v. *East India House Estate Co. Ltd* (1863) 3 DeG J & S 263, discussed at p. 178 below.

[20] It has been pointed out that the name 'restitution' suggests 'giving *back*' rather than 'giving up' and in order to avoid this implication some writers prefer the word 'disgorgement'. See E. A. Farnsworth, 'Your Loss or my Gain? The Dilemma of the Disgorgement Principle in Breach of Contract' (1985) 94 *Yale Law Journal* 1339, L. Smith, 'Disgorgement of the Profits of Breach of Contract: Property, Contract, and Efficient Breach' (1994) 24 *Canadian Business Law Journal* 121, S. Worthington, 'Reconsidering Disgorgement for Wrongs' (1999) 62 *Modern Law Review* 218, and M. McInnes, 'The Canadian Principle of Unjust Enrichment', note 14 above, at 24. J. Edelman, *Gain-based Damages* (Oxford, 2002), uses both 'restitution' and 'disgorgement', but confines the former to instances of wrongful 'transfer' to which word he also gives a specialized meaning. Beatson retains the term 'restitutionary damages', J. Beatson (ed.), *Anson's Law of Contract* (27th edn, Oxford, 1998), p. 614; so does the Law Commission, *Report No 247: Aggravated, Exemplary and Restitutionary Damages* (London, 1997); see also on this point M. McInnes, 'Restitution, Unjust Enrichment and the Perfect Quadration Thesis' [1999] *Restitution Law Review* 118 at 121–2. Birks (see also note 12 above) and Mitchell also retain 'restitution' in this context: P. Birks (ed.), *English Private Law* (Oxford, 2000), para. 15.176. Virgo accepts 'disgorgement' but regards it as 'falling within the law of restitution', *Principles*, pp. 5, 449.

[21] For example, whether a subjective or an objective measure of value is to be used, and whether change of position is a defence. See *Kuwait Airways Corp.* v. *Iraqi Airways Co. (Nos 4 and 5)* [2002] 2 WLR 1353, HL, para. 79 (Lord Nicholls).

is classified as strictly one of unjust enrichment, it will continue to be the case, as Francis Rose has said of general average and maritime salvage, that 'many of the same principles that govern the law of restitution [unjust enrichment] also operate [there]'.[22] These considerations tend to qualify the assertion that the issue 'has nothing to do with unjust enrichment'. We may take the issue out of unjust enrichment, but it is not so easy to take unjust enrichment out of the issue.

Where the courts have allowed a tort to be 'waived', the plaintiff has been permitted to recover a reasonable fee from the defendant as though the plaintiff had authorized the wrongful conduct in advance. To say that this line of reasoning contains an element of fiction is true, but this does not establish that it is accidental or irrelevant. To insist that cases of this sort have been concerned *only* with wrongdoing, and have had nothing to do with unjust enrichment, or contract, or other legal concepts, is to oversimplify, for the contract that might have been made if the defendant had acted lawfully has often been an important consideration. In the Kentucky cave case, for example, where the result was based on accounting of profits (not waiver of tort), the court said, 'In substance...their [plaintiffs'] action is ex contractu and not, as appellants contend, simply an action for damages arising from a tort.'[23] The court's conclusion was plainly influenced not only by considerations of wrongdoing, but also by the concepts that the defendant had taken something that belonged to the plaintiff,[24] had been unjustly enriched,[25] had wrongfully deprived the plaintiff of an opportunity to bargain for rent,[26] and had acted in a manner contrary to public policy.[27]

It is well established that profits derived from breach of fiduciary duty must be given up. These cases cannot be entirely explained as compensatory, for the defaulting fiduciary is bound to account even if the plaintiff has suffered no loss, and could not have realized the profit herself.[28] They have

[22] F. D. Rose, 'Restitution and Maritime Law' in E. J. H. Schrage (ed.), *Unjust Enrichment and the Law of Contract* (The Hague, 2001), p. 367 at p. 380.
[23] 96 SW 2d, at 1030. Similarly in *Olwell* v. *Nye & Nissen Co.* 26 Wash 2d 282 (1946) expenses saved by wrongful use of the plaintiff's egg-washing machine were allowed, even though the award exceeded the full apparent value of the machine.
[24] 'actually used the property of Lee to make a profit', 'there was a taking of esthetic enjoyment', 96 SW 2d at 1030.
[25] 'real basis of recovery is the profits received', *ibid.*, at 1031; 'benefits accruing', at 1032. The draft of what was then called the *Restatement of Restitution and Unjust Enrichment* was cited, at 1032.
[26] 'rental value', *ibid.*, at 1031, 1032.
[27] 'a wrongdoer shall not be permitted to make a profit from his own wrong', *ibid.*, at 1032.
[28] See *Boardman* v. *Phipps* [1967] 2 AC 46, HL.

been treated by some writers as instances of unjust enrichment,[29] but they do not fall within those definitions of unjust enrichment that require the claimant to establish a loss corresponding to the defendant's enrichment,[30] and they have been excluded from unjust enrichment by those writers who exclude all claims that depend on proof of wrongdoing.[31] Very often the underlying relations between the parties involve a contract, but, as we shall see, breach of contract has not in itself been recognized as sufficient reason to require an accounting of profits.[32]

These cases, though not involving an infringement of a strict property right, have had strong proprietary links.[33] A trustee who profits from trust property in a sense takes something of the plaintiff's. In *Reid Newfoundland Co. v. Anglo-American Telegraph Co. Ltd*[34] the defendant used the plaintiff's telegraph wire to transmit unauthorized messages, and was held accountable as a trustee for the profits so made:

> When and as often as the appellants used the special wire for the transmission of unprivileged messages an obligation in the nature of a trust arose.[35]

Similarly an agent who receives a bribe or secret commission profits in a general sense from his principal's enterprise. A striking example is *Reading v. Attorney General*,[36] where a British army sergeant accepted bribes to accompany contraband goods wearing his uniform, thus deterring police inspection. The Crown was held to be entitled to the money. Although the Crown could not have profited itself in this way it is true to say that the profit was, in a real sense, derived from what belonged to the Crown, notably Reading's position and rank, and the uniform of the British army.[37] However, on strict property principles alone the Crown did not have title to the money.[38] Considerations of deterrence were strongly influential in the

---

[29] Goff and Jones, *The Law of Restitution*, ch. 35, Maddaugh and McCamus, *The Law of Restitution*, ch. 25, G. Palmer, *The Law of Restitution* (4 vols., Boston, 1978), ch. 2.

[30] L. Smith, 'Three-Party Restitution: A Critique of Birks's Theory of Interceptive Subtraction' (1991) 11 *Oxford Journal of Legal Studies* 481 at 514–16.

[31] P. Birks, 'The Concept of a Civil Wrong', note 14 above, pp. 35–7, Virgo, *Principles*, p. 285.

[32] In *Reading* v. *Attorney General* [1951] AC 507, HL, at 517 Lord Oaksey relied on the concept of implied contract.

[33] E. Weinrib, 'Restitutionary Damages as Corrective Justice' (2000) 1 *Theoretical Inquiries in Law* 1 at 32.

[34] [1912] AC 555, PC.   [35] Lord Robson, *ibid.*, at 559.

[36] [1951] AC 507, HL.   [37] Denning J. quoted *ibid.*, at 514 (Lord Porter).

[38] S. Worthington, 'Justifying Claims to Secondary Profits' in Schrage (ed.) *Unjust Enrichment and the Law of Contract*, p. 451 at p. 462.

Reading case, as it has been in other cases of fiduciaries.[39] It was said in a case of 1874, of a secret profit made by an agent, that 'the safety of mankind requires that no agent shall be able to put his principal to the danger of such an inquiry as that [whether the principal suffered actual loss]'.[40]

In respect of breach of contract, the acceptance of a general principle that all benefits must be given up would have had far-reaching effects on well-established legal doctrines.[41] For example, the principle of mitigation would be subverted if a disappointed buyer, having failed to purchase substitute goods on a rising market, could sue the defaulting seller for the judgment date value of the goods.[42] Again, in a contract for personal services, if there is no loss to the employer, because an equally competent employee can be found for the same price, the courts have not held the employer entitled to the benefits derived by the employee from the alternative use of time, albeit in breach of contract. To permit such a claim would be to give the employer a sort of proprietary interest in the employee's services: this concept has, since the nineteenth century, been generally unacceptable, and that is one reason why contracts of personal services have not usually been specifically enforceable against employees, and why there have usually been no exemplary damages for breach by the employee.

Where the cost of substitute performance of a contract exceeds the economic benefit of performance to the plaintiff, the court must answer the question whether the plaintiff is entitled to the cost of substitute performance or only to the actual economic loss. Cases of this sort may arise where the promise is to operate an enterprise for a long period of time and operation becomes costly, but of little value to the promisee, or where the promise is to make extensive renovations to a building that is later scheduled for demolition, or to restore a mining site where the cost of restoration greatly exceeds the value to be added by it to the land. A vivid example is supplied by the 1963 Oklahoma case of *Peevyhouse* v. *Garland Coal & Mining Co.*,[43] where the cost of restoring a mining site, as promised by a lessee of land, was nearly one hundred times the value to the landowner of effecting

---

[39] See chapter 4 above.
[40] James LJ in *Parker* v. *McKenna* (1874) LR 10 Ch App 96. See *Keech* v. *Sandford* (1726) Cas t. King 61.
[41] See S. Waddams, 'Profits Derived from Breach of Contract: Damages or Restitution' (1997) 11 *Journal of Contract Law* 127, S. Waddams, 'Breach of Contract and the Concept of Wrongdoing' (2000) 12 *Supreme Court Law Review (2d)* 1.
[42] See *Asamera Oil Corp. Ltd* v. *Sea Oil & General Corp.* [1979] SCR 633.
[43] 382 P 2d 109 (Okla SC) cert. den. 375 US 906 (1963).

restoration, assuming (as appeared to be the fact) that the landowner had no genuine non-economic interest in actually doing the work. The court awarded the smaller sum only. There has been considerable difference of judicial and academic opinion on this question,[44] but most cases have held that in such circumstances the plaintiff is only entitled to the actual economic loss unless she actually intends to purchase substitute performance, and a decision to do so is not wholly unreasonable. If this conclusion stands, it must follow that the landowner cannot evade it by demanding an accounting of the money saved by the lessee in failing to restore the site. In a well-known hypothetical example Justice Cardozo said:

> Specifications call, let us say, for a foundation built of granite quarried in Vermont. On the completion of the building, the owner learns that through the blunder of a sub-contractor part of the foundation has been built of the same quality quarried in New Hampshire. The measure of allowance is not the cost of reconstruction.[45]

Let us consider a variation of this example, where after the contract is made there is a transport strike in Vermont that causes the cost of Vermont granite to double. The contractor decides to use New Hampshire granite of equal quality. No doubt the contractor here saves money by deliberately breaking the contract, but it has not been held that the owner is in such circumstances entitled to the money saved. The owner is not deprived of any valuable opportunity to bargain for a price reduction, because the builder cannot (unless there is a right to specific enforcement) be prevented from using New Hampshire stone. Even if the builder's conduct amounted to a material breach that entitled the owner to terminate the contract, there would be no substantial damages, because the cost of substitute performance would

---

[44] *Groves v. John Wunder Co.* 205 Minn 163 (1939), *Ruxley Electronics and Construction Ltd* v. *Forsyth* [1996] 1 AC 344, HL, *Jacob & Youngs Inc.* v. *Kent* 230 NY 239 (1921), *Moss* v. *Christchurch RDC* [1925] 2 KB 750, *Joyner* v. *Weeks* [1891] 2 QB 31, *Miles* v. *Marshall* (1975) 55 DLR (3d) 664, Ont. HC, *Wigsell* v. *School for the Indigent Blind* (1880) 8 QBD 357, *Radford* v. *deFroberville* [1977] 1 WLR 1262, *Tito* v. *Waddell* [1977] Ch 106, *Hollebone* v. *Midhurst and Ferhurst Builders Ltd* [1968] 1 Lloyds Rep 38, *Attica Sea Carriers Corp.* v. *Ferostaal Poseidon Bulk Reederei GmbH* [1976] 1 Lloyds Rep 250, CA, *C. R. Taylor (Wholesale) Ltd* v. *Hepworths Ltd* [1977] 1 WLR 659. See writers cited in S. Waddams, 'Restitution as Part of Contract Law', in A. Burrows (ed.), *Essays on Restitution* (Oxford, 1991), p. 197 at p. 208. D. Friedmann, 'The Performance Interest in Contract Damages' (1995) 111 *Law Quarterly Review* 628, B. Coote, 'Contract Damages, *Ruxley*, and the Performance Interest' [1997] *Cambridge Law Journal* 537.

[45] *Jacob & Youngs Inc.* v. *Kent* 230 NY 239, 129 NE 889 (1921). The same conclusion was reached by the House of Lords in *Ruxley Electronics and Constructions Ltd* v. *Forsyth*, note 44 above.

normally be measured by the reasonable cost of building with New Hampshire stone, and (assuming all else were unchanged) there would be no difference between the contract price and the cost of substitute performance. The fact that the breach of contract is deliberate makes no difference to this conclusion.

Practical and administrative considerations have also played a part. Let us suppose a case in which the defendant is offered a bargain opportunity for an immediate cash investment, and he postpones payment of all his current financial obligations to take advantage of it. The opportunity materializes and the defendant becomes wealthy in consequence. Could it be contemplated that the creditors could claim a portion of the enrichment? The answer must surely be no. The creditors are amply compensated by payment of their debts with interest and costs of collection, if any. The intractable problems of tracing what money had produced what profit, and allocating the profit among various creditors, suggest strong practical reasons for restricting the creditors to their usual compensatory remedies.

Where the plaintiff can be said to have something like a proprietary interest in the subject matter of the contract, an accounting of profits has often been, by various techniques, imposed. These are cases in which it can be said that the wrongdoer has derived a profit from something that, in a sense, belonged to the plaintiff, as in the cases of trespass like the Kentucky cave case. An analogous contractual example has arisen where the plaintiff is a purchaser of land with a right to specific performance.[46] It is not always clear, however, when it can appropriately be said that a promisee has a proprietary interest in the subject matter of a contract. This question is linked with the availability of specific performance, for an interest may be characterized as proprietary partly because it is protected by the court's willingness to grant specific relief.[47]

In a number of cases money awards have been made for breaches of covenants restricting uses of land. In *Wrotham Park Estate Co. Ltd* v. *Parkside Homes Ltd*[48] (1974) a sum of money was awarded corresponding to what would have been a reasonable licence fee for relaxation of the covenant. In the later case of *Surrey County Council* v. *Bredero Homes Ltd*,[49] the defendant

---

[46] *Lake* v. *Bayliss* [1974] 1 WLR 1073, *Webb* v. *Dipenta* [1925] SCR 565 (on theory of specific performance cy près). See *British Motor Trade* v. *Gilbert* [1951] 2 All ER 641, and Lord Nicholls in *Attorney General* v. *Blake*, note 2 above.

[47] See chapters 3 above, and 9 below.   [48] [1974] 1 WLR 798.

[49] [1993] 1 WLR 1361 (CA).

had, in breach of a covenant, built seventy-seven houses in a housing development, instead of the seventy-two permitted, the breach of covenant causing no diminution in the value of the plaintiff's own property. The Court of Appeal held that the plaintiff was entitled to nominal damages only. The argument that the plaintiff had been deprived of an opportunity to bargain was dismissed by Steyn LJ as 'a fiction',[50] and the *Wrotham Park* case[51] was explained as 'only defensible on the basis of the . . . restitutionary principle [i.e., unjust enrichment]'.[52] The court, unwilling to extend restitution to breach of contract generally, thought it inapplicable in the *Bredero* case, which was characterized simply as a case of 'breach of contract'.[53] The English Court of Appeal subsequently reconsidered the question in *Jaggard* v. *Sawyer*,[54] and held that the *Wrotham Park* case was rightly decided, and was, after all, rightly to be understood as resting on compensatory not restitutionary principles. Sir Thomas Bingham, MR, said that the '*Wrotham Park* approach was appropriate even on pure compensatory principles'.[55] The House of Lords later (2000) approved the result in the *Wrotham Park* case, preferring it to the *Bredero* case, and mentioning *Jaggard* v. *Sawyer* also with approval.[56] This fluctuation of judicial opinion supports the suggestions, earlier mentioned,[57] that the resolution of this issue has combined *simultaneously* elements both of compensation for wrongs and of unjust enrichment. The land covenant cases also have strong proprietary overtones: the beneficiary of a restrictive covenant has often been described as having a property interest in the land affected.[58]

It might be said that some of the principles mentioned earlier by way of objection to requiring an accounting of profits derived from breach of contract are compensatory principles that become irrelevant when the case is categorized as one of unjust enrichment: to establish that the plaintiff has suffered no loss does not establish that the defendant has not been enriched. If legal principles were derived from independent sources on purely logical grounds this point might have force, but it has not been a satisfactory practical answer where exclusion of the principles of compensation would lead to results generally perceived to be extravagant and unjust. The legal problems that have to be resolved (must the employee, or the debtor, pay over the profits; must the lessee of the mining site pay the cost of restoration;

[50] *Ibid.*, at 1369.   [51] [1974] 1 WLR 798.   [52] *Ibid.*, per Steyn LJ.
[53] *Ibid.*, at 1371 (Steyn LJ), 1364 (Dillon LJ).   [54] [1995] 1 WLR 269.
[55] *Ibid.*, at 283.   [56] *Attorney General* v. *Blake*, note 2 above, at 281.
[57] P. 112 above.   [58] See pp. 43–4 above.

must the seller pay the increase in the value of the goods between date of breach and date of judgment?) do not alter by being recharacterized. The questions of what is fair to the plaintiff, whether there is an unjust enrichment of the defendant, whether the defendant has taken something of the plaintiff's, and what public policy requires are aspects of a single legal problem, and cannot be resolved in isolation from each other.

From the perspective of unjust enrichment the crucial question has appeared in the form of whether the enrichment has been shown to be 'at the plaintiff's expense',[59] or that the plaintiff has suffered 'a corresponding deprivation'.[60] In the examples just discussed this feature is lacking: the skilled employee who finds a more valuable use for his time than house-painting is enriched by his breach of contract, but he cannot be said to be enriched 'at the employer's expense', nor does the employer suffer 'a corresponding deprivation' because in no sense does the employee take anything that can be said to belong to the employer.[61] Neither does the debtor (where there is no sort of trust), or the lessee of the mining site (where the actual cost of performance was not foreseen and taken into account at the time of the contract and where the lessor's interest is purely commercial), or the defaulting seller of goods (where the contract is not specifically enforceable) take anything that can be said to belong to the creditor, lessor, or buyer. The introduction to the argument here of proprietary concepts is not accidental, and is closely related (as the qualifications in parentheses indicate) to other concepts such as trust and specific enforcement. Legal reasoning has not always been strictly logical,[62] and legal results have often been supported by mutually interdependent concepts.

Those arguing for a rule that profits made in breach of contract must be given up have supported their argument with the assertion that the contract breaker should not be permitted to 'expropriate' the plaintiff's

---

[59] This is generally stated as one of the fundamental elements of restitution for unjust enrichment, e.g. *Restatement of Restitution* s. 1, Goff and Jones, *Law of Restitution*, p. 16, Palmer, *Law of Restitution*, s. 2.10, Birks, *Introduction to the Law of Restitution*, p. 21. See S. Worthington, 'Reconsidering Disgorgement for Wrongs' (1999) 62 *Modern Law Review* 218 at 225–6.

[60] *Pettkus v. Becker* [1980] 2 SCR 834 at 848, 117 DLR (3d) 257 at 273–4. The latter formulation has been said to be 'awkward' in the context of restitution for wrongs, M. McInnes, 'The Canadian Principle', note 20 above, at 25.

[61] It is otherwise where the employer has invested heavily in the enterprise of marketing the services of the particular employee. See discussion of *Lumley* v. *Wagner* at p. 120 below, and in chapter 2 above.

[62] G. Samuel, *The Foundations of Legal Reasoning* (Maastricht, 1994), pp. 278–9. See p. 2 above.

rights.[63] This is a telling phrase, but has not supported the conclusion that all profits made by breach of contract should be given up, precisely because not every contractual right can be characterized as proprietary, nor every breach of contract as 'expropriation'. The points are interconnected. It is in just the kind of (exceptional) case in which specific performance is available that the courts have categorized the plaintiff's interest as proprietary; it is in such a case that profits derived from breach have usually been required to be given up, and where it could be said that the contract breaker had been enriched at the other party's expense, and had deprived the other party of an opportunity to bargain;[64] and it is in just this kind of case that the courts have contemplated an award of exemplary damages, and the possibility of self-help, and where the ordinary measure of compensatory damages has been perceived as inadequate.[65]

Interdependence of legal concepts, as we have seen elsewhere, has often given an appearance of circularity to legal reasoning, but this does not show that the conclusions reached have been accidental, arbitrary, or unprincipled. In the case of the purchase of a unique piece of land, the court's willingness to grant an injunction or a decree of specific performance, binding on third parties, from one point of view creates and from another point of view protects the purchaser's proprietary interest in the land. By contrast, an employer does not usually have a proprietary interest in an employee's services, and neither has the court usually restrained the freedom of the employee, or that of third parties, by specific remedies. The distinction is relevant to the present enquiry: the purchaser, but not the employee, has usually been obliged to account for profits derived from the breach of contract.

From the point of view of loss of opportunity to bargain, the concept of proprietary interest, and its link with specific relief, is significant. In the Kentucky cave case, had the defendant respected the plaintiff's rights, he would have approached him for permission to admit the tourists into the plaintiff's property, and the plaintiff would have been in a position to demand, in return, a share of the profits. But in the case of an employee who quits a job in breach of contract, it cannot be said that the breach deprives the employer of any opportunity to bargain. It has been suggested, in order to disparage the significance of compensation for loss of opportunity

---

[63] See, for example, L. Smith, 'Disgorgement', note 20 above, at 129, 132 and 140.
[64] See pp. 108–9 above. [65] See chapter 8, below.

to bargain, that 'in theory every time there is a breach of contract the injured party is deprived of his "bargaining power" to negotiate for a financial consideration a variation of the contract which would enable the party who wants to depart from its terms to do what he wants to do'.[66] But this line of reasoning seeks to force all contracts into a single category to the exclusion of other legal concepts. Where there is no right of specific enforcement, breach of contract does not deprive the employer of any opportunity to bargain. Suppose that the employee, before the breach of contract, announces an intention of resigning in order to earn more money elsewhere. If substitute employees are available to do the contract work at the contract price (or less), the employer has no bargaining power. Whether the employer agrees or not, there will be no substantial damages. To this extent, there is force in Holmes' proposition (1881) that the common law (Holmes excluded equity) leaves a promisor 'free to break his contract if he chooses'.[67] The same idea is reflected in the economic concept of 'efficient breach'.[68] The employee who makes a profit by breach of an ordinary employment contract, therefore, has not been held liable to account, and one of the reasons is that she has not deprived the employer of any valuable opportunity.

But it is otherwise where the courts will issue an injunction against a defaulting employee. These are the (comparatively rare) cases of 'star' employees, opera singers in one era, as in *Lumley* v. *Wagner*[69] (1852), movie actors in another,[70] and athletes in a third.[71] In cases of this sort an employee who profits by breach of contract *can* be said to deprive the employer of a valuable opportunity, for the employer could have restrained the employee by injunction. Even in these cases, the injunction has not been given in terms that restrain the employee from any other profitable activity whatever, though such a restraint might have been contractually agreed.[72] In *Warner Bros.* v. *Nelson* (1937) a film actress was restrained by injunction

[66] *Surrey County Council* v. *Bredero Homes Ltd* [1993] 1 WLR 1361, CA, at 1368 (Dillon LJ).
[67] O. W. Holmes, *The Common Law*, ed. M. Howe (Boston, 1963 [1881]), p. 236.
[68] Approved by the Supreme Court of Canada in *Bank of America Canada* v. *Mutual Trust Co.* (2002) 211 DLR (4th) 385 at 394–5. See R. A. Posner, *Economic Analysis of Law* (Boston, 1972), pp. 55–6, and subsequent editions.
[69] (1852) 1 De G M & G 604. See chapter 2, above.
[70] *Warner Bros Pictures Inc.* v. *Nelson* [1937] 1 KB 209.
[71] See *Flood* v. *Kuhn* 407 US 258 (1971), *Detroit Football Co.* v. *Dublinski* (1956) 4 DLR (2d) 688, revd on other grounds 7 DLR (2d) 9.
[72] *Warner Bros* v. *Nelson*, note 70 above.

from working as an actress for a film company which could be said to be a competitor of the plaintiff.[73] If, in such a case, the defendant had managed to beat the injunction by filming the necessary sequences without the plaintiff's knowledge, it could be said that the plaintiff had been deprived of an opportunity to bargain, and there would therefore be a strong case for requiring the defendant to account for part at least of the profits derived from the breach of contract. On the other hand, if the employee, in breach of contract, had abandoned film acting altogether, and taken up, let us say, landscape painting, the plaintiff would not have been deprived of a bargaining opportunity, because no injunction would have been issued restraining the defendant from painting, or restraining a third party from commissioning a painting. Profits derived from painting, therefore, would, partly for these reasons, not be payable to the plaintiff.[74]

More common have been cases in which injunctions have been issued against employees, or former employees, to restrain competition, or to restrain the use of confidential information. In such cases, if the employee engages in competition, or sells the confidential information before the plaintiff can act to obtain an injunction, it can again be said that the plaintiff is deprived by the defendant's wrong of an opportunity to bargain. It may often also be said in cases of this sort that the defendant has infringed something closely analogous to a proprietary interest of the plaintiff, for, as we have seen, the concept of proprietary interest has often been linked with the availability of specific relief. In *United States Surgical Corp.* v. *Hospital Products International Pty Ltd*[75] (1984) the Australian High Court held that a distributor of products was not a fiduciary, and therefore not bound to account for profits made by competing, in breach of contract, with its supplier. It may be suggested that if the distributor could have been restrained by injunction from competing, or from using secret information, it could be said that the supplier had lost an opportunity, the value of which could be measured by a reasonable fee that the supplier might have charged to license the defendant's activity. On the other hand, if the distributor, albeit in breach of contract, had wholly neglected surgical products, and

---

[73] This was considered to be a crucial point by McRuer CJHC in *Detroit Football Club v. Dublinski*, note 71 above, where an injunction was refused precisely because the defendant's new employer was not a competitor of the plaintiff.
[74] See *Attorney General v. Blake*, note 2 above, where the test suggested was whether the plaintiff had a legitimate interest in preventing the defendant's profit-making activity.
[75] (1984) 156 CLR 41.

had made profits in another field altogether, there would (in the absence of proof of loss) be no case for substantial damages.

Contracts of the kind considered in the preceding paragraphs are contracts in restraint of trade, and generally, therefore, they have been subject to stringent tests of enforceability. In view of the link between the concept of proprietary interest and the availability of specific relief it is not surprising to find that, in seeking to establish criteria for enforceability of contracts in restraint of trade, the courts have distinguished between proprietary interests (which can be protected, often by injunction) and the employee's personal skills (the exercise of which should not be unduly restrained).[76] The distinction between proprietary and non-proprietary interests, though elusive and to some extent circular, is not accidental, and corresponds to the same important distinction that is required in the present context. Considerations of public policy have also played an important role where an employee's freedom to work is at stake.

Several cases have considered the question of profits made by publication of memoirs by former members of the secret services in breach of contractual obligations of confidentiality. In the most recent of these cases, *Attorney General* v. *Blake* (2000), the House of Lords held that an accounting of profits may be required as a discretionary and exceptional remedy for breach of contract.[77] Lord Nicholls, who gave the principal speech, was careful to emphasize the exceptional nature of this remedy, and careful not to make a definitive ruling on when it was available. He said:

> a useful general guide, although not exhaustive, is whether the plaintiff had a legitimate interest in preventing the defendant's profit-making activity and, hence, in depriving him of his profit

adding immediately that 'It would be difficult and unwise to attempt to be more specific.'[78] The use of the words 'discretionary' and 'exceptional' indicate rejection of a simple or universal rule in terms only of breach of contract, and shows that there were other dimensions to the question: one of the principal reasons given by the court was the idea (not derived solely from contract) that Blake's duty was 'closely akin to a fiduciary obligation'.[79] The concept of the claimant's 'legitimate interest in preventing the defendant's profit-making activity' signified activities likely to cause damage to

---

[76] See M. J. Trebilcock, *The Common Law of Restraint of Trade* (Toronto, 1986), though criticizing the way in which the distinction has been applied (pp. 146–7).

[77] *Attorney General* v. *Blake*, note 2 above.

[78] *Ibid.* at 285.   [79] *Ibid.* at 287, 292 (Lord Steyn).

the government (for example, memoir writing) independent of what would have been caused by simple neglect of contractual duties (for example, premature resignation from the public service to take up landscape painting).[80] Such independent damage is likely to occur in precisely those cases where the plaintiff suffers a loss of opportunity to bargain, where damages measured by the plaintiff's loss will be perceived as inadequate, where the obligation is likely to be specifically enforceable, where the defendant can be said to have infringed a proprietary interest, where the defendant can be said to be unjustly enriched, and where there is a perceived public policy in deterring the wrong. Not all these factors have been present in every case, nor can they be considered in isolation from each other, for, as in many of the cases considered in this study, the various concepts have tended to support each other with cumulative effect. They are mutually interdependent to such a degree that they are, in the context of certain legal issues, different ways of saying the same thing.

The proposition that no one should profit from his or her own crime has an attractive ring. It has played a part in legal reasoning, but rather as a maxim than as an actual working rule.[81] In penal law the maxim certainly has been influential in sentencing for crime, but even there it is not an overriding principle, for it must be balanced against other considerations. It was held in *Attorney General* v. *Blake*, discussed above, that the courts had no inherent jurisdiction to confiscate the proceeds of crime, and the attempt of the Court of Appeal to achieve that result by issuing an interlocutory injunction restraining the publisher from paying royalties was held to be improper. Arguments have been made in favour of forfeiture of profits derived from publications describing crime, and legislation to this effect has been proposed and enacted in some jurisdictions, but there are strong countervailing policy arguments, and New York legislation of this sort was held unconstitutional as abridging free speech.[82] It has not been established that the courts have any inherent jurisdiction, in the absence of valid legislation, to effect such a forfeiture to the state as a matter of public law; a private law obligation has not been found appropriate without a convincing link between the defendant's profits and some kind of entitlement in the plaintiff.[83]

---

[80] See pp. 35 above and 154 below.
[81] See P. Stein and J. Shand, *Legal Values in Western Society* (Edinburgh, 1972), pp. 100–01.
[82] *Simon & Schuster, Inc.* v. *New York State Crime Victims Board* 502 US 105, 112 S Ct 501 (1991).
[83] See E. Weinrib, *The Idea of Private Law* (Cambridge, Mass., 1995).

In a number of instances such a link has been established. Thus it has been held in most Anglo-American jurisdictions that a murderer is not entitled to succeed to the victim's property by contract, by will, by right of survivorship, or by the law of intestacy.[84] These cases have often been treated as part of the law of unjust enrichment,[85] despite the absence of one of the usual requirements of unjust enrichment, namely a loss on the plaintiff's side corresponding to the defendant's gain.[86] Nevertheless the successful claimants in these cases were not total strangers: they were the persons who stood to receive the property when the murderer was disqualified, and usually they could have shown that they would probably have acquired an interest in the property if the murderer had predeceased the victim.

The maxim that no one should profit by wrongdoing has been cited in many of these cases, but the courts have not accepted it elsewhere as an actual legal rule. Lord Goff said, in 1990:

> The statement that a man shall not be allowed to profit from his own wrong is in very general terms, and does not of itself provide any sure guidance to the solution of a problem in any particular case.[87]

In the *Blake* case, Lord Nicholls said:

> The broad proposition that a wrongdoer should not be allowed to profit from his wrong has an obvious attraction. The corollary is that the person wronged may recover the amount of this profit when he has suffered no financially measurable loss . . . [T]he corollary is not so obviously persuasive.[88]

As we have seen, the House of Lords in this case rejected a principle that profits derived from crime were liable to forfeiture for that reason alone, and accepted only in limited circumstances an obligation to account for profits derived from breach of contract.

---

[84] *Re Sigsworth* [1935] Ch 89, *Riggs* v. *Palmer* 115 NY 506 (1889), *Re Crippen* [1911] P. 108, *Cleaver* v. *Mutual Reserve Fund Life Assurance* [1992] 1 QB 147.

[85] Goff and Jones, *The Law of Restitution*, ch. 34, Maddaugh and McCamus, *The Law of Restitution*, ch. 22.

[86] Andrew Burrows for this reason excludes these cases from unjust enrichment: Burrows, *The Law of Restitution*, p. 380. Graham Virgo treats them as cases of 'restitution' but not of 'unjust enrichment', Virgo, *Principles*, p. 570.

[87] *Attorney General* v. *Guardian Newspapers (No. 2)* [1990] 1 AC 109, HL.

[88] *Attorney General* v. *Blake*, note 2 above, at 278, with reference to *Halifax Building Society* v. *Thomas* [1996] Ch 217 at 229.

In 1982 a notorious murderer in British Columbia arranged, in exchange for giving information to the police, that a sum of money would be paid into a trust for his wife and child. This money was subsequently claimed by the parents of the murder victims. The claim succeeded before the judge of first instance, who relied on the 'well-established principle of our law that it is contrary to public policy that a man should be allowed to claim a benefit resulting from his own crime'.[89] But the decision was reversed in the British Columbia Court of Appeal, in substance because the plaintiffs had not established a ground for any private law claim: there was no claim for unjust enrichment because the enrichment of the murderer's wife and child had not occurred at the plaintiffs' expense.[90] The payment was not compensation, and the plaintiffs would not have received it if the arrangement with the murderer had not been made.

Contracts that are illegal have often been held to be unenforceable, but this is not to say that all benefits derived from illegal contracts are necessarily forfeited. In *St John Shipping Corp.* v. *Joseph Rank, Ltd*[91] (1957) a shipper of goods that had been safely carried to their destination sought to withhold payment of part of the freight on the ground that the carrier had overloaded the ship. But it was held that the contract was enforceable and that the freight was payable in full, Devlin J resting his conclusion mainly on the consideration that the carrier's right to the freight had not arisen 'directly' from the overloading. The defendant had withheld the amount of payment that it calculated to be equivalent to the profit derived from the overloading:

> The fact is that the defendants ... have ... withheld money, not on a basis that is proportionate to the claim against them, but so as to wipe out the improper profit on the whole of the cargo.[92]

But if the defendant could withhold part of the freight on this ground, it could withhold it all, and if one cargo owner had that right, all must have had the same right, for there was nothing to connect the illegal profit to any particular cargo. This would be excessive, but no principle was apparently at hand to support a proportionate deduction:

> I do not, however, think that the defendants' position would be any better if they had deducted no more than the sum attributable to their freight

---

[89] *Rosenfeldt v. Olsen* (1984) 16 DLR (4th) 103, BCSC, at 125.
[90] *Rosenfeldt v. Olsen* (1986) 25 DLR (4th) 472, BCCA.
[91] [1957] 1 QB 257.   [92] *Ibid.* at 293.

on a pro rata basis. There is no warrant under the principle for a pro rata division. . . . The fact is that in this type of case no claim or part of a claim for freight can be clearly identified as being the excess illegally earned.[93]

This is to say, in effect, that the necessary link between the illegal gain and the defendant was absent: principles of private law should not be employed solely for the purpose of augmenting the penal provisions of the statute governing the loading of ships, inadequate though those provisions might be. Another way of putting this conclusion would be that, if the shipper were to be excused from its contractual obligation to pay the agreed freight, the effect would be unjustly to enrich the shipper, who would receive the benefit of the carriage of its goods without paying the price. Considerations of unjust enrichment in such cases have thus cut in both directions, as they have also in the analogous case of gratuitous transfers of property for illegal purposes.[94]

The question of profits derived from wrongdoing has become a kind of test case for classification in private law, with some writers seeking to incorporate it entirely into unjust enrichment, and others seeking rigorously to exclude it. As we have seen, the issue is one that has been resolved neither wholly in terms of unjust enrichment, nor wholly in terms of compensation for loss, nor in terms that entirely exclude considerations of either. The additional influence, in many of the cases, of concepts of contract, property, and public policy shows why no single home can be found for them on legal maps, or in taxonomic schemes.

---

[93] Ibid.   [94] Tinsley v. Milligan [1994] 1 AC 340, HL.

7

Domestic obligations

Domestic obligations must rank among the most important of personal obligations, whether importance is judged by social significance, by the number of persons affected, or (in recent decades) by volume of litigation. They are private legal obligations in the strictest sense of each of these words, yet they have usually been marginalized in or omitted entirely from accounts of the law of obligations.

Anglo-American law, unlike some other systems, has not formally separated family relationships from the rest of private law. In the past some features have tended towards a separation, such as the exclusive matrimonial jurisdiction of the English ecclesiastical courts[1] (abolished in 1857), the rule of interspousal immunity in tort law (abolished in the twentieth century), and a presumption against binding contractual relations in family agreements[2] (never more than a presumption). In the second half of the twentieth century any possibility of a formal separation receded as property disputes between spouses were adjudicated by applying general principles of property law, contracts, torts, trusts, and unjust enrichment; sharp distinctions based on the status of marriage became untenable as the same principles were then extended to non-matrimonial relationships.

The omission of domestic obligations from accounts of private law cannot therefore be justified on formal grounds. They can neither be subordinated to any of the concepts just mentioned nor wholly separated from them. As we shall see, the ideas of contract, wrongdoing, unjust enrichment, and property are readily discernible both in the old ecclesiastical law, and in the dramatic changes that occurred in the second half of the twentieth century. Considerations of public policy can also be seen to have been highly influential in both periods, but this neither distinguishes domestic

---

[1] For a fuller account, see S. Waddams, 'English Matrimonial Law on the Eve of Reform' (2000) 21 *Journal of Legal History* 59.
[2] *Balfour* v. *Balfour* [1919] 2 KB 571, CA.

obligations from other obligations, nor establishes that public policy has operated in isolation from the other concepts. Statutes affecting domestic obligations have been enacted in all jurisdictions, but this fact does not exclude those obligations from the scope of the present enquiry. The obligations enforced by the ecclesiastical courts were not statutory in origin, and the twentieth-century changes were led, as we shall see, by judicial employment, sometimes in conjunction with statutory reform but often in advance of it, of the concepts with which this study has been mainly concerned, namely, contract, wrongdoing, unjust enrichment, and property, combined with considerations of public policy.

By English matrimonial law, as it was until the middle of the nineteenth century, a wife had the right to reside in her husband's home. She also had the right, if her husband was proved guilty of adultery or cruelty, to live apart from him if she chose to do so, in which case he was obliged to support her by payments, usually between one-third and a half of the parties' joint income, called alimony.[3] These rights were not derived from the common law or equity, and in places where English law had been received, but ecclesiastical courts had not been instituted, special provisions were necessary to introduce them.[4] Though the rights were personal, they had proprietary consequences. The husband's obligations to receive his wife in his home, and to pay alimony, were enforceable by imprisonment for contempt of court, and so had some affinities with orders of the court of Chancery. Though not property rights, they were personal rights that directly affected the husband's property.

The right to alimony was often regarded as a kind of substitute for a married woman's loss of ownership of property. In defending the rule that husbands were obliged to pay the costs of matrimonial litigation, win or

---

[3] R. Roper, *A Treatise of the Law of the Property arising from the Relation between Husband and Wife* (2 vols., London, 1841), vol. II, p. 310n., L. Shelford, *A Practical Treatise on the Law of Marriage and Divorce* (London, 1841), pp. 592–3, *Cooke* v. *Cooke* (1812), 2 Phil 40, *Otway* v. *Otway* (1813) 2 Phil 109, J. Barton, 'The Enforcement of Financial Provisions', in R. Graveson (ed.), *A Century of Family Law* (London, 1957), pp. 352, 353.

[4] In Nova Scotia the power was exercised by the Governor in Council, K. S. Maynard, 'Divorce in Nova Scotia 1750–1890', in P. Girard and J. Phillips (eds.), *Essays in the History of Canadian Law* (Toronto, 1990), pp. 232, 233, 257. In Upper Canada statute gave the power to the Court of Chancery, 7 Wm IV c.2, s.3 (1837). In some American jurisdictions courts of equity asserted an inherent power to award alimony, J. Story, *Commentaries on Equity Jurisprudence* (13th edn, 2 vols., Boston, 1886), vol. II, p. 757, para. 1323a, and see comments of Blake C in *Severn* v. *Severn* (1852) 3 Grant's Ch R 431 at 432–4.

lose, Robert Phillimore, one of the leading nineteenth-century ecclesiastical lawyers, made the connexion:

> if the law of the land gives all her fortune to the husband, surely it is only just that he should be compelled to allow her the means of defending herself from a charge by which he is to deprive her of the means of subsistence...[5]

Alimony was usually measured by the husband's income, but all his property was affected, because he was not permitted to evade payment by investing in non-income producing assets. In a case (1828) where the husband owned shares, Dr Stephen Lushington, judge of the London Consistory (diocesan) Court established the point in this way:

> Though it might be true, the shares...might not...be available as income, yet if the Court were to allow this exemption, a husband might so invest his income as to evade all claims upon him for the support and maintenance of his wife.[6]

Thus, though the wife did not have a property right in the husband's assets, the extent of her personal right varied according to their value.

Matrimonial obligations differed in many respects from ordinary contracts: they could not be varied, modified, or rescinded by the parties, and they were enforceable by imprisonment for contempt of court, not by payment of damages or recovery in debt.[7] Nevertheless contractual links were strong: matrimony was regarded as (among many other things) a contract,[8] and one of the general reasons for enforcement of matrimonial obligations was that matrimony was a kind of bargain. Considerations of wrongdoing were also relevant. Though alimony was not, conceptually speaking, compensation for loss caused by wrongdoing, the obligation to pay it only arose in consequence of the husband's wrongdoing (cruelty or adultery); the wife then became entitled to live apart, and alimony was a substitute for the support that she would (in the absence of the wrong) have received in her husband's home.

---

[5] R. Phillimore, *Thoughts on the Law of Divorce in England* (London, 1844), p. 45.
[6] *Harris* v. *Harris* (1828) 1 Hagg Ecc 351, at 352–3.
[7] Barton, 'The Enforcement of Financial Provisions', note 3 above, at p. 353.
[8] W. Blackstone, *Commentaries on the Laws of England* (4 vols., London, 1765–69), vol. I, p. 421, *Hyde* v. *Hyde* (1866) LR 1 PD 130.

Alimony also had important, though secondary, punitive and deterrent aspects.[9] The burdens imposed by ecclesiastical law were perceived as the natural legal consequences of misconduct, and were closely associated with strong considerations of public policy. Sir John Nicholl, Dean of the Arches (judge of the court of appeal for the ecclesiastical province of Canterbury), said in *Cooke* v. *Cooke* (1812) that it was 'the duty of every court of justice to guard the public morals of society', adding that

> this principle has been fully established, and forcibly applied to cases where the husband is the injured party – on this principle pecuniary damages are awarded in other courts [i.e. at common law against another man guilty of adultery with the plaintiff's wife] – and where the husband is the delinquent, and the wife the injured party, the same principle may be justly applied [i.e., by ecclesiastical courts], not vindictively, nor excessively, but reasonably and moderately.[10]

The general idea of unjust enrichment also played an important part. In the legal and social circumstances of the first half of the nineteenth century a woman who married, and was then compelled to leave her husband because of his cruelty or adultery, suffered an irreparable loss. She was unable to remarry or to own personal property, and might often be unable in practice to return to her parents' home. Husbands derived many benefits from marriage, including, as the common law then stood, the benefits of property brought into the marriage by the wife,[11] and custody of the children. The idea that a husband could retain these benefits at the expense of his wife, and, having compelled her by his own misconduct to leave his house, deprive her of the means of subsistence, was antithetical to general considerations of justice. In a case of 1836, where the wife, having obtained a divorce (separation) from the ecclesiastical court on the ground of her husband's adultery, took her children abroad in defiance of the common law order of habeas corpus (for custody of the children), the husband sought to withhold alimony. The ecclesiastical court judge (Dr Lushington), showing little sympathy with the then prevailing common law of child custody, refused to reduce the alimony:

---

[9] Alimony could be increased on account of very bad conduct: Barton, 'The Enforcement of Financial Provisions', note 3 above, at p. 353.
[10] *Cooke* v. *Cooke* (1812) 2 Phil 40 at 45.   [11] A point stressed in *Cooke* v. *Cooke*, note 10 above.

I am at a loss to know why I should, by starving an innocent wife, compel obedience to the orders of other tribunals [i.e. the common law court] to render up to the guilty husband the offspring of that union, the obligations of which he has grossly violated.[12]

After the Married Women's Property Acts (1870–93) married women were legally capable of owning property, but often in practice the legal title to valuable property, including the matrimonial home, was vested in husbands. The English courts for a period of about twelve years (1952–64) under the leadership of Lord Denning developed a new proprietary interest in favour of married women. The effect of this interest, known as the deserted wife's equity, was to prevent a husband who had deserted his wife from selling the matrimonial home without her consent. The reasons given included contract ('the husband is presumed to have given authority to his wife to remain in the matrimonial home'),[13] wrongdoing ('he cannot take advantage of his own wrong – of his own desertion – and use it as a ground for ejecting her'),[14] unjust enrichment ('if such a transaction were permitted, the husband would benefit greatly because he would get a high price at the wife's expense'),[15] and public policy ('it would be shocking to contemplate that a husband could put his wife and children into the street, so that he could himself return to live in the home perhaps with another woman').[16]

The cumulative effect of these considerations was to create a proprietary interest in the wife that would bind a purchaser from the husband, unless the latter could claim to have purchased in good faith without notice of the wife's interest. This line of cases was not enthusiastically received by English property lawyers,[17] and was overruled by the House of Lords in 1965,[18] but its cumulative use of legal concepts, and the interrelation of personal and proprietary claims are significant to the theme of the present study. Equally significant is the sequel: Lord Denning was in a sense vindicated,

---

[12] *Greenhill v. Greenhill* (1836) 1 Curt 462 at 467 (Dr Lushington). See *R v. Greenhill* (1836) 4 Ad & E 627, for the common law decision.

[13] *National Provincial Bank v. Hastings Car Mart* [1964] Ch 655, CA, at 684.

[14] *Ibid.*, at 683.   [15] *Ibid.*, at 685.

[16] *Ibid.*, at 684, quoting *Report of Royal Commission on Marriage and Divorce*, Cmnd 9678 (London, 1956), at p. 180.

[17] R. Megarry and H. Wade, *The Law of Real Property* (2nd edn, 1959), pp. 748–50, and articles cited there.

[18] *National Provincial Bank v. Ainsworth* [1965] AC 1175, HL.

for broadly similar protection was soon afterwards given to married women by legislation in England[19] and in many other jurisdictions.[20]

One of the most important and difficult issues faced by all common law jurisdictions in the second half of the twentieth century was the resolution of property claims on the dissolution of domestic (matrimonial and quasi-matrimonial) partnerships. These were claims based both on property concepts and on private law obligations in the strictest sense of those words, but they cannot conveniently be allocated exclusively to property, or to any division of the law of obligations.[21]

These cases have raised issues of high controversy in an area of rapidly changing social attitudes. Substantially it was a new problem for private law, and, if useful maps had been available, this would have surely been the time to consult them. The variety of approaches and solutions in different common law jurisdictions, and within jurisdictions over time, shows that no usable map has been available: any map that could have been envisaged in 1850, 1900, or even 1950, would have led to results wholly unacceptable in 2000.

The resolution of this legal issue has involved, simultaneously and cumulatively, a variety of legal concepts, including contractual or contract-like expectations, reliance, trusts, property, wrongdoing, unjust enrichment, and public policy. In most cases there has been insufficient common intention to satisfy the requirements of contract formation or of express or implied trusts. Title to property has been typically vested in the defendant. A rigorous investigation of the extent of enrichment would often have yielded little to the claimant.[22] But the claims have succeeded. The arguments are cumulative: the claimant has a reasonable and justified expectation,[23] in

---

[19] Matrimonial Homes Act, 1967 (UK).

[20] E.g., Family Law Act (Ontario) RSO 1990 c. F-3, Part II, ss. 19, 24(1).

[21] P. Birks (ed.), *English Private Law* (Oxford, 2000), treats family law, with corporations, as part of the law of persons, separately from property and obligations, an arrangement derived from Blackstone, and, more remotely, Gaius.

[22] See Ontario Law Reform Commission, *Report on Family Law* (Toronto, 1993), p. 39: 'The doctrine of unjust enrichment has serious limitations as a tool for the fair allocation of property between spouses or others who have integrated their economic lives as part of an intimate relationship. The doctrine rests on a transfer of wealth . . . [which] may not be easily demonstrated on the evidence.'

[23] *Sorochan v. Sorochan* [1986] 2 SCR 38 at 52–3, 29 DLR (4th) 1 at 12, *Peter v. Beblow* [1993] 1 SCR 980 at 990, 101 DLR (4th) 621 at 645 ('in every case the fundamental concern'). P. Maddaugh and J. McCamus, *The Law of Restitution* (Toronto, 1990), p. 667, make an analogy with frustration of a joint venture.

reliance on which she has changed her position;[24] she ought to receive a fair share of the property which in a real sense belongs to a joint venture,[25] and is partly 'hers'; otherwise the defendant would be doing her a wrong,[26] and would be unjustly enriched; and public policy[27] supports sharing of property between life partners.

The idea that this important issue can be allocated to one of these legal concepts to the exclusion of the others is contradicted by the varying experience of different common law jurisdictions. As Jack Beatson has pointed out,

> out of the same underlying material, different jurisdictions have emphasized and acted on different principles. In dealing with the ownership of property occupied by spouses and cohabitees, in England courts have predominantly used an estoppel doctrine which emphasizes reliance, in Canada they have relied on unjust enrichment, in Australia on unconscionability, and in New Zealand on the protection of reasonable expectations.[28]

Though different concepts have predominated in different jurisdictions at various times, they are closely interrelated, and may indeed be regarded as complementary aspects of the same question.[29]

American law has reflected the same concurrence of concepts. June Carbone, writing of the American Law Institute's principles of the law of family dissolution, has said that they 'combine property and contract, expectation and restitution...'.[30] In *Marvin* v. *Marvin* (1976) the California

---

[24] *Gillies* v. *Keogh* [1989] 2 NZLR 327.   [25] *Muschinski* v. *Dodds* (1985) 160 CLR 583.

[26] The Australian cases have based similar results on a principle of unconscionability, with some doubt as to whether it is the defendant's conduct, or the denial of a remedy that is unconscionable: see *Baumgartner* v. *Baumgartner* (1987) 164 CLR 137, and D. W. Waters, 'Where is Equity Going? Remedying Unconscionable Conduct' (1988) 18 *University of Western Australian Law Review* 3. See also *Soulos* v. *Korkontzilas* [1997] 2 SCR 217 at 240, 146 DLR (4th) 214 at 229 ('good conscience'), M. Halliwell, *Equity and Good Conscience in a Contemporary Context* (London, 1997), pp. 73–103.

[27] *Peter* v. *Beblow*, note 23 above, at 991 (SCR), 646 (DLR).

[28] J. Beatson, *The Use and Abuse of Unjust Enrichment: Essays on the Law of Restitution* (Oxford, 1991), p. 248. See also C. Rotherham, 'The Contribution Interest in Quasi-Matrimonial Property Disputes' (1991) 4 *Canterbury Law Review* 407, R. Stenger, 'Cohabitants and Constructive Trusts – Comparative Approaches' (1988) 27 *Journal of Family Law* 373.

[29] See Cooke P in *Gillies* v. *Keogh*, note 24 above, at 330–1, suggesting that the various approaches are substantially equivalent, C. Rotherham, *Proprietary Remedies in Context* (Oxford, 2002), pp. 208–9.

[30] J. Carbone, 'The Futility of Coherence: the ALI's Principles of the Law of Family Dissolution, Compensatory Spousal Payments' (2003) *Utah Journal of Law and Family Studies* (forthcoming).

Supreme Court, in upholding the possibility of a claim by an unmarried co-habitant, relied on concepts of contract, unjust enrichment, and property. As Carol Bruch, who submitted an amicus curiae brief to the court, put it, the delineation in such cases of legal doctrines 'as distinct categories ... is inevitably blurred'.[31] She emphasized also the blurring of the line between law and equity: 'Perhaps the most useful remedy – the imposition of a trust upon property – may accordingly be requested in a case in which trust theory does not provide the underlying cause of action'.[32] The California court adopted these views:

> In the absence of an express contract, the courts should inquire into the conduct of the parties to determine whether that conduct demonstrates an implied contract, agreement of partnership or joint venture, or some other tacit understanding between the parties. The courts may also employ the doctrine of quantum meruit, or equitable remedies such as contract or resulting trust, when warranted by the facts of the case.[33]

Many other American jurisdictions have adopted similar reasoning while weighing also changing perceptions of public policy – a consideration that formerly excluded enforcement of contracts between unmarried cohabitants.[34]

Canada has, as Beatson's words earlier quoted suggest, adopted a distinctive approach, resting the results on a broad concept of unjust enrichment, combined with a flexible use of proprietary concepts to reach what have been considered to be just conclusions.[35] Thus the Supreme Court of Canada has said that 'acceptance of the notion of restitution and unjust enrichment in Canadian jurisprudence has opened the way to recognition of the constructive trust as an available and useful remedial tool in resolving matrimonial property disputes',[36] and that 'the great advantage of ancient principles of

---

[31] C. Bruch, 'Property Rights of De Facto Spouses Including Thoughts on the Value of Homemakers' Services', in S. N. Katz and M. L. Inker (eds.), *Fathers, Husbands and Lovers* (Chicago, 1979), p. 283 at p. 308.
[32] *Ibid.*   [33] 18 Cal 3d 660, 557 P 2d 106, 134 Cal Rptr 815, 819.
[34] See *Hewitt v. Hewitt* 394 NE 2d 1204, 1209–11 (Ill, 1979), M. L. Inker, 'Changes in Family Law: A Practitioner's Perspective' (1999) 33 *Family Law Quarterly* 515 at 520, E. S. Scott and R. E. Scott, 'A Contract Theory of Marriage', in F. H. Buckley (ed.), *The Fall and Rise of Freedom of Contract* (Durham, N. C., 1999). See chapter 10 below.
[35] *Rathwell v. Rathwell* [1978] 2 SCR 436, *Pettkus v. Becker* [1980] 2 SCR 834, *Sorochan v. Sorochan*, note 23 above.
[36] *Rathwell v. Rathwell*, note 35 above, at 444, repeated in *Sorochan v. Sorochan*, note 23 above, at 43 (SCR), 4 (DLR).

equity is their flexibility: the judiciary is thus able to shape these malleable principles so as to accommodate the changing needs and mores of society, in order to achieve justice. The constructive trust has proven to be a useful tool in the judicial armoury.'[37]

This is not the language of map-reading, nor of map-making in the sense of describing pre-existing terrain.[38] Some commentators have, partly for these reasons, been critical of these tendencies. Mitchell McInnes, for example, makes the point that 'while bearing the language of unjust enrichment, the Supreme Court of Canada's decisions in cohabitational property disputes arguably have little to do with restitutionary relief and much to do with the court's desire to achieve fairness between former parties to spousal-like relationships'.[39] Joachim Dietrich considers that 'the results of many Canadian cases are not consistent with unjust enrichment analysis'.[40] David Stevens has similarly suggested that 'the co-option of private law doctrine in the matrimonial or quasi-matrimonial union cases has done a great deal of substantive damage to both family law and private law'.[41]

There is certainly some force in these points. It may be accepted that unjust enrichment, viewed in isolation from other concepts, could not support the results reached in many of these cases. But it does not follow either that the cases were wrongly decided or that considerations of unjust enrichment can be wholly excluded.[42] As with the legal issues considered in earlier chapters, the various concepts mentioned, though each insufficient when considered in isolation, have operated effectively in combination.

---

[37] *Pettkus* v. *Becker*, note 35 above, at 847–8, repeated in *Sorochan* v. *Sorochan*, note 23 above, at 43 (SCR), 4–5 (DLR), and affirmed in *Peter* v. *Beblow* note 23 above, at 987–8 and 990 (SCR), 643 and 645 (DLR).

[38] R. Probert, Book Review (1999) 19 *Legal Studies* 591 at 595 ('the conclusion that the new developments cannot be reconciled with orthodox equitable doctrines is a predictable one . . . [and] the disparity . . . was only to be expected').

[39] M. McInnes, 'Reflections on the Canadian Law of Unjust Enrichment' (1999) 78 *Canadian Bar Review* 416 at 426. See also S. Gardner, 'Rethinking Family Property' (1993) 109 *Law Quarterly Review* 263, D. Stevens and J. W. Neyers, 'What's Wrong with Restitution?' (1999) 37 *Alberta Law Review* 221 at 240.

[40] J. Dietrich, *Restitution: A New Perspective* (Sydney, 1998), p. 166.

[41] D. Stevens, 'Restitution, Property, and the Cause of Action in Unjust Enrichment: Getting by with Fewer Things' (1989) 39 *University of Toronto Law Journal* 258, at 282. See also R. Scane, 'Relationships "Tantamount to Spousal", Unjust Enrichment, and Constructive Trusts' (1991) 70 *Canadian Bar Review* 260.

[42] See S. Gardner, 'Rethinking Family Property', note 39 above, combining considerations of unjust enrichment with those of fiduciary obligation.

It is impossible to doubt the influence of considerations of public policy. In 1975 the Supreme Court of Canada, in *Murdoch* v. *Murdoch*,[43] dismissed the claim of a woman for a share in her former husband's ranch. Four of the five judges who heard the case, following English law,[44] dismissed the claim on the ground that there was 'no common intention that the beneficial interest in the property in issue was not to belong solely to the [husband], in whom the legal estate was vested'.[45] Laskin J dissented on the ground that the wife's contribution to the ranch had been 'extraordinary', and that she was entitled to the benefit of a constructive trust. The majority decision caused an unprecedented storm of public protest, and put the court (which then included no women members) at the centre of a highly political controversy.[46]

Three years later the case of *Rathwell* v. *Rathwell*[47] came before a nine-judge court, of which Laskin was now the Chief Justice. The wife's claim to a half share succeeded by a bare majority, but the majority was itself divided, and so the basis of the decision was difficult to determine. Dickson J (for himself, Laskin CJ, and Spence J) made it very clear that he was strongly influenced by the kinds of issues that had been aired in the public debate following the *Murdoch* case:

> The introduction generally of the Married Women's Property Acts made it possible for wives to hold separate property but did little to improve the lot of married women. The custom by which real estate acquired by a married couple was taken in the name of the husband, coupled with the reverence paid to registered title, militated against wives . . . Many factors, legal and non-legal, have emerged to modify the position of earlier days. Among these factors are a more enlightened attitude toward the status of women, altered life-style, dynamic socio-economic changes. Increasingly, the work of a woman in the management of the home and rearing of children, as wife and mother, is recognized as an economic contribution to the family unit.[48]

This language plainly indicated a willingness to alter the law in order to conform with an 'enlightened attitude', and to improve the status of women by redistribution of property. The reference to property acquired

[43] [1975] 1 SCR 423.
[44] Summarized by Scane, 'Relationships "Tantamount to Spousal", note 41 above, at 268–70.
[45] [1975] 1 SCR 423 at 439.
[46] A. H. Young, 'The Changing Family, Rights Discourse, and the Supreme Court of Canada' (2001) 80 *Canadian Bar Review* 749 at 755.
[47] [1978] 2 SCR 436.   [48] *Ibid.*, at 442.

by a married couple, together with the disparaging reference to the 'reverence' paid to 'registered' title shows the influence of property concepts, the implication being that (whatever the registered title might be) *in reality* the property ought to be recognized as jointly owned. The two points (policy and property) are strongly interconnected. These three judges held that the plaintiff's claim might be made effective either by finding a resulting trust, or by finding a constructive trust in order to avoid an unjust enrichment. The view of these judges, however, was not then established as law, because the two other members of the majority (Ritchie and Pigeon JJ) supported the result on a different ground, finding that on the particular facts there was a joint venture between the spouses; four judges dissented in part, denying any principle of equal sharing.

Two years later, the question came again before the Supreme Court in *Pettkus* v. *Becker*,[49] (1980) where the cohabitants had not been married. Again the case was heard by a full nine-judge court, but this time they were unanimous in the result with a clear majority as to the reasoning. Dickson J, giving the judgment of six members of the court, took the opportunity 'to clarify the equivocal state in which the law of matrimonial property was left, following *Rathwell* v. *Rathwell*'[50]and rested the claimant's right to a half share of the property not on the basis of any actual intention (which he called a 'phantom intent'[51]), but on the basis of a constructive trust imposed by the court in order to avoid unjust enrichment. Dickson J introduced also the concepts of reliance and expectation:

> Miss Becker supported Mr Pettkus for 5 years. She then worked on the farm for about 14 years. The compelling inference from the facts is that she believed that she had some interest in the farm and that that expectation was reasonable in the circumstances.[52]

There was a suggestion also, as in the estoppel cases discussed in an earlier chapter, of wrongdoing on the part of the defendant:

> Mr Pettkus would seem to have recognized in Miss Becker some property interest, through the payment to her of compensation, however modest. There is no evidence to indicate that he ever informed her that all her work performed over the 19 years was being performed on a gratuitous basis. He freely accepted the benefits conferred upon him through her financial support and her labour.[53]

---

[49] [1980] 2 SCR 834. [50] *Ibid.*, at 841–2. [51] *Ibid.*, at 843.
[52] *Ibid.*, at 849. [53] *Ibid.*

The concepts of expectation, reliance, estoppel, and wrongdoing thus combined with those of property, unjust enrichment, and public policy to supply an argument sufficiently persuasive to attract the support of the six judges. As we have seen elsewhere, such ideas may be mutually interdependent: in the present context they not only support each other, but each is an aspect of the others; they are mutually complementary in that each fills out the meaning of the others.

The effect of these cases was a significant redistribution of wealth, openly made on broad grounds of social policy, from one class of persons to another. It has often been suggested that redistributions of this sort are proper rather to the legislature than to the courts. This suggestion, which has powerful academic support,[54] corresponds in part to the distinction between private and public law, in part to that between law and politics, and in part to that between corrective and distributive justice. Martland J touched on the point in his dissenting judgment in *Pettkus* v. *Becker*:

> In my opinion, the adoption of this concept [remedial constructive trust] involves an extension of the law as so far defined in this Court. Such an extension is, in my opinion, undesirable. It would clothe judges with a very wide power to apply what has been described as 'palm tree justice' without the benefit of any guidelines. By what test is a judge to determine what constitutes unjust enrichment? The only test would be his individual perception of what he considered to be unjust.[55]

This line of thinking has always carried some weight in Anglo-American legal reasoning. These cases show that the weight has not always been decisive, even on a question of high political controversy where legislation had, by 1980, already been enacted in some provinces, and was pending in others.[56] In the very short space of five years, Martland J's view had been reduced from that of the clear majority of the court to that of a small minority.[57]

The intersection of judicial and legislative development of the law gave rise to an important and interesting question in *Rawluk* v. *Rawluk* (1990).[58] The Ontario Family Law Act, 1986, provided for an equal division of family property on separation, and set the date for valuation of the property at

[54] E. Weinrib, *The Idea of Private Law* (Cambridge, Mass., 1995).
[55] [1980] 2 SCR 859.
[56] Young, 'The Changing Family', note 46 above, at 756.
[57] Beetz J joined his dissent in *Pettkus* v. *Becker*, note 35 above.
[58] [1990] 1 SCR 70, 65 DLR (4th) 161.

the date of separation. Property held in the husband's name rose in value after that date, and the question was whether the wife was entitled to a share of that increase in value. Here it was possible to argue that this was a case not of mere legislative silence, but of a specific legislative provision that determined the very point in issue. The majority of the court held, however, that the wife was entitled to the benefit of a constructive trust, which gave her a property interest in the disputed assets, and therefore a right to a share of their present value. To the argument that the legislature had determined the date for valuation, Cory J said:

> The Family Law Act, 1986, does not constitute an exclusive code for determining the ownership of matrimonial property. The legislators must have been aware of the existence and effect of the constructive trust remedy in matrimonial cases when the Act was proposed. Yet neither by direct reference nor by necessary implication does the Act prohibit the use of the constructive trust remedy.[59]

Thus, the constructive trust, conceived ten years earlier as a remedial device at the court's disposal in order to reverse an unjust enrichment established on grounds *other than* ownership of property, had taken on the characteristics of an independent vested property right, which it was to be presumed that the legislature did not intend to remove. The counter-argument, forcefully expressed by the three dissenting judges, was summed up in the words that the constructive trust 'is not a doctrine of substantive law, but a remedy'.[60] As appears elsewhere in this study,[61] and as the decision in this case confirms, the constructive trust has had, in practice, both aspects.

On the question of the deference due by the court to the legislature, the majority of the court had no hesitation in giving effect to its own view of desirable social policy:

> The application of the remedy [constructive trust] in the context of the Family Law Act, 1986, can achieve a fair and just result. It enables the courts to bring that treasured and essential measure of individualized justice and fairness to the more generalized process of equalization provided by the Act. That vital fairness is achieved by means of a constructive trust remedy and recognition of ownership. In this case fairness requires that the dedication and hard work of Jacqueline Rawluk in acquiring and maintaining the properties in issue be recognized.[62]

---

[59] *Ibid.*, at 97 (SCR), 180–1 (DLR).   [60] *Ibid.*, at 107 (SCR), 188 (DLR).
[61] Pp. 63 and 78 above and 181–3 below.   [62] *Ibid.*, at 97–8 (SCR), 181 (DLR).

Despite the reference to 'individualized' justice, there is no mention of factors that might distinguish this case from any other in which the value of the property had risen after the equalization date: the effect was therefore to substitute a different general rule from that prescribed by the legislation. It may not be without significance that by this date the Canadian Charter of Rights and Freedoms was in operation, and the court had become accustomed to modifying and supplementing legislation in the public sphere on the basis of very general considerations of social policy.[63]

The concepts of ownership of property and of personal obligation of support are distinct, and have different legal origins, but they have not operated in isolation from each other. Future earning capacity may, for various legal purposes, be visualized as a capital asset.[64] If a claimant, entitled to an equal share of assets, received half the capital value of a spouse's future earning capacity she could not, *on grounds of equal sharing*, be entitled in addition to half the spouse's future earnings, for this would be to create an unequal division of assets. On the other hand, if property rights and support obligations were conceptually distinct, there would be no reason why the claimant should not receive all the property to which she was entitled at one date and, in addition, the support to which she was also entitled at a later date.

When this issue arose in respect of a pension in *Boston* v. *Boston* (2001), the Supreme Court of Canada was divided.[65] The dissenting judges (it may be significant that both were civilians) made a sharp conceptual distinction between property rights and personal obligation, holding that a prior division of property could not diminish the husband's personal obligation (itself dependent on a variety of factors) to pay support out of actual current income. The case was (for the dissenting judges) 'a very straightforward matter of assessment of the needs and means of the former spouses'.[66] In this view, 'the equalization of net family property differs fundamentally from the determination of the quantum of support payments'.[67] On the other hand, the majority of the court accepted the idea that property and

---

[63] See Young, 'The Changing Family', note 46 above.
[64] This is done for several purposes in awarding compensation for personal injury. See S. Waddams, *The Law of Damages* (3rd edn, Toronto, 1997), para 3.710.
[65] *Boston* v. *Boston* [2001] 2 SCR 413, 201 DLR (4th) 1.
[66] *Ibid.*, at 445 (SCR), 24 (DLR) (LeBel J, L'Heureux Dube J concurring).
[67] *Ibid.*, at 446 (SCR), 25 (DLR).

support obligations were 'intertwined',[68] with the consequence that the prior division of the capitalized pension as property necessarily modified the obligation to pay support. Related to this division of opinion was an important and controversial question of public policy, unresolved in Canadian law: to what extent can future support obligations be excluded or modified in the settlement of a matrimonial dispute?

Domestic obligations have been found difficult to classify because they can be neither subordinated to nor separated from concepts of contract, wrongdoing, and unjust enrichment, nor from concepts of property and public policy. The profound changes, institutional, social, and political, that have affected the issues discussed in this chapter over the past century and a half exclude the idea of a single timeless scheme. Suggestions have been to assign domestic obligations to a residual or miscellaneous category within the law of obligations,[69] or to assign them to a separate 'law of persons' outside the law of obligations.[70] Either of these ideas (though not both together) might claim the merits of convenience, simplicity, logic, coherence, elegance, or compatibility with other legal systems, but neither could derive support from the actual past practice of Anglo-American law.

---

[68] *Ibid.*, at 432 (SCR), 14–15 (DLR) ('somewhat intertwined': *Shadbolt* v. *Shadbolt* (1997) 32 RFL (4th) 253 at para. 35).

[69] W. Anson, *Principles of the English Law of Contract* (Oxford, 1879), pp. 7–8, P. Birks, 'Definition and Division: A Meditation on *Institutes* 3:13', in P. Birks (ed.), *The Classification of Obligations* (Oxford, 1997), p. 19.

[70] P. Birks (ed.), *English Private Law* (Oxford, 2000), recognizing this as an 'impurity', p. 1 (i.e., 50), n.23.

8

Interrelation of obligations

In law, as in history, there is a complex interdependence between the particular and the general. Particular instances are analysed and understood in the light of general concepts, but the general concepts themselves have drawn their form and substance from the aggregation of particular instances. The preceding chapters have shown that many legal issues have been resolved not by subordination to a single concept but by the concurrent influence of several. This does not by any means show that concepts have been unimportant (indeed it shows the opposite) nor that they are reducible to a single inscrutable mass, but it does show that they have often interacted with each other, and that they cannot therefore be fully understood without attention to their mutual interdependence. The concepts are distinct, but in respect of many issues they have operated concurrently, influencing each other. Thus, breach of contract has been treated in Anglo-American law (differing in this respect from many other systems) as a wrong, but it cannot be entirely subordinated to the idea of wrongdoing. Even where there is no contract, the disappointment of economic expectations has sometimes been treated as a wrong, but it is not a wrong that can be understood in isolation from other concepts. Taking undue advantage of an inequality of bargaining power, or of a fundamental mistake, or retaining a benefit without rendering an anticipated benefit in exchange may cause unjust enrichments, but the law on these questions cannot be understood in terms of unjust enrichment alone. In this chapter it will be seen that the relation to each other of the concepts of contract, wrongdoing, and unjust enrichment can be envisaged neither in terms of mutual isolation nor in terms of subordination of one to any other.

The origins of modern contract law lay in the concept of breach of contract as a species of wrongdoing. This has made it impossible to avoid overlapping liability, for there has been no contractual 'domain' exclusive of tort.[1] Where the same facts give rise to claims both in contract and in tort, Anglo-American law, with few exceptions,[2] has admitted concurrent liability.[3] No convincing argument has been adduced in support of the idea that the simultaneous commission of two wrongs means that one must be excused.[4]

Breach of contract, though in its origin a wrong, has not shared all the characteristics of other wrongs.[5] Non-contractual wrongs usually have the following legal consequences: they may be restrained by judicial order; they may be abated where practicable by self-help; profits derived from them must be given up; benefits obtained by threat of a wrong must be restored; persuading another to commit a wrong will itself be a wrong. In addition, non-contractual wrongs usually are contrary to public policy, they attract moral disapprobation, and sometimes they may be deterred by penal money awards. Anglo-American law has not attached all these consequences to all breaches of contract. Logic, simplicity, and consistency might seem to favour the attribution to all legal wrongs (contractual and non-contractual) of similar consequences. But other values have been at stake. It cannot be established by logic that a contract for personal services should not be enforceable by a decree of specific performance. But such a rule has not been generally adopted because it would sometimes (it is not necessary to say 'always', or even 'usually') have led to consequences generally regarded as extravagant, oppressive, and unjust.

It is evident that actions categorized as legal wrongs cover a wide range of conduct, attracting very varied degrees of moral disapprobation. It is quite possible to imagine circumstances in which a breach of contract might attract more censure than a tort, but in general it is true to say that there are

---

[1] S. Whittaker, 'The application of the "Broad Principle of Hedley Byrne" as between Parties to a Contract' (1997) 17 *Legal Studies* 169.

[2] Solicitors' liability in England was, for many years, restricted to contract, *Howell* v. *Young* (1826) 5 B & C 259, *Groom* v. *Crocker* [1939] 1 KB 194, *Clark* v. *Kirby-Smith* [1964] 1 Ch 506, *Cook* v. *Swinfen* [1967] 1 WLR 457, CA. See also *Bagot* v. *Stevens Scanlon & Co.* [1966] 1 QB 197, *McLaren Maycroft & Co.* v. *Fletcher Devt Co.* [1973] 2 NZLR 100, *Nunes Diamonds Ltd* v. *Dominion Electric Protection Co.* [1972] SCR 769, 26 DLR (3d) 699.

[3] *Flint & Walling Manufacturing Co.* v. *Beckett* 79 NE 503 (Indiana SC, 1906), *Central Trust Co.* v. *Rafuse* [1986] 2 SCR 147, *Henderson* v. *Merrett Syndicates Ltd* [1995] 2 AC 145, HL, *BC Checo Int. Ltd* v. *BC Hydro & Power Authority* [1993] 1 SCR 12.

[4] *Winterbottom* v. *Wright* (1842) 10 M & W 109, which Pollock said was 'perfectly correct', *The Law of Torts* (London, 1887), p. 449, held only that a contract to which the plaintiff was not a party could not *enlarge* the plaintiff's rights.

[5] For a fuller account, see S. Waddams, 'Breach of Contract and the Concept of Wrongdoing' (2000) 12 *Supreme Court Law Review (2d)* 1.

many breaches of contract that have not attracted moral censure, and that have not been treated as contrary to public policy. Examples are breaches of contract by employees and residential tenants who leave their jobs or their homes without notice, consumer buyers who change their minds, and debtors who postpone payment of their debts. A breach of contract by a business person has not usually been considered morally objectionable, if coupled with an offer to pay full compensation; it follows that the morally objectionable feature of a breach of contract without such an offer has been not the breach of contract itself, but the failure to offer compensation for it.[6] On the other hand there are some cases where the plaintiff has more than a purely financial interest in contractual performance, and these are likely to be the cases where an injunction or a decree of specific performance is available, where the plaintiff can be said to have a proprietary interest, where supra-compensatory remedies might be appropriate, and where moral disapprobation of breach is appropriate.

It has sometimes been maintained that breach of contract is *never* a wrong. Holmes said that there was no legal duty to perform a contract, but only to perform or to pay damages at the promisor's option,[7] and his published correspondence with Pollock shows that Holmes adhered to this opinion throughout his life despite cogent arguments to the contrary adduced by Pollock.[8] A modern version of Holmes' view has appeared in the shape of the economic doctrine of 'efficient breach', to the effect that breach of contract may be economically efficient, since the contract breaker is made better off by it, and the other party no worse off on receipt of full compensation.[9] Holmes' view has been called heretical,[10] and the concept

---

[6] A distinction is often made in this context between 'primary' and 'secondary' obligations. See, for example, P. Birks, 'The Concept of a Civil Wrong', in D. Owen (ed.), *Philosophical Foundations of Tort Law* (Oxford, 1995), pp. 50–51.

[7] O. W. Holmes, *The Common Law*, ed. M. D. Howe (Boston, 1963 [1881]), p. 236, O. W. Holmes, 'The Path of the Law' (1897) rep. (1998) 78 *Boston University Law Review* 699 at 702.

[8] These were that Holmes' view was incompatible with the historical origins of assumpsit, with the availability of specific performance, with the tort of inducing breach of contract, with the doctrine of frustration, and with the ordinary expectations of contracting parties, *Holmes–Pollock Letters: The Correspondence of Mr Justice Holmes and Sir Frederick Pollock 1874–1932*, ed. M. D. Howe (2 vols., Cambridge, Mass., 1941), I, pp. 79–80 [1894], II, pp. 201–2 [1927]. See P. S. Atiyah, 'Holmes and the Theory of Contract', in P. S. Atiyah, *Essays on Contract* (Oxford, 1986), p. 57, at p. 59.

[9] R. Posner, *Economic Analysis of Law* (5th edn, Boston, 1998), pp. 131–4, accepted by the Supreme Court of Canada in *Bank of America Canada* v. *Mutual Trust Co.* (2002) 211 DLR (4th) 385, para. 31.

[10] G. Calabresi, 'Remarks: the Simple Virtues of *The Cathedral*', (1997) 106 *Yale Law Journal* 2201 at 2204.

of efficient breach fallacious,[11] but the ideas underlying these concepts have played a significant role. As with many heresies and fallacies, error lies not so much in the basic idea (which may tend, if not overstated, to illuminate an aspect of the truth) but in supposing that this one aspect is the only aspect, and that it overrides all other considerations.

Sometimes arguments have been adduced in favour of a general right to specific performance of contracts,[12] but no such right has developed in Anglo-American law.[13] The principal cases where specific performance has been refused are contracts for personal services, non-payment of debts, and long-term contracts where orders of specific performance might have unexpected and oppressive consequences. Other considerations have been that the rules governing mitigation would be undercut by a general right to specific performance; that a decree of specific performance would often have the effect of prolonging a dispute, and creating new occasions for conflict between hostile parties; that where the cost of performance greatly exceeds the economic benefit of the performance, a decree of specific performance would be oppressive to the defendant and would give undue bargaining power to the plaintiff; and that rights of third parties would sometimes be affected.

These arguments may be summarized by saying that specific remedies are orders of the court, enforced by the court, by machinery under its control, and by the strictest sanctions available to the community against its members (i.e., imprisonment for disobedience); experience has shown that such orders are liable to operate in ways that had not been foreseen at the time of the contract, that they may operate in the future in ways that cannot be foreseen at the time of the order, that they are potentially oppressive to defendants and to third parties, and that they may impose on the court a heavy burden of supervision. In these circumstances the court has refused to put out of its own ultimate control the power to withhold such orders where they were not, in the traditional phrase, 'just or convenient'. This is fundamentally the effect of saying that equitable remedies are discretionary, or that, unlike money remedies, they are never available as of right, or that they are not available unless damages are shown to be inadequate or inappropriate.

[11] D. Friedmann, 'The Efficient Breach Fallacy' (1989) 18 *Journal of Legal Studies* 1.
[12] F. Lawson, *Remedies of English Law* (2nd edn, London, 1980), 211, A. Schwartz, 'The Case for Specific Performance' (1979) 89 *Yale Law Journal* 271.
[13] S. Waddams, 'The Choice of Remedy for Breach of Contract', in J. Beatson and D. Friedmann (eds.), *Good Faith and Fault in Contract Law* (Oxford, 1995).

It may be urged that this feature is not unique to contracts: there has been no absolute right, either, to an injunction to restrain non-contractual wrongs. Injunctions have been refused, for example, in a variety of tort cases, including nuisance, inducing breach of contract, and infringements of intellectual property rights.[14] The whole range of legal wrongs, contractual and non-contractual, might thus be conceived as arranged on a scale according to the readiness of the court to restrain them by specific remedies. This way of looking at the matter would not be wholly erroneous, but it would be necessary to add that most deliberate non-contractual wrongs and most breaches of what have been characterized as property rights have qualified for injunctive relief, and that most breaches of contractual rights have not. There is a familiar link here: if a non-contractual wrong is not restrainable by injunction we may say, for that very reason, that the plaintiff's interest should not be called 'proprietary';[15] on the other hand, if a contract is specifically enforceable and third parties are affected, we may say, partly for those reasons, that the plaintiff's interest is, or is analogous to, a property right. Though the reasoning is to some extent circular, the results, as we saw in relation to profits derived from breach,[16] are not accidental or arbitrary. An employee cannot be compelled to perform personal services, and one very good reason for this has been that, if she could be so compelled, the employer would have something like a proprietary interest in her services. Since that proposition is (in most cases) unacceptable, the rule denying specific performance has been perceived to be soundly based. On the other hand, the purchaser of a unique parcel of land for personal use is entitled to enforce the contract by decree of specific performance binding on third parties, and, partly for that very reason, has been said to have a proprietary interest in the land.[17]

As we have seen in a variety of non-contractual settings, a right to compensation may arise from conduct that is not wrongful in any ordinary sense, and is sometimes justifiable and even laudable.[18] In the contractual context this phenomenon is well illustrated by *Wells* v. *Newfoundland*[19] (1999), where the question at issue was the Crown's liability for breach of an employment contract with a civil servant who had been appointed to a senior tenured position (until age 70 and 'during good

[14] See *Microsoft* v. *Plato*, *The Times*, 17 Aug. 1999 (CA).
[15] See G. Calabresi and A. Melamed, 'Property Rules, Liability Rules, and Inalienability: One View of the Cathedral' (1972) 85 *Harvard Law Review* 1089. See chapters 3, above, and 9, below.
[16] See p. 122 above.   [17] *Rose* v. *Watson* (1864) 10 HLC 672.
[18] See pp. 82–106 above.   [19] *Wells* v. *Newfoundland* [1999] 3 SCR 199.

behaviour').[20] About four years later the position was abolished by new legislation restructuring the board to which he had been appointed. The government offered no compensation, and Wells brought an action. The action failed in the Newfoundland Supreme Court, but succeeded in the Court of Appeal and in the Supreme Court of Canada. Restructuring the board was perfectly legal, the court held, and the legislation valid. The actions of the executive and of the legislature were, in other words, immune to any public law challenge. But nevertheless the Crown was in breach of its contract and was bound to pay reasonable compensation. This was a right that could have been removed, but only by express legislative provision: there being no such express provision, an abrogation of Wells' right to compensation was not to be implied.

This decision illustrates that a breach of contract may give rise to a right of compensation even though the contract breaker had, in a sense, a right to act as it did pursuant, in this case, to valid legislation. The traditional words denoting a tenured appointment ('during good behaviour') must (the court said) mean something. Tenure in this context meant that, while the government was free to eliminate the position, it was bound to pay compensation. This interpretation protected the plaintiff's expectations (to the extent that a money award could do so) while preserving the government's freedom to act in the public interest, a freedom that must imply immunity from punitive damages, specific performance,[21] and from any attempt by the plaintiff to force his unwanted services on the Crown. If payment of compensation were really deemed contrary to the public interest, the court pointed out, adopting a suggestion of Professor Peter Hogg, there was always the possibility of legislation specifically abrogating the plaintiff's rights.[22] The fact that a breach of contract is authorized, by statute or by the constitution, need not exclude an obligation to pay compensation, just as statutory authority to commit a nuisance has not always excluded payment of compensation.[23]

Where practicable, many wrongs may be abated by self-help, as, for example, in the cases of recapture of chattels, re-entry on to land, and abatement

---

[20] The age of Wells on appointment is not given in the Supreme Court reasons. The Newfoundland Court of Appeal said early 50s, [1997] NJ 250, para 61, but the *Encyclopedia of Newfoundland and Labrador* (online) gives his birthdate as 1944, making him 41 on appointment.

[21] Assuming that specific performance is available against the Crown; see I. Spry, *The Principles of Equitable Remedies* (3rd edn, Sydney, 1984), p. 331, R. Sharpe, *Injunctions and Specific Performance* (2nd edn, Toronto, 1995), paras. 3.1030–1150.

[22] P. Hogg, *Liability of the Crown* (2nd edn, Toronto, 1989), pp. 171–2.

[23] See *Tock* v. *St John's Metropolitan Area Board* [1989] 2 SCR 1181, and chapter 5 above.

of nuisance. In the contractual context the equivalent question (though it has not usually been framed in these terms) is whether a party to a contract may impede or prevent a breach by forcing on the other party an unwanted performance. Generally speaking, the answer has been no. An employee who is wrongfully dismissed does not have the right to ignore the dismissal and force his services on the employer;[24] still less does an employer have a right to conscript a defaulting employee. When property in goods has not passed to the buyer, the seller generally does not have the right to deliver the unwanted goods and compel the buyer to pay the price,[25] nor would a buyer usually have the right to use self-help to take possession of goods that the seller had refused to deliver. The owner of a picture who agrees to have it cleaned may effectively withdraw permission, albeit in breach of contract,[26] and, by stronger reasoning, it cannot be doubted that a patient who agrees to undergo a surgical operation may effectively (though in breach of contract) withdraw permission. In a nineteenth-century railway construction case a dispute arose between the railway company and the contractor, each blaming the other for delay. The company attempted to terminate the contract but the contractor refused to quit the work. The dispute threatened to bring the work to a standstill as each impeded the other's employees. The court granted an injunction to exclude the contractor, subject to terms and conditions devised to protect his legitimate interests.[27]

There are some cases that have tended in the opposite direction. One is the House of Lords decision in *White & Carter (Councils) Ltd* v. *McGregor* [28] (1962), where an advertiser, in the face of a repudiation of the contract by the other party, exhibited unwanted advertisements and was permitted to sue for the full agreed price. The case has been subjected to heavy academic criticism;[29] it has been departed from by subsequent courts,[30] and its effect is weakened by the suggestion in the leading speech (by Lord Reid) that the

---

24 *Vine* v. *National Dock Labour Board* [1956] 1 QB 658 at 674, *Denmark Productions Ltd* v. *Boscobel Productions Ltd* [1969] 1 QB 699 at 726, 737, *Gunton* v. *Richmond upon Thames Rural London Borough Council* [1981] Ch 448.
25 *Sells* v. *Thomson* (1914) 17 DLR 737, BCCA, *Campbell* v. *Mahler* (1918) 47 DLR 722, Ont. SC App. Div.
26 *Clark* v. *Marsiglia* 43 Am Dec 670 (NYSC, 1843).
27 *East Lancashire Railway Co.* v. *Hattersley* (1849) 8 Hare 72.
28 [1962] AC 413, HL(Sc).
29 A. Goodhart, 'Comment' (1962) 78 *Law Quarterly Review* 263.
30 *Finelli* v. *Dee* (1969) 67 DLR (2d) 393, Ont. CA, *Attica Sea Carriers Corp* v. *Ferrostaal Poseidon Bulk Reederei GmbH* [1976] 1 Lloyd's Rep 250, CA, *Clea Shipping Corp* v. *Bulk Oil International Ltd (No 2)* [1984] 1 All ER 129.

result would have been different if the pursuer had had 'no substantial or legitimate interest in carrying out the work rather than accepting damages'.[31] It is by no means clear how this suggestion was applied to the facts of the case itself, since it did not appear that the pursuer had any interest, other than financial, in exhibiting the advertisements. Another case tending to permit self-help is the decision of the English High Court in *Hounslow London Borough Council* v. *Twickenham Garden Developments Ltd*[32] (1971), where a building contractor refused to accept the owner's attempt, in breach of contract, to exclude the contractor from the building site. The court declined to grant an injunction to the owner, thus enabling the contractor to bring pressure on the owner by occupying its property, with the probable practical consequence of excluding other contractors. The effect was indirectly to restrain the owner from engaging another contractor, and so to give a kind of indirect specific performance to the contractor. This has not been the usual practice of the courts where the promisee has no such special interest as would justify specific enforcement:[33] an employee who refuses to leave the employer's premises can (in the absence of very exceptional circumstances) be lawfully excluded, with the support of an injunction if necessary, even if the termination of employment is in breach of contract. In general, therefore, the courts have not permitted a party to abate a breach of contract by self-help. The exception has been in cases where, to use Lord Reid's expression, a party has had a substantial and legitimate interest in actual performance, of a kind that the court would recognize and enforce by decree or injunction, and where irreparable loss would have resulted from submitting to the breach of contract.

Profits derived from wrongs must usually be given up to the person wronged, but, as appears from the discussion in chapter 6, this principle has not been applied in its full force to profits derived from breach of contract. The exceptional cases where profits derived from breach of contract have been required to be given up have tended to be cases where the plaintiff has suffered a corresponding loss, or where there has been an infringement of some interest akin to a proprietary interest, or where disbursement is favoured by strong public policy considerations. As we have seen, this question has been found difficult to classify, and several

---

[31] [1962] AC at 413 at 431.   [32] [1971] 1 Ch 233.
[33] *Mayfield Holdings Ltd* v. *Moana Reef Ltd* [1973] 1 NZLR 309, refusing to follow *Hounslow* v. *Twickenham*, note 32 above.

variations of division and nomenclature have been proposed.[34] It was earlier suggested that it is neither necessary nor desirable nor even possible to
make a definitive selection among them: each offers its own perspective and
insight. Whatever names are used the issue remains: in what circumstances
has a contract breaker been permitted to retain the benefits derived from
the breach? It is not so much a question of allocating this issue to one or
another category[35] as of perceiving that several concepts, incommensurable
and not all pointing in the same direction, have been simultaneously in play.
They include concepts of wrongdoing, compensation for loss, expectation,
unjust enrichment, property, and public policy.

A contract procured by a threat to commit a tort is generally unenforceable, and restitution is generally available of benefits so obtained,[36] but the
same cannot always be said of a contract procured by a threat to break an
earlier contract. This raises the much-debated question of the enforceability
of contractual modifications. It has often occurred that during performance
of a contract circumstances change so that one party finds itself in a position
to demand from the other a higher payment than that originally agreed. A
number of nineteenth-century cases involved sailors, who, having agreed
to serve for the whole of a voyage at a certain wage, subsequently demanded
a higher wage when the ship was at a place where substitute services were
not readily obtainable. The renegotiated contracts were generally set aside.
According to one of the reports in the leading case of *Stilk* v. *Myrick*[37]
(1809), the reason for this result was that performance of a pre-existing
contractual duty could not constitute consideration. Thus, where a contract had been entered into at a fixed price, a subsequent renegotiation or
variation consisting of an agreed increase in the price was unenforceable.

The rule in *Stilk* v. *Myrick* was much criticized on the grounds that it did
not correspond to commercial understanding, that it failed to recognize
that actual performance was of greater real practical value than a legal right
to performance, and that it was easily circumvented by the parties or by a
court desirous of enforcing the variation.[38] But criticism was often tempered
with the observation that the rule, though difficult to defend in terms of
consideration, was yet serving a useful purpose in offering, albeit indirectly,

---

[34] See note 20, p. 111 above.   [35] See p. 118 above.
[36] P. Birks, *An Introduction to the Law of Restitution* (Oxford, 1985), p. 177.
[37] (1809) 2 Camp 317, 6 Esp 129.
[38] B. Reiter, 'Courts, Consideration, and Common Sense' (1977) 27 *University of Toronto Law
Journal* 439.

some legal protection against taking undue advantage of economic pressure. *Stilk* v. *Myrick* itself was a case in point, where sailors, having agreed to serve on a voyage for certain wages, were promised higher wages in order to induce them not to desert during the course of the voyage. It is evident that one of the reasons for the decision was to protect the shipowner from a potentially extortionate threat by the crew to desert the ship in a distant place where there was no ready supply of substitute labour. One of the reports of the case gives 'just and proper policy' as the reason for the decision,[39] and in a subsequent decision in the Admiralty Court (*The Araminta*, 1854) where the sailors had secured payment in gold of the extra money in advance of the extra performance (they were tempted to desert to gold diggings in Australia in 1852) and so the doctrine of consideration was of no assistance, *Stilk* v. *Myrick* was interpreted as holding that the variation in the contract was 'illegal'.[40]

In *Williams* v. *Roffey Bros & Nicholls (Contractors) Ltd*[41] (1990) the English Court of Appeal held that a renegotiation was enforceable if there was no duress. In that case, a subcontractor had contracted to perform carpentry work at an agreed price. When the work was partly done it became clear that he would not complete it at the contract price, and the head contractor, who was subject to a penalty clause in the main contract for delay in completion, agreed to pay a higher price for the carpentry work. This latter agreement was held to be enforceable. The court said that performance of an existing obligation might constitute consideration, though the renegotiation would be liable to be set aside if there were economic duress.

Many have welcomed the demise of consideration in this context, but it is not easy to say precisely what has replaced it. What exactly, in the court's view, was the governing concept of enforceability and how did it apply in practice to contractual renegotiations? These questions are not very easily answered.[42] One approach has been to attempt to distinguish between a 'threat' and a mere 'offer to renegotiate', on the ground that there is something wrongful about a threat but not about an offer.[43] In *Williams*

---

[39] 6 Esp 129, 130. 'Espinasse did not have a very high reputation as a reporter, but on the other hand he was one of the counsel in the case and had the means of knowledge.

[40] *The Araminta* (1854) 1 Sp Ad & Ecc 224, Adm. Ct.   [41] [1991] 1 QB 1, CA, at 10, 19.

[42] For a fuller discussion see S. Waddams, 'Commentary on "The Renegotiation of Contracts"' (1998) 13 *Journal of Contract Law* 199, S. Waddams, 'Unconscionable Contracts: Competing Perspectives' (1999) 62 *Saskatchewan Law Review* 1.

[43] See S. Smith, 'Contracting under Pressure: a Theory of Duress' [1997] *Cambridge Law Journal* 343.

v. *Roffey* it was suggested that there was no duress because the proposal for renegotiation emanated from the head contractor. Purchas LJ thought this a conclusive point,[44] but it is evident that the subcontractor had indicated, by conduct if not by words, that he was not likely to complete the work on time at the contract price. It cannot be crucial that the threat not to complete was implicit rather than explicit. Indeed, it may be in the very cases where there is no real choice that it is unnecessary to spell out the threat, or even to make what could readily be called a 'threat' at all. In *The Araminta*, the case of the payment to the ship's crew at the Australian gold diggings in 1852, it was the master who, after several desertions, took the initiative and called together the rest of the crew, offering them increased wages if they would work the ship short-handed. Dr Lushington said, of the master's payment, that it was made voluntarily, adding:

> I have used the expression *voluntarily*, because I think the effect of the evidence is, that the crew exercised no compulsion towards him, though, perhaps, in another sense of the word, such payment was not voluntary, and the more apt expression may be, and the one nearest to the truth, that he was compelled by circumstances to make that payment.[45]

This is indeed very often an apt expression to describe such circumstances, and for this reason it is doubtful whether the conclusion can be resisted that in *Williams* v. *Roffey Bros*, as in most cases of this sort, there was a threatened breach of the first contract. The decision that the modified contract was nevertheless enforceable lends support to the view that, where the pressure on the other party is not excessive,[46] many courts have accepted that it is legitimate to gain an advantage in this way.

In *Rookes* v. *Barnard*[47] (1963) a labour union threatened (in breach of contract) to strike unless the employer dismissed the plaintiff. The House of Lords held that this constituted the tort of intimidation, so as to give rise to an action by the plaintiff, who had lost his job. As a matter of employment law and policy it may be debated whether or not compensation should have been required in the circumstances of *Rookes* v. *Barnard*. But the suggestion that every threat of a breach of contract potentially constitutes a tort does

---

[44] [1991] 1 QB 1 at 21.   [45] 1 Sp Ad & Ecc 224 at 229 (emphasis in original).

[46] S. 89 of *The Restatement of Contracts (2d)* (St Paul, 1979) provides that modifications are enforceable if 'fair and equitable' in view of unexpected circumstances. The Uniform Commercial Code, s. 2-209, makes modifications enforceable, explicitly subject, however, by comment 2, to a test of good faith.

[47] [1964] AC 1192, HL.

not correspond with the past practice of the courts. Even an actual breach of contract has not normally given rise to an action by a third party,[48] and it has been common in many commercial contexts for one person to pay another in order to induce the other to perform a contract with a third person.[49]

In the context of the issues addressed here it tends sometimes to be assumed that the normal measure of damages for breach of contract is something comparatively trivial, the choice being between 'mere' compensatory damages, and some more extensive remedy. But it should not be forgotten that the normal measure of compensatory damages imposes a substantial burden on the contract breaker. Indeed, the more usual question discussed in relation to the normal measure of contract damages has been whether it is not too generous to the plaintiff.[50] The normal measure of compensatory damages aims at putting the plaintiff in the position it would have occupied if the contract had been performed, that is, it secures to the plaintiff the benefit of the bargain, or the 'expectation'. This has the effect of operating as an effective deterrent to breach in the great majority of cases, where the cost to the defendant of performance approximates the value of it to the plaintiff. One of the arguments in favour of the general rule and against a rule measuring damages only by the plaintiff's reliance is that a rule protecting only reliance would fail to deter breach in a large number of cases where the defendant calculated that the plaintiff's provable losses were less than the cost of performance.[51] It may properly be said, therefore, that, though deterrence is not a primary or overriding objective, nevertheless an element of deterrence has been an aspect of the normal measure of damages for breach of contract.

In most Anglo-American jurisdictions exemplary (punitive) damages are not available for breach of contract.[52] In English law awards of exemplary

---

[48] *Winterbottom v. Wright*, note 4 above.

[49] An example would be other tenants of a shopping centre agreeing to pay a grocery store to continue its business there in accordance with its lease. The continuing in business, or the promise to do so, would be sufficient consideration for the promises to pay, which would be enforceable, subject to duress. See *Pao On v. Lau Yiu Long* [1980] AC 614, PC, *Restatement of Contracts (2d)*, s. 73, comment *d*.

[50] L. Fuller and W. Perdue, 'The Reliance Interest in Contract Damages' (1936) 46 *Yale Law Journal* 52, P. Atiyah, 'Contracts, Promises and the Law of Obligations', (1978) 94 *Law Quarterly Review* 193. See chapter 4 above.

[51] Fuller and Perdue, 'The Reliance Interest in Contract Damages', note 50 above.

[52] *Addis v. Gramophone Co. Ltd* [1909] AC 488, HL, *Peso Silver Mines Ltd (NPL) v. Cropper* [1966] SCR 673.

damages have, since 1963, been restricted to torts committed by the government, and torts committed for financial gain,[53] and there has been no judicial movement towards awarding exemplary damages for breach of contract.[54] The American Law Institute's *Second Restatement of Contracts* (1979) provides that 'punitive damages are not recoverable for a breach of contract unless the conduct constituting the breach is also a tort.'[55] The Supreme Court of Canada, on the other hand, has held (2002) that punitive damages may, in exceptional cases, be awarded for breach of contract.[56] The general refusal of exemplary damages for breach of contract corresponds to the reluctance to decree specific performance or to order an accounting of profits, a matter discussed in an earlier chapter.[57] An employee who leaves his employment without notice in order to take a better position has not been held liable for more than compensatory damages, even if his motive is to earn a higher salary. Where the cost of performing a contract greatly exceeds the economic benefit of performance the usual position is that the contract breaker has not been required to account for the costs saved by the breach.[58]

It cannot be claimed that Anglo-American law has been entirely consistent on the question of the wrongfulness of breach of contract. One kind of case that has tended in the direction of treating breach of contract as a wrong in the full sense is that of inducing breach of contract, discussed in earlier chapters.[59] But it is significant in the present context to note that in practice the courts have not always attached all the usual consequences of torts to inducing breach of contract, and that various restrictions have been placed on its scope by the requirements of intention and by the evolution of special defences of privilege and justification,[60] and in the field of industrial relations by specific legislation.[61] In a modern case (1989), where a professional boxer endeavoured in breach of contract to engage a new manager, an injunction was sought by the old manager to restrain the new manager

---

[53] *Rookes* v. *Barnard* [1964] AC 1129, HL.
[54] Law Commission, *Report No 247: Aggravated, Exemplary and Restitutionary Damages* (London, 1997), para. 1.112.
[55] *Restatement of Contracts (2d)*, s. 355.
[56] *Vorvis* v. *Insurance Corp. of British Columbia* [1989] 1 SCR 1085, *Royal Bank of Canada* v. *W Got & Associates Electric Ltd* [1999] 3 SCR 408, *Whiten* v. *Pilot Insurance Co.* (2002) 209 DLR (4th) 257.
[57] Chapter 6 above.   [58] *Ibid.*   [59] See pp. 35 and 123 above.
[60] See J. Fleming, *The Law of Torts* (Sydney, 1957), pp. 718–21, (9th edn, 1998) pp. 762–65.
[61] Trade Disputes Act (UK), 1906, s. 3. See H. Glasbeek, 'Lumley v. Gye. The Aftermath: An Inducement to Judicial Reform' (1975) 1 *Monash University Law Review* 187.

from inducing breach of the prior contract. The injunction was refused by the English Court of Appeal on the ground that it would be an undue restraint on the boxer's freedom to compel him to retain a manager in whom he had lost confidence.[62] The refusal of the injunction in effect protected the boxer's freedom to break his contract with the first manager. If inducing breach of contract were treated in all cases as tortious, the managing officers and employees of a corporation who caused it to break a contract would be personally liable in tort. The undoubted need to create an exception here from ordinary principles of tort liability shows that not every inducement of breach of contract has been treated as wrongful.[63]

'Wrong', in the context of contractual breach, has not been a unitary concept, and neither has been the concept of contractual 'right'. No simple scheme of sub-classification has been adopted. The consequences of a breach of contract have depended on a number of interrelated factors, involving the concepts of reasonable expectations, wrongdoing, unjust enrichment, property, and public policy. In very many cases of breach of contract no remedy has been considered appropriate beyond the normal measure of compensatory damages. Of these cases it is not entirely erroneous to say that there has been, in practice, a degree of freedom to break contracts, subject to payment of compensatory damages. But there is another dimension, because there have been exceptional cases that have evoked a supra-compensatory response of one sort or another. Various interrelated factors considered throughout this study have been relevant to this question. It is in just those cases in which the courts have given a specific remedy that they have been inclined to say that the plaintiff has a proprietary interest and it is in just those cases that they have been most ready to look with favour on a claim to recover profits derived from the breach, and to consider that there is a public interest in deterring breach.[64] A conclusion

---

[62] *Warren* v. *Mendy* [1989] 1 WLR 853, CA. See also *Page One Records Ltd* v. *Britton* [1968] 1 WLR 157, refusing an injunction to restrain breach of contract in similar circumstances.

[63] *Said* v. *Butt* [1920] 3 KB 497, *ADGA Systems Int. Ltd* v. *Velcom Ltd* (1999) 168 DLR (4th) 351, Ont. CA. Consider in this context the cases, discussed at pp. 114–16 above, where the cost of performance greatly exceeds the benefit of it. Assuming, for present purposes, that the proper measure of damages for breach of contract is the economic value of performance to the plaintiff, it would be highly anomalous to allow this result to be circumvented by permitting the plaintiff to sue the managing officers of the corporation personally in tort and to recover damages measured in effect by the cost of performance, or exemplary damages.

[64] P. Cane, 'Exceptional Measures of Damages: A Search for Principles', in P. Birks (ed.), *Wrongs and Remedies in the Twenty-first Century* (Oxford, 1996), p. 301 at pp. 322–3, links damages for profits derived from wrongs with the question of deterrence.

on one of these factors affects the others, and often more than one has been present simultaneously, though they have not all been present in every case. These conclusions are conceptually untidy and imprecise, but, as we have seen, tidiness and precision have not been the overriding characteristics of the Anglo-American legal system.

The scope for concurrent liability in contract and tort was very much enlarged by the admission of the principle that negligently caused economic loss might give rise to tortious liability. As has been shown in earlier chapters,[65] this kind of liability has resisted assimilation into the general law of negligence. The courts have required proof of an 'assumption of responsibility'[66] and have restricted liability to losses within the range of risks appropriate to that assumption.[67] Several writers[68] have suggested that tort and contract may be distinguished on the basis of the kind of loss claimed. It is true that, in general, contracts have dealt with expectations and torts with harms, but this has never been adopted as an actual rule restricting recovery in either. Damages for personal injury have been recoverable for breach of contract, and expectations have often been protected by means of actions in tort, as is illustrated by a number of instances discussed earlier.[69]

The admission in English law of negligence liability for economic loss opened the door to the possibility of a claim to an expectation-based benefit that the plaintiff had not contracted for and that the defendant had not promised. Before 1963 in English law,[70] as generally in American jurisdictions,[71] such claims were excluded by the principle that there was no liability for pure economic loss caused by negligence. The problem may be illustrated by considering the defective performance of building contracts and the closely related question of the supply of defective products. In the case of building contracts English law oscillated from one extreme

---

[65] Chapters 3 and 4 above.

[66] For the difficulties of this concept see K. Barker, 'Unreliable Assumptions in the Modern Law of Negligence' (1993) 109 *Law Quarterly Review* 461.

[67] *Banque Bruxelles Lambert SA* v. *Eagle Star Ins. Co. Ltd* [1997] AC 191, HL.

[68] See S. Whittaker, 'Application of the "Broad Principle"', note 1 above.

[69] Chapter 3 above. And see J. Stapleton, 'The Normal Expectancies Measure in Tort Damages' (1997) *Law Quarterly Review* 257.

[70] *Hedley Byrne & Co. Ltd* v. *Heller & Partners* [1964] AC 465, HL.

[71] *Robins Dry Dock Co.* v. *Flint* 275 US 303 (1927), *East River SS Corp.* v. *Transamerica Delaval Inc.* 476 US 858 (1986), B. Feldthusen, *Economic Negligence* (4th edn, Toronto, 2000), pp. 194–5, 237.

to the other between 1976 and 1981, holding first that there was no rule excluding economic loss,[72] and then that there was such a rule.[73] It was the attempt to resolve this question in terms exclusively of tort and economic loss that led to this intellectual impasse,[74] creating the apparent necessity of an all-or-nothing choice between extreme opposite views.

A Canadian decision shows that the issue has other dimensions. In *Winnipeg Condominium Corporation No. 36 v. Bird Construction Co.*[75] (1995) the plaintiff became the owner, in 1978, of a building constructed in 1972. In 1989 a section of exterior stone cladding collapsed. No one was injured, but the plaintiff claimed the cost of repairs from (among others) the general contractor who had constructed the building in 1972. The Manitoba Court of Appeal, on an appeal from a motion for summary dismissal of the action, held that the claim disclosed no cause of action. The plaintiff's appeal was allowed by the Supreme Court of Canada.

The decision of the Supreme Court was that the plaintiff was entitled to recover from the defendant the reasonable cost of making the building safe. La Forest J, giving the judgment of the Court, relied primarily on a consideration of public policy. He said that repair of dangerous defects was a means of mitigating a larger loss (by averting the danger of personal injury), and that 'allowing recovery against contractors in tort for the cost of repair of dangerous defects thus serves an important preventative function by encouraging socially responsible behaviour'.[76]

The Supreme Court of Canada had previously held that there was no absolute rule, in the common law of Canada, precluding recovery of economic loss for negligence,[77] but it does not follow from this decision that all kinds of economic loss caused by defective buildings or products should be recoverable. Stamp LJ had said, in 1972,

---

[72] *Anns v. Merton London Borough Council* [1978] AC 728, HL, *Junior Books Ltd v. Veitchi Co. Ltd* [1983] 1 AC 520, HL (Sc).

[73] *Leigh & Sillivan Ltd v. Aliakmon Shipping Co. Ltd* [1986] AC 785, HL, *D & F Estates Ltd v. Church Commissioners for England* [1989] AC 177, HL, *Murphy v. Brentwood District Council* [1991] 1 AC 398, HL.

[74] R. Cooke, 'An Impossible Distinction' (1991) 107 *Law Quarterly Review* 46.

[75] [1995] 1 SCR 85, 121 DLR (4th) 193, cited with approval by the High Court of Australia in *Bryan v. Maloney* (1995) 182 CLR 609, 629, 664, a decision that goes further, in allowing recovery in respect of a defect not shown to be dangerous.

[76] Note 75 above, at 118 (SCR), 213 (DLR).

[77] *Canadian National Railway v. Norsk Pacific Steamship Co.* [1992] 1 SCR 1021, 91 DLR (4th) 289.

I have a duty not carelessly to put out a dangerous thing which may cause
damage to one who may purchase it, but the duty does not extend to putting
out carelessly a defective or useless or valueless thing.[78]

This dictum, approved by the House of Lords in *Murphy* v. *Brentwood
District Council*[79] represents an important line of thought that may carry
weight[80] despite the rejection by the Supreme Court of Canada of other
aspects of the *Murphy* decision. The argument is, in substance, that if the
plaintiff's complaint is that too high a price has been paid, that complaint
should be made to the person to whom the price was paid. This point,
sometimes put in terms of claims appropriate to contract as opposed to
tort,[81] may be more forcefully formulated in terms of responsibility for
expectations: unless the defendant misrepresents the quality of the product
in some way, there is no sufficient reason to impose tortious liability for
disappointed expectations of quality.[82] Recovery would be denied in the case
supposed by Stamp LJ of manufacture of a safe but low-quality product,
not because the loss claimed was economic, but for a more basic reason,
namely, that the loss claimed was for disappointed expectation of quality,
and the manufacturer of the product (in the case supposed, where there
was no misrepresentation and no contract between the parties) was not
responsible for the plaintiff's expectation. Recognition (as in Canada) that
economic loss is in principle recoverable need not lead to the imposition
of liability in this sort of case.

In the *Winnipeg Condominium* case the Court did not have to assess the
damages because the case was decided on an appeal from an interlocutory
motion. La Forest J indicated, however, that he did not intend that, in
general, a builder or manufacturer should be liable in tort for the plaintiff's
disappointed expectations of quality. He said, on this point:

---

[78] *Dutton* v. *Bognor Regis United Building Co.* [1972] 1 QB 373, CA, at 415.

[79] Note 73 above.

[80] But it has not prevailed in New Zealand or Australia, *Bowen* v. *Paramount Builders (Hamilton)
Ltd* [1977] 1 NZLR 394, *Bryan* v. *Maloney*, note 75 above.

[81] See Lord Bridge in *Murphy* v. *Brentwood District Council*, note 73 above, at 475, *Marigold Holding
Ltd* v. *Norem Construction Ltd* [1988] 5 WWR 710, Alta QB, at 751.

[82] The actual result in *Junior Books Ltd* v. *Veitchi Ltd*, note 72 above, may be supported on the basis
that the defender was responsible for the pursuer's expectation. See Lord Bridge in *Murphy*
v. *Brentwood District Council*, note 73 above, at 481, and Lord Keith at 466, and see *Robert
Simpson Co. Ltd* v. *Foundation Co. of Canada Ltd* (1982) 36 OR (2d) 97, Ont. CA (negligent
misrepresentation).

I note that the present case is distinguishable on the policy level from cases where the workmanship is merely shoddy or substandard but not dangerously defective. In the latter class of cases tort law serves to encourage the repair of dangerous defects and thereby to protect the bodily integrity of inhabitants of buildings. By contrast, the former class of cases bring into play the questions of quality of workmanship and fitness for purpose. These questions do not arise here. Accordingly, it is sufficient for present purposes to say that, if Bird is found negligent at trial, the Condominium Corporation would be entitled on this reasoning to recover the reasonable cost of putting the building into a non-dangerous state, but not the cost of any repairs that would serve merely to improve the quality, and not the safety, of the building.[83]

This distinction, though tenable for the reasons mentioned above, is likely to cause difficulties in practice. One such difficulty lies in the concept of 'defect' in this context. How is it to be established that the original building was defective? It may be thought obvious that a building is defective if slabs of stone fall off, but this will not be so in all cases. If a building required a new roof after ten years, it would not be assumed that the original roof was defective in the absence of proof that roofs were expected to have a longer life than ten years. The fact that the roof, if left unrepaired, might become dangerous does not affect this point. It is possible that on facts like those in the *Winnipeg* case, the contract between the builder and the first owner might have stipulated for cladding with a ten-year life expectancy only. It is not difficult to imagine a case where the builder expressly warns the original owner that the cladding will require replacement after ten years. If the original owner contracts on that basis, choosing in effect to pay only for a low-quality product, there is no breach of contract by the builder, and no ground for complaint against the builder by a subsequent owner, though there might, possibly, be a ground for complaint by a person injured by falling masonry.

A related point, perhaps even more basic, lies in the question of whether the plaintiff can be said to have suffered a 'loss'. On the bare facts that the plaintiff has purchased a building or a product less valuable than expected, no loss is established. It is essential to know what price the plaintiff paid, for the price might not have exceeded the value of what was received. It is possible, and by no means unrealistic, to imagine that the true facts were accurately disclosed to the plaintiff (by the first owner, or by an engineer's

---

[83] Note 75 above, at 120 (SCR), 215–16 (DLR).

survey) before the sale. In that case it could be justly said that the price agreed took into account the anticipated cost of repair. The point made in this and the preceding paragraph is that in situations where a second owner of a building sues the builder there are two transactions that cannot be ignored in considering the question of the builder's liability to the second owner: that between the builder and the first owner, and that between the first owner and the plaintiff.

Another point is that it is anomalous to make liability for one kind of loss (the cost of repairs) depend on the possibility of another kind of loss (personal injury) that has not occurred and has not been complained of.[84] Much repair and maintenance of buildings might be justified for safety reasons, and it would be strange to make the builder's liability dependent on whether a risk of personal injury could be imagined in hypothetical circumstances. Moreover such a legal rule would create an incentive for the plaintiff to delay repair and maintenance until the repairs became urgently necessary for safety reasons, the very opposite kind of incentive to that desired by La Forest J. Furthermore, there would be a serious conflict of interest between the plaintiff and the defendant in selecting the standard of repairs, the plaintiff's interest being in extensive and aesthetically pleasing repairs that would improve the capital value of the building, and the defendant's interest in repairs that would make the building safe at minimal cost.

Another difficulty is that often the cost of repair represents simply a convenient measure of the degree to which a product is worth less than the plaintiff expected. If the plaintiff claims the difference in value between the product she owns, and the product she expected to own, there is no obvious ground on which a builder or manufacturer (not being responsible for the plaintiff's expectation) can be liable in tort or on any other basis. Where the building or product is worth repairing, the reasonable cost of repair is simply a way of measuring the difference between the value of the product as it is, and the value that it would have had if it had answered to the plaintiff's expectations. On the principle discussed above, and apparently accepted by La Forest J in the passage just quoted, therefore, the builder or manufacturer ought not to be liable for this loss. This conclusion accords with the view of the majority of the Supreme Court of Canada in the earlier

---

[84] See *Murphy v. Brentwood District Council*, note 73 above, at 470 (Lord Keith), and 488 (Lord Oliver).

case of *Rivtow Marine Ltd* v. *Washington Iron Works* (1974), where the cost of repairing a dangerously defective crane was held not to be recoverable in tort from the manufacturer.[85] Though, in the *Winnipeg Condominium* case, the Court preferred the dissenting judgment of Laskin J in *Rivtow*, the majority view has not been, and cannot be, entirely discarded, so long as the principle is maintained that the defendant is not to be made responsible for the plaintiff's disappointed expectations of quality.

This view does not require the abandonment of the public policy consideration that weighed with La Forest J: the defendant could be held liable for the reasonable cost of averting a safety risk, for the reasons given in the *Winnipeg Condominium* case, but only on the condition that any improvement in the capital value of the building caused by the repairs should be taken into account to the defendant's credit. In this way the plaintiff would be encouraged to avert danger, but would, on the other hand, have no incentive to commission costly repairs at the defendant's expense in order to improve the capital value of the building. The plaintiff would recover the full cost of 'mitigating' the larger loss, but only the net cost, that is, the expense incurred minus the value to the plaintiff of the improvement. The defendant would thus be made liable for the cost of averting the danger, but not for the plaintiff's disappointed expectations of quality.

Considerations of unjust enrichment, though not expressly mentioned by the court, have played an important part here, as Mayo Moran has pointed out:[86] the plaintiff, in repairing the building, confers a benefit on the defendant by relieving it of the risk of incurring more extensive liability for physical damage, should such damage materialize. This perspective supplies a powerful additional reason both for allowing the cost of repair, and for limiting recovery to the *net* cost incurred by the plaintiff, for the defendant would not be enriched by improvements to the capital value of the plaintiff's building. Indeed, the *plaintiff* would be unjustly enriched if the defendant were compelled to pay for such improvements. It has proved impossible to assign these cases exclusively to the law of contracts, or of torts, and it would equally be impossible to assign them exclusively to unjust enrichment,[87] but,

[85] [1974] SCR 1189, 40 DLR (3d) 530.

[86] M. Moran 'Rethinking *Winnipeg Condominium:* Restitution, Economic Loss, and Anticipatory Repairs' (1997) 47 *University of Toronto Law Journal* 115.

[87] See J. Neyers, 'Donoghue v. Stevenson and the Rescue Doctrine: A Public Justification of Recovery in Situations involving the Negligent Supply of Dangerous Structures' (1999) 49 *University of Toronto Law Journal* 475 at 513, doubting that the benefit can be measured by the cost of repair.

as with other questions considered in this study, these concepts, combined as in the *Winnipeg Condominium* case with considerations of public policy, have operated cumulatively and in combination.

The principle of reversal of unjust enrichment was formulated by Lord Mansfield in *Moses* v. *Macferlan*[88] (1760), and expressly adopted by Blackstone, writing shortly afterwards.[89] Lord Mansfield said:

> This kind of equitable action, to recover back money, which ought not in justice to be kept, is very beneficial, and therefore much encouraged. It lies only for money which, ex aequo et bono [in good conscience], the defendant ought to refund... [I]t lies for money paid by mistake; or upon a consideration which happens to fail; or for money got through imposition, (express, or implied); or extortion; or oppression; or an undue advantage taken of the plaintiff's situation, contrary to laws made for the protection of persons under those circumstances. In one word, the gist of this kind of action is, that the defendant, upon the circumstances of the case, is obliged by the ties of natural justice and equity to refund the money.[90]

This expansive view came later to be regarded with suspicion,[91] but was revived in the twentieth century following the writings of Warren Seavey and Austin Scott and the American Law Institute's *Restatement of Restitution* (1937) and, in England, the writings of Robert Goff and Gareth Jones.

Goff and Jones, in *The Law of Restitution* (1966), writing the first English book on the subject, naturally took an expansive view of unjust enrichment.[92] Their object, very successfully accomplished, was to remind or persuade the reader that the concept of unjust enrichment had played an important (though often unacknowledged) role in the resolution of many issues throughout English law. For this purpose a large variety of issues supplied convincing illustrations, even though they did not depend *solely* on unjust enrichment: cases of prevention, as well as of reversal of unjust enrichment, were included, as were many instances where concepts of wrongdoing, contract, property, and public policy were also involved.

---

[88] (1760) 2 Burr 1005.
[89] W. Blackstone, *Commentaries on the Laws of England* (4 vols., London, 1765–9), vol. III, p. 163.
[90] (1760) 2 Burr 1005 at 1012.
[91] *Bayliss* v. *Bishop of London* [1913] 1 Ch 127 at 140, *Holt* v. *Markham* [1923] 1 KB 504 at 513 ('well-meaning sloppiness of thought': Scrutton, LJ).
[92] R. Goff and G. Jones, *The Law of Restitution* (London, 1966). See J. McCamus, 'Unjust Enrichment: Its Role and Its Limits', in D. Waters (ed.), *Equity, Fiduciaries and Trusts, 1993* (Toronto, 1993), p. 129.

Existing English law was taken as a given, and from it was derived the con-clusion that principles of unjust enrichment were to be found frequently in operation there. The phrase 'unjust enrichment' was given a relatively wide meaning, the reader being invited to join the authors in making a judgment that many rules of English law could be so explained even though the phrase 'unjust enrichment' had not, in most cases, previously been used in con-nexion with them. Since the publication in 1985 of Peter Birks' *Introduction to the Law of Restitution*, there has been a tendency to look at the matter from the other direction: 'unjust enrichment' has been used as a term of art, equivalent to 'reversible' or 'legally disapproved' enrichment;[93] the princi-ples of unjust enrichment have then been defined, and from that definition has been derived the conclusion that many claims, not being dependent *solely* on unjust enrichment, must be excluded from the subject. This mode of analysis has led various writers to exclude from the law of unjust en-richment claims based on wrongs,[94] claims for breach of fiduciary duty,[95] claims based on infringement of proprietary interests,[96] claims based on contract law,[97] claims for the value of services that do not produce residual wealth,[98] and claims dependent on public policy.[99] If all these matters were excluded, many of the leading unjust enrichment cases, including *Moses v. Macferlan* itself,[100] would have to be excluded. To say that these were not cases of pure autonomous unjust enrichment is true, but to say that they have had nothing to do with unjust enrichment (in the general sense of those words) would be to press the point too far.[101] From a historical

---

[93] P. Birks, *An Introduction to the Law of Restitution* (Oxford, 1985), p. 19.

[94] See pp. 109–10 above.

[95] See P. Birks, *Introduction*, pp. 331, 338–43, P. Watts, 'Accounting for Profits' [1992] *Lloyd's Maritime and Commercial Law Quarterly* 439 at 441, R. Chambers, 'Constructive Trusts in Canada' (1999) 37 *Alberta Law Review* 173 at 177–8, P. Birks and C. Mitchell, in P. Birks (ed.), *English Private Law* (Oxford, 2000), paras 15.04–08, 15.180n.

[96] Virgo, *Principles*, pp. 12, 592–4.

[97] I. Jackman, 'Restitution for Wrongs' [1989] *Cambridge Law Journal* 302 at 318, A. Burrows, *The Law of Restitution* (London, 1993), p. 403, D. Stevens and J. Neyers, 'What's Wrong with Restitution?' (1999) 37 *Alberta Law Review* 221 at 240.

[98] J. Beatson, 'Benefit, Reliance, and the Structure of Unjust Enrichment', in J. Beatson, *The Use and Abuse of Unjust Enrichment* (Oxford, 1991), pp. 21–44.

[99] Including salvage. See chapter 9, below, and Virgo, *Principles*, p. 321.

[100] See P. Birks, 'Misnomer', in W. R. Cornish et al. (eds.), *Restitution: Past, Present and Future* (Oxford, 1998), p. 1, at p. 13, P. Birks, 'At the Expense of the Claimant: Direct and Indirect Enrichment in English Law' [2000] *Oxford University Comparative Law Forum* 1 at 4, P. Birks, 'Unjust Enrichment and Wrongful Enrichment', (2001) 79 *Texas Law Review* 1769, at 1790.

[101] See p. 110 above.

perspective it is not necessary or even possible to formulate the question in terms of rigorous inclusion or exclusion. In an uncodified system both answers may be right, in that each emphasizes a different dimension of a complex interrelationship.

Contracts have, in a wide variety of circumstances, been set aside for what may broadly be called reasons of unfairness. The cases include relief on account of duress, undue influence, and unconscionability, and from forfeitures, penalties, limitations of liability, and grossly improvident trans-actions of various kinds.[102] These cases cannot be wholly explained by theories of consent because in most of them there is consent to the terms of the transaction in every ordinary sense of the word. Nor can they be explained in terms of wrongdoing, for often the party advantaged has committed no wrong,[103] except in the specialized equitable sense of failing to do what the court later declares to be just.[104] Neither can they be wholly explained in terms of public policy, for the primary focus has been on justice between the contracting parties. Not every case can be explained in terms of unjust enrichment because a transaction may be set aside even though, objectively speaking, there is an equal exchange of values. Yet the concepts of consent, wrongdoing, public policy, and especially unjust enrichment have been highly relevant in these cases. Relief from contractual liability for mistake in basic assumptions and for frustration may be similarly analysed.[105]

The relation between contract and unjust enrichment is of interest in this context. Where the issue has arisen as a defence to an action to enforce the contract, unconscionability and mistake have evidently been part of con-tract law: the question is of the extent and limits of contractual obligation, and 'rescission' (setting aside the contract) is a contractual question. On the other hand, if the contract has been executed and the values exchanged, an action by the party disadvantaged by the transaction is an action for restitution of an unjust enrichment, and 'rescission' is part of the law of un-just enrichment. But the issue is the same, and requires the same answer, in

---

102 For a fuller discussion, see S. Waddams, 'Unconscionability in Contracts' (1976) 39 *Modern Law Review* 369, S. Waddams, *The Law of Contracts* (4th edn, Toronto, 1999), ch. 14, S. Waddams, 'Unconscionable Contracts: Competing Perspectives' (1999) 16 *Saskatchewan Law Review* 1.

103 'The use of economic duress to induce another person to part with property or money is not a tort per se', *Universe Tankships Inc. of Monrovia* v. *International Transport Workers Federation* [1983] 1 AC 366, HL, at 385 (Lord Diplock), R. Grantham and C. Rickett, 'On the Subsidiarity of Unjust Enrichment' (2001) 117 *Law Quarterly Review* 273 at 279.

104 See chapter 4 above.

105 G. Palmer, *Mistake and Unjust Enrichment* (Columbus, Ohio, 1962).

both cases: if the contract is enforceable there can be no unjust enrichment in carrying it out; on the other hand, if the transaction, when executed, gives rise to an immediate claim for unjust enrichment, the contract must be unenforceable.[106] A map of concepts necessarily separates contract from unjust enrichment – rightly for some purposes for they are distinct concepts, but not for the purpose of assigning facts, or legal issues, or legal rules to one category exclusively. In respect of unconscionability and mistake the issue may be envisaged as simultaneously one of contracts and of unjust enrichment; alternatively it might be said that the issue has been part of contract law when it has appeared as a defence but part of unjust enrichment law when it has been a cause of action. Neither proposition is readily reducible to a schematic map or diagram.[107]

To assign unjust enrichment and contracts to separate 'areas' of a conceptual map is to introduce the possibility – indeed the certainty – of conflict between them,[108] and to make it necessary to determine if and when one of them is supplemental, subordinate, secondary or subsidiary to the other,[109] or when they may be combined.[110] This would require a complex new set of terminology that would be by no means self-applying, and not obviously necessary or desirable in an uncodified system.

Nor is it quite satisfactory to say that unjust enrichment is excluded until the contract has 'first' been set aside. Tests commonly used for setting aside a contract for unconscionability are whether the party with superior bargaining power has taken an 'undue advantage', or derived an 'immoderate gain'. These are not tests to be distinguished or applied separately from unjust enrichment; they *are* tests of unjust enrichment. Unfairness and mistake are reasons for reversing enrichments, but these are not principles that can be applied independently of contract law, for almost every disadvantageous contract may be said to be unfair, or to involve a mistake of some kind by the party disadvantaged. The contractual view of the matter and the unjust enrichment view are different aspects of the same question.

---

[106] See S. Waddams, 'Restitution as Part of Contract Law', in A. Burrows (ed.), *Essays on the Law of Restitution* (Oxford, 1991), p. 197, *North Ocean Shipping Co. Ltd* v. *Hyundai Construction Co. Ltd* [1979] QB 705, *Stocznia Gdanska SA* v. *Latvian Shipping Co.* [1998] 1 WLR 574.

[107] See S. Waddams, 'Restitution as Part of Contract Law', note 106 above.

[108] See K. Barker, 'Unjust Enrichment: Containing the Beast' (1995) 15 *Oxford Journal of Legal Studies* 456.

[109] See Grantham and Rickett, 'On the Subsidiarity of Unjust Enrichment', note 103 above.

[110] See J. Beatson, 'Restitution and Contract: Non-cumul?' (2000) 1 *Theoretical Inquiries in Law* 83.

Another way of putting this point is that *prevention* of unjust enrichment cannot be separated from *reversal* of it.[111] It was for many years asserted as a rule of English contract law that economic duress was no defence to contractual obligation.[112] On the other hand, it had been established that where a benefit was actually conferred in consequence of economic duress, restitution was available on principles of unjust enrichment.[113] As Jack Beatson pointed out,[114] these rules were incompatible, and eventually the rule of unjust enrichment prevailed.[115] It might be concluded from this that (so far from unjust enrichment being subordinate or subsidiary, as has been suggested[116]) contract law is subsidiary to unjust enrichment, and in a sense this is true: it is a defence to a contractual obligation to show that the obligation, were it to be performed, would lead to an immediate right in the other party to restitution. But it would be more accurate to conclude that neither concept has been subordinate or subsidiary to the other, for unjust enrichment may be both a cause of action and a defence.

A similar analysis may be made of rectification (reformation). On sufficient proof that an agreement had been erroneously recorded in writing, the courts of equity have ordered the reformation or rectification of the writing. The effect of this was to prevent an unjust enrichment, as would clearly ensue if a contractual price were to be increased tenfold by the accidental misplacing of a decimal point. So rectification is part of the law of unjust enrichment, and has been so treated by many writers on the subject;[117] on the other hand it is equally a part of contract law, and any examination of the effect of written documents on contractual obligations that lacked a discussion of the subject would be deficient.

One kind of case in which contractual relief has been given for mistake is where the mistake has been induced by the misrepresentation of another

---

[111] Virgo, *Principles*, p. 30, R. Goff and G. Jones, *The Law of Restitution* (5th edn, London, 1998) p. 802n., *Banque Financière de la Cité* v. *Parc (Battersea) Ltd* [1999] 1 AC 221, HL. This is one reason why 'restitution' is not an entirely satisfactory name for unjust enrichment. See Birks, 'Misnomer', note 100 above.

[112] *Skeate* v. *Beale* (1841) 11 Ad & E 983 at 990.

[113] *Maskell* v. *Horner* [1915] 3 KB 106, CA, *Astley* v. *Reynolds* (1731) 2 Str 915.

[114] J. Beatson 'Duress as a Vitiating Factor in Contract' [1974] *Cambridge Law Journal* 97 at 106–8, J. Beatson, 'Comment' (1976) 92 *Law Quarterly Review* 496.

[115] Virgo *Principles*, p. 199, *Pao On* v. *Lau Yiu Long* [1980] AC 614, PC, at 636.

[116] Grantham and Rickett, 'On the Subsidiarity of Unjust Enrichment', note 103 above.

[117] Goff and Jones, *Law of Restitution* (London, 1966), pp. 135–9, G. Palmer, *The Law of Restitution* (4 vols., Boston, 1978), vol. III, ss. 13.1, 18.7, American Law Institute, *Restatement of the Law of Restitution and Unjust Enrichment, Tentative Draft No. 1* (Philadelphia, 2001), p. 155.

party to the contract. As we saw in the discussion of reliance in an earlier chapter,[118] the concept of unjust enrichment here has operated in combination with that of reliance. Unjust enrichment standing alone would not suffice, unless the mistake were sufficiently fundamental to justify setting aside the contract, nor does innocent misrepresentation constitute a wrong, but when the element of reliance is added there has been found sufficient reason to prevent a person from enforcing an advantage procured by that person's own misrepresentation (albeit innocent).

In many kinds of case restitution has been given of the value of benefits conferred under a contract, where for some reason the party conferring the benefit has been deprived of the anticipated contractual exchange. These are cases of contracts terminated for breach by either party,[119] and contracts, or supposed contracts, that turn out for some reason to be unenforceable. The concepts of contract and unjust enrichment have clearly been distinct in this context, but they have not operated in isolation from each other.[120]

The basic measure of damages for breach of contract has regularly and effectively operated in most cases to prevent unjust enrichment, by compelling one who has received contractual benefits to pay the agreed price for them. This is one of the reasons that may be adduced in support of the normal measure of damages, and tends to prevent unjust enrichment by a contract breaker. Conversely, the courts have often leaned against permitting termination of a contract for breach, thereby giving some *protection* to a contract breaker, precisely because they have recognized that the right to enforce the contract is itself a valuable benefit that will be forfeited if termination is permitted, and that if forfeiture is allowed for an insufficient reason an unjust enrichment of the *innocent* party (the party not in breach of contract) will ensue;[121] even when termination has been permitted, the proper measure of restitution may be affected by the terms of the contract.[122]

---

[118] Chapter 4 above.
[119] See S. Waddams, 'Restitution for the Part Performer', in B. Reiter and J. Swan (eds.), *Studies in Contract Law* (Toronto, 1980), p. 155.
[120] J. Beatson, 'Restitution and Contract: Non-Cumul?', note 110 above.
[121] S. Waddams, 'Restitution as Part of Contract Law', note 106 above, at pp. 205–6.
[122] Goff and Jones, *The Law of Restitution* (5th edn, London, 1998), p. 534, J. Beatson, *The Use and Abuse of Unjust Enrichment* (Oxford, 1991), p. 13; but other writers disagree: P. Maddaugh and J. McCamus, *The Law of Restitution* (Toronto, 1990), p. 429.

Where the contract is terminated, or is unenforceable, the claim for restitution rests on the assertion that a benefit was conferred on the defendant in the expectation of receiving an agreed exchange for it, but, by reason of some legal rule, neither the expected exchange nor its money equivalent has been forthcoming. The claim is not based primarily on the contract,[123] but neither is it entirely independent, for the existence of the contract is an essential part of the claim, and the terms of the contract remain relevant.[124] In the simple case of advance payment of money for a performance that the defendant then wrongfully fails to render, the plaintiff is entitled to restitution of the money. The question, 'is this the correction of a wrong, or is it the avoidance of an unjust enrichment?' is unanswerable, for both concepts have been influential.[125]

It is, indeed, the very impurity, or mixture, of concepts that has enabled the courts in many cases to reach the results they have considered just. The leading Canadian case on unjust enrichment (1954), for example, involved services performed by a nephew for his aunt in exchange for the aunt's promise to leave him her house in her will. The nephew performed valuable services, but when the aunt died she had not made the promised will, and her contractual promise to do so was found to be unenforceable by reason of the Statute of Frauds,[126] requiring a contract to sell land to be evidenced in writing.[127] The Supreme Court of Canada held that, though the contract could not be enforced, the nephew was entitled to restitution of the value of his services. This result was based on restitution of an unjust enrichment. Proof of the contract and of its non-performance were essential parts of the nephew's claim because they were necessary to rebut the inference that he had performed the services gratuitously, but the concept of unjust enrichment was equally an essential part of the court's reasoning, because it enabled it to circumvent the apparent consequences of the

---

[123] *Fibrosa Spolka Akcyjna* v. *Fairbairn Lawson Combe Barbour, Ltd* [1943] AC 32, HL.

[124] See J. Beatson, 'Restitution and Contract: Non-Cumul?' note 110 above, Waddams, 'Restitution for the Part Performer', note 119 above, S. Waddams, *The Law of Contracts* (4th edn, Toronto, 1999), p. 724.

[125] See *Greville* v. *Da Costa* (1797) Peake Add Cas 113 at 114 ('the defendant held this money against conscience'), *Fitt* v. *Cassanet* (1842) 4 Man & G 898 at 905 ('I think the evidence does not show that the defendant has done any thing wrong . . . and consequently the present action for money had and received cannot be maintained').

[126] 29 Car II, c.3. See chapter 4 above.

[127] *Deglman* v. *Guarantee Trust Co. of Canada* [1954] SCR 725. The leading Australian case, *Pavey & Matthews Pty Ltd* v. *Paul* (1987) 162 CLR 221, involves somewhat similar facts.

statute. To insist that the claim should have been classified exclusively as a contract claim[128] would be to insist that the nephew should have had no remedy, for the court was not prepared to invalidate the Statute of Frauds.

Where money is paid in advance by a party who later defaults, the payor, unless it has been effectively agreed that the money should be forfeited, is entitled to recover back the payment, subject to any valid claim by the recipient for compensation for loss caused by the default. The claim of repayment in these circumstances has often been categorized as based on unjust enrichment rather than contract, but in the leading case on the point, *Dies* v. *British & International Mining & Finance Corp.*[129] (1939) the court said that 'the real foundation of this right is not a total failure of consideration but the right of the purchaser [the payor] derived from the terms of the contract and the principle of law applicable to recover back his money'.[130] Jack Beatson and Gregory Tolhurst, commenting on this case, wrote that 'if the law "confers" the right to recovery and it is not based on a term of the contract or a restitutionary right based on unjust enrichment, the interpretation of this case as contractual would amount to a return to implied contract theory.'[131]

Those concerned to emphasize the autonomy of unjust enrichment are naturally apprehensive, in view of the past links between unjust enrichment and implied contract, about admitting obligations based on implied contractual terms. But implied terms have played an important part in contract law, and avoidance of unjust enrichment has been one of the commonest and strongest reasons for them. Thus terms have often been implied in order to avoid an unconscionable result.[132] The emergence of unjust enrichment as an autonomous legal principle has not meant that the concept of unjust enrichment (in its general sense) has ceased to play a role in the implication of contractual terms. Implied terms give effect to the presumed intentions of the contracting parties, but ascertaining such intentions is not a simple factual inquiry: it includes what the parties, as reasonable persons, might be presumed to have intended, and it has usually been presumed that they intended to avoid an unjust enrichment.

---

[128] Stevens and Nyers, 'What's Wrong with Restitution?', note 97 above, at 240.
[129] [1939] 1 KB 724.
[130] *Dies* v. *British & International Mining & Finance Corp.* [1939] 1 KB 724, Beatson, *Use and Abuse*, ch. 3, J. Beatson and G. Tolhurst, 'Comment' [1998] *Cambridge Law Journal* 253 at 256–7.
[131] *Ibid.*, at 257.
[132] Waddams, *The Law of Contracts*, paras. 494–508.

The claim in the *Dies* case contained elements both of contract and of unjust enrichment. To categorize such claims as based exclusively on unjust enrichment would admit a defence of change of position, but this would produce anomalous results. Where a person overpays a 'running account' it is a reasonable interpretation that the recipient agrees *in fact* (even if not expressly) to a full accounting: return of the overpayment is owed as a debt, and cannot be affected by the debtor's change of position.

It has sometimes been suggested that unjust enrichment is subsidiary, secondary, subordinate, or supplementary to other legal principles.[133] These concepts have been much debated by civilian jurists,[134] and some such idea may be necessary in certain codified systems in order to reconcile the effect of code provisions that would otherwise be in conflict. But in Anglo-American law there has been no such necessity. A plaintiff who has transferred benefits under a valid contract cannot generally assert a claim for restitution of them on the ground of unjust enrichment so long as the contract remains open for performance by the other party, but this is because, so long as the anticipated exchange may be forthcoming, the claim of unjust enrichment is incomplete: it is only the failure of the anticipated exchange that makes retention of the benefits by the defendant unjust. It is not necessary to explain this by any formal principle of subsidiarity, or 'non-cumul', though it would be true to say, in a general sense, that a claim for unjust enrichment has not been available where the retention of the benefit has been justified by another valid legal principle.

The examination of the various legal issues considered in this and other chapters shows that the concept of unjust enrichment has played an important part – often the principal part – in the resolution of many legal issues that cannot, however, be assigned exclusively to unjust enrichment as a distinct branch or area of the law. Prevention of unjust enrichment has been as important as reversal of it, and the principle has often operated as a defence, rather than as a source of obligations. The consideration that a proposed rule of law, if adopted, would cause an unjust enrichment, has been a persuasive argument against adoption of such a rule. The concepts of contract, wrongdoing, and unjust enrichment are distinct, but they have been interrelated in operation. Contract law has sometimes worked to prevent wrongdoing, tort law has sometimes worked to protect expectations, and

---

[133] Grantham and Rickett, 'On the Subsidiarity of Unjust Enrichment', note 103 above.
[134] See the references mentioned by Grantham and Rickett, note 103 above, at 297n.

both have sometimes worked to prevent unjust enrichment. Most modern writers on unjust enrichment have, naturally enough in view of the subject's earlier subordination to contract, insisted on its independence;[135] others, however, have stressed the interdependence of unjust enrichment with other legal concepts.[136] From a historical perspective both views may, if not overstated, be right, for each illuminates a different aspect of a complex interrelationship. Similarly inconclusive results would attend debates on whether contract, wrongdoing, and property were fully autonomous in respect of each other and of unjust enrichment. Unjust enrichment has been an independent concept, as much as the others, but it has also been interdependent, as they too have been interdependent.

---

[135] Goff and Jones, *The Law of Restitution* (1966), Birks, *Introduction* (1985), A. Burrows, *The Law of Restitution* (London, 1993), Virgo, *Principles*, Maddaugh and McCamus, *The Law of Restitution*.

[136] S. Stoljar, *The Law of Quasi-Contract'* (Sydney, 1964), P. Atiyah, *The Rise and Fall of Freedom of Contract* (Oxford, 1979), pp. 767–8, S. Hedley, 'Unjust Enrichment as the Basis of Restitution – an Overworked Concept' (1985) 5 *Legal Studies* 56 at 66, S. Hedley, *A Critical Introduction to Restitution* (London, 2001), S. Hedley, *Restitution: Its Division and Ordering* (London, 2001).

9

Property and obligation

An essential part of any account of private law must be the relation between property and obligation. Sometimes property is thought of as inherently separate from obligations. Thus a distinction is often made between ownership and obligation,[1] or between being an owner and being a creditor,[2] which corresponds to some degree with the distinction between rights 'in rem' (against a thing) and rights 'in personam' (against a person). These latter expressions, however, lack consistent meaning in Anglo-American law,[3] and often both have been applicable simultaneously. Equity, for example, always acts 'in personam', but equitable rights and interests, because they bind third parties, are frequently described as proprietary and therefore may be, and often are, called rights 'in rem'.[4] An obligation owed to persons generally is called by some writers an obligation 'in rem', but an action for personal injury or for defamation is an action against a person.[5]

---

[1] *Lister & Co.* v. *Stubbs* (1890) 45 Ch D 1, CA, at 15 (Lindley LJ).

[2] Sometimes stated as a distinction between owning and owing, which sounds well, but is not what is intended.

[3] '[T]here has never been a clear distinction in English law between actions *in rem* and actions *in personam*', G. Samuel, *The Law of Obligations and Legal Remedies* (2nd edn, London, 2001), p. 13. 'The words as to an action being *in rem* or *in personam* . . . are apt to be used by English lawyers without attaching any definite meaning to these phrases', *Castrique* v. *Imrie* (1870) 4 LR HL 414 at 429. They may refer to the old forms of action (real, personal, mixed), to the distinction between real and personal property, to the distinction between proprietary (as opposed to money) claims, to the maritime lien in admiralty (as opposed to the common law), or to the distinction between duties owed by everyone (as opposed to those owed by identifiable individuals). The phrase 'in personam' may refer to the equitable power to demand instant personal compliance with court orders. None of these usages corresponds to the Roman law division between *actiones in personam* and *actiones in rem*: T. C. Williams, 'The Terms Real and Personal in English Law' (1888) 4 *Law Quarterly Review* 394, G. Samuel, *Foundations of Legal Reasoning* (Maastricht, 1994) pp. 71–2.

[4] But Maitland went only so far as to say that a right under a trust was 'very like' *jus in rem* and '*almost equivalent* to a right good against all', F. W. Maitland, *Equity* (Cambridge, 1910), p. 23 (emphasis added).

[5] See P. Birks, 'Definition and Division: A Meditation on *Institutes* 3.13', in P. Birks (ed.), *The Classification of Obligations* (Oxford, 1997), p. 10. In *English Private Law* (Oxford, 2000), p. xxxix, Birks allocates these cases to a third class to be called 'superstructural' rights.

Maritime law permits an action to be brought against a thing itself (a ship, or goods found at sea), with no person named as defendant, the decision of the admiralty court binding every potential claimant. This is, in a strict sense, an action 'in rem', but outside admiralty such a process is very rare: property claims are almost always vindicated by actions against persons. This fact has led some writers to subordinate property to obligations by suggesting that property is a 'bundle of rights' and so a shorthand term for describing obligations of many persons.[6] On the other hand, some writers have moved in the opposite direction by seeking to explain obligations in terms of property.[7] Some others again have pointed out that there is an inextricable circularity in legal language, because it is frequently impossible to say whether the law protects property, or whether 'property' is the name given to what the law protects.[8] Another suggestion is that property is not so much a source of rights as a legal response to events that constitute the source.[9] It is not likely that any of these various views of the relation of property to obligation can be shown to be exclusively correct as an explanation of past judicial decisions. Each captures a different aspect of a complex interrelation: as we have seen in the instances discussed in other chapters, property rights may be simultaneously both the cause and the effect of obligations. The idea that progress has been made towards discovering the 'true' nature of property is not one in support of which historical evidence can be adduced. As James Harris has written (1996), 'any general notion of

---

[6] Holmes said that 'all proceedings like all rights are really against persons. Whether they are proceedings or rights in rem depends on the number of persons affected,' *Tyler v. Court of Registration* (1900) 175 Mass 71, 76, W. Hohfeld, 'Some Fundamental Legal Conceptions as Applied in Judicial Reasoning' (1913) 23 *Yale Law Journal* 24.

[7] P. Benson, 'The Basis for Excluding Liability for Economic Loss in Tort Law', in D. Owen (ed.), *Philosophical Foundations of Tort Law* (Oxford, 1995), p. 427 at p. 456; P. Benson, 'The Unity of Contract Law' in P. Benson (ed.), *The Theory of Contract Law* (Cambridge, 2001), p. 118.

[8] 'It is incorrect to say that the judiciary protected property; rather they called that property to which they accorded protection', W. H. Hamilton and I. Till, 'Property', in *Encyclopaedia of the Social Sciences* (15 vols., New York, 1963), vol. XI, p. 536. 'Property is itself merely the label for that crystallized bundle of economic interests which the law deems worthy of protection. When intangibles such as information and opportunity are at stake, affixing the label of property constitutes a conclusion not a reason.' E. Weinrib, 'The Fiduciary Obligation' (1975) 25 *University of Toronto Law Journal* 1 at 10–11. A similar point is often made in discussion of *International News Service v. Associated Press* 248 US 215 (1918) (injunction against selling news reports copied from rival service), discussed in chapter 3 above.

[9] P. Birks, 'Property and Unjust Enrichment: Categorical Truths' [1997] *New Zealand Law Review* 623 at 631, P. Birks (ed.), *English Private Law* (Oxford, 2000), p. xlii.

property is notoriously elusive'.[10] More recently (2000) an English casebook on personal property similarly concluded, perhaps a little bleakly:

> At the end of all the readings in this book, it is necessary to ask what is really meant by the word 'property'. Is it simply a label which the law attaches to achieve a desired end? Is it a word which describes a unified concept, or does it have different meanings in different contexts? The extracts in this [concluding] chapter will not necessarily provide answers; they may add uncertainty rather than remove it.[11]

Once the concept of property has been extended beyond land and tangible things, there is no way of saying what is property, or what is not property, without consulting a particular system of law at a particular time.[12] 'Property', R. H. Tawney said,

> is the most ambiguous of categories. It covers a multitude of rights which have nothing in common except that they are exercised by persons and enforced by the state. Apart from these formal characteristics, they vary indefinitely in economic character, in social effect, and in moral justification . . . [T]hings are not similar in quality, merely because they are identical in name.[13]

'In the past', he went on to point out, speaking of English law, 'human beings, roads, bridges and ferries, civil, judicial and clerical offices, and commissions in the army have all been private property.'[14]

Property may be abolished by changes in the law, as Tawney's examples show, and equally property may be newly created. Copyright, patents, trade marks, and registered designs are now regarded as property, but they are all comparatively recent creations. Debates on the desirable extent of such rights are awash with property rhetoric, but the proposition that the law should protect property cannot in itself support the enlargement of property rights, for that would be to beg the question at issue. Against the merits of enlarging the property rights of one person or class of persons must always be set the loss of freedom of action that such enlargement inevitably causes to others.[15] The case will be recalled of *International News Service* v.

---

[10] J. Harris, *Property and Justice* (Oxford, 1996), p. 6.
[11] S. Worthington, *Personal Property Law: Text and Materials* (Oxford, 2000), p. 665.
[12] K. Gray, 'Property in Thin Air' [1991] *Cambridge Law Journal* 252, C. Rotherham, 'Conceptions of Property in Common Law Discourse' (1998) 18 *Legal Studies* 41 at 43.
[13] R. Tawney, *The Acquisitive Society* (New York, 1920), pp. 53–4.   [14] *Ibid.*, p. 73.
[15] See J. Band and M. Katoh, *Interfaces on Trial: Intellectual Property and Interoperability in the Global Software Industry* (Boulder, 1995).

Associated Press,[16] discussed in an earlier chapter, where the court granted an injunction to restrain the copying and reselling of published news derived from the plaintiff's news service. There had been no prior legal recognition of the interest claimed by the plaintiff, for most commentators would have said that published news was in the public domain. It is easy to say, after the event, that the court was 'simply' protecting the plaintiff against one who was trying to 'steal' its property, but the conclusion was neither simple nor obvious: it was only the decision of the United States Supreme Court in this case that established that the plaintiff had a proprietary interest in the news. Had the decision been otherwise its effect could and probably would have been summarized by saying that there could be no property in published news.[17] Justice Brandeis, dissenting in *International News Service v. Associated Press*, distinguished earlier cases[18] as depending on breach of contract or trust, and precisely on the ground that they had not recognized 'a general property right in news'.[19] Analogous cases include the taking of unauthorized photographs, unauthorized rebroadcasting of television signals, use of confidential information, or the copying of a design where there is no copyright or registration protection. When such an issue arises, the claimant is always eager to categorize the claim as proprietary. Thus the conduct of the defendant is apt to be described by claimants as piracy, highway robbery, and brazen theft.[20] This is rhetoric: the taking of a photograph, the rebroadcasting of television signals, the use of confidential information, or the copying of a design cannot, in fact or in law, be piracy, robbery (on or off the highway), or theft,[21] and if it were any of these things the rhetoric would be unnecessary. But the choice of rhetoric is significant, showing

---

[16] 248 US 215 (1918).

[17] Compare *Victoria Park Racing Co.* v. *Taylor* (1937) 58 CLR 479 (observation and broadcasting of horse races).

[18] *Exchange Telegraph Co. Ltd* v. *Gregory & Co.* [1896] 1 QB 147, *Exchange Telegraph Co.* v. *Central News Ltd* [1897] 2 Ch 48, *Exchange Telegraph Co. Ltd* v. *Howard* (1906) 22 TLR 375, *Board of Trade of the City of Chicago* v. *Christie Grain & Starch Co.* 198 US 236 (1905), *National Telegraph News Co.* v. *Western Union Telegraph Co.* 119 F 294 (1902), *Hunt* v. *New York Cotton Exchange* 205 US 322 (1907).

[19] *International News Service* v. *Associated Press*, note 16 above, at 251.

[20] The rebroadcast of television signals was described as 'one of the most brazen thefts of intellectual property ever committed . . . The simplest way of putting this is that they are stealing and we are going to put a stop to it.' *Globe and Mail* (Toronto), 21 Jan. 2000.

[21] See *R* v. *Stewart* [1988] 1 SCR 963 (information not a 'thing' for purposes of criminal law of theft).

the persuasive power of proprietary concepts,[22] and where the claimant has succeeded in obtaining an injunction to restrain the defendant's conduct, or an accounting of the profits derived from use of the matter claimed, the court has been perceived, not without justification, to have recognized or created a proprietary interest or something very like it. As Peter Stein and John Shand wrote in 1974,

> it may be inappropriate to ascribe to an abstraction, such as confidential information, the quality of property, but the common law has been able to do so by reason of its willingness to recognise equitable or beneficial entitlements quite independent of a possessory interest... It is essentially the common lawyer's instinctive understanding of property as a bundle of rights that makes this flexibility possible.[23]

A person who takes or otherwise deals with another's goods is liable for conversion. This has been treated in Anglo-American law as a tort, but it does not depend on proof of fault. A converter is liable to pay damages even though acting reasonably and in good faith. In the absence of an action (as exists in some other systems) for vindication of property rights, disputes over title to goods have been resolved in Anglo-American law by actions in tort. These actions (conversion, detinue, and trover) may be said to have been as much a part of the law of property as of the law of personal obligations or of wrongs. The reasons for imposing liability include concepts of property and unjust enrichment. Andrew Tettenborn has written that

> Conversion is one of the mysteries, or perhaps embarrassments, of English law... True it is classified as a tort; but that is only for historical reasons and for lack of anywhere else to file it. In fact it is trying to do not one, but three very different jobs at the same time; it is (1) standing in as a kind of surrogate *vindicatio*, allowing owners to get back their property or its value from a

---

[22] Thus reputation has often been treated as analogous to property. See *Othello*, III, iii, 155 ('Who steals my purse steals trash ... but he that filches from me my good name robs me of that which not enriches him, and makes me poor indeed'). In *De Crespigny* v. *Wellesley* (1829) 5 Bing 392 at 405–6, Best CJ said, 'he had no more right to take away the character of the plaintiff ... than to take his property'.

[23] P. Stein and J. Shand, *Legal Values in Western Society* (Edinburgh, 1974), p. 217. See also G. Jones, 'Restitution of Benefits Obtained in Breach of Another's Confidence' (1970) 86 *Law Quarterly Review* 463 at 464 ('confidential information is conceptually very much *sui generis*'), P. North, 'Breach of Confidence: Is there a New Tort?' (1972) 12 *Journal of the Society of Public Teachers of Law* 149 (analogy with property).

wrongful possessor; (2) acting to compensate owners for losses caused by past misdealing with their property (tort proper); and (3) on occasion reversing unjust enrichment arising from the property or its proceeds which have got into the wrong hands (restitution).[24]

Where goods of one person are wrongfully sold by another to a third person, the owner, or other person with a right to possession, has a personal right to damages against the seller, as well as continuing ownership of the goods. If there were a strict separation between proprietary and personal rights a claimant could recover damages from the seller amounting to the full value and in addition could assert continuing proprietary rights against the buyer. In order to prevent this consequence it has been uniformly held that satisfaction of a judgment for damages for conversion has the effect of vesting the property in the defendant:

> by a former recovery in trover, and payment of the damages, the plaintiff's right of property is barred and the property vested in the defendant in that action.[25]

The principle is akin to election:

> though the conversion by the defendant is different from the conversion [by the earlier wrongdoer], and may make either the one or the other liable to the plaintiff, at his election, yet satisfaction for one is a defence for the other.[26]

Thus, satisfaction of a personal claim against one person has had the effect of extinguishing a proprietary claim against another, and partial recovery has reduced the claim proportionately, making the assertion of property rights dependent on proof of actual loss.[27] These consequences are incompatible with a strict conceptual separation of property from obligations, and Lionel Smith has, in this context, praised 'the wisdom of the common law in refusing to give the owner of a thing an unqualified right to recover possession of it'.[28]

There is nothing new in the observation that there is a complex interrelation between right and remedy, but this has particular implications for the relation between property and obligation. A right that can never be

---

[24] A. Tettenborn, 'Conversion Tort and Restitution', in N. Palmer and E. McKendrick (eds.), *Interests in Goods* (2nd edn, London, 1998), p. 825.

[25] *Cooper* v. *Shepherd* (1846) 3 CB 266 at 272.   [26] *Ibid.*

[27] *Burn* v. *Morris* (1834) 2 C & M 579, *Rice* v. *Reed* [1900] 1 QB 54, CA, esp. at 58, 64.

[28] L. Smith, *The Law of Tracing* (Oxford, 1997), p. 379.

enforced by injunction might plausibly be classified as something less than a proprietary right in the full sense. Conversely, the willingness of the court to grant specific remedies, binding on third parties, may itself supply the principal reason for calling the plaintiff's interest 'proprietary'. Thus, where a contractual licence for the use of land is enforceable by injunction the licensee's interest has been categorized as proprietary;[29] conversely, the fear of prejudicing the interests of third parties, especially creditors of the seller, by creating a proprietary interest in the buyer has been a principal reason for the reluctance of the courts to decree specific performance of contracts for the sale of goods.[30]

The proposition that interference with a property interest should be prevented by injunction has the appearance of a logically compelling syllogism: all who infringe property interests are to be restrained by injunction; the defendant infringes a property interest; therefore the defendant is to be restrained by injunction. In some cases the courts have invoked this appearance of logic,[31] but the appearance is misleading, because the courts have reserved a general power to withhold injunctions, like other equitable remedies, where they would operate unfairly against the defendant or against third parties. Thus in *Isenberg* v. *East India House Estate Co. Ltd*,[32] where an injunction was sought to prevent the construction of a building that would interfere with a right to light, Lord Westbury said:

> I hold it to be the duty of the Court in such a case as the present not, by granting a mandatory injunction, to deliver the defendants over to the plaintiff bound hand and foot, in order to be made subject to any extortionate demand that he may by possibility make.[33]

It is not possible, therefore, to assert that property interests are always protected by injunctions, unless indeed the speaker or writer has chosen to define property rights as 'rights protected by injunction'. In that case the assertion would be true by definition, but *only* by definition. It could not determine whether an injunction should be issued in any particular case; it

---

[29] See *Millennium Productions Ltd* v. *Winter Garden Theatre (London) Ltd* [1948] AC 173, HL. See also pp. 30–1 and 116 above.
[30] *Re Wait* [1927] 1 Ch. 606, CA.
[31] *Goodson* v. *Richardson* (1874) LR 9 Ch App 221, *Krehl* v. *Burrell* (1878) 7 Ch D 551, *John Trenberth Ltd* v. *National Westminster Bank* (1979) 39 P & CR 104.
[32] (1863) 3 De G J & S 263.   [33] *Ibid.*, at 271.

could only support the linguistic point that, if an injunction were withheld, the plaintiff's right should be called something other than a property right. The point nevertheless has rhetorical force. Thus where courts have refused injunctions to protect rights to light,[34] or rights in air space,[35] or rights to be free of nuisance,[36] or rights in confidential information,[37] a commentator may justly say that those rights have been treated as something less than property rights in the fullest sense; but it does not follow that therefore they *ought to be* treated as full property rights.

In English law and in systems derived from it orders of the court (injunctions and decrees of specific performance) have an immediate and drastic impact, demanding, as is not the case in many other legal systems, immediate obedience on pain of imprisonment for contempt of court. There are often good reasons for withholding or modifying such orders, but it is not possible to state all of these reasons fully and precisely in advance, and therefore the court retains a power to withhold its orders in appropriate circumstances. This feature of equitable remedies is usually summarized by saying that they are 'discretionary'.

The word 'discretionary' is somewhat misleading in this context. What is meant is that it is not possible to define in advance the precise circumstances in which judicial orders will be made, but the use of the word might be taken to imply, and has often been taken to imply, that some special deference is due by an appellate court to the judge of first instance, and that the powers of appellate courts to clarify and settle the law are therefore restricted. In *Elsom* v. *Elsom*, for example, dealing with a statutory provision for variation of division of spousal property where 'unfair', the Supreme Court of Canada said that 'Courts of Appeal should be highly reluctant to interfere with the exercise of a trial judge's discretion. It is he who has the advantage of hearing the parties and is in the best position to weigh the equities of a case.'[38] The reason given here in the second sentence quoted is persuasive only where the 'advantage of hearing the parties' is really relevant. On some matters

---

[34] *Isenberg* v. *East India House Estate Co. Ltd* (1863) 3 De G J & S 263.

[35] See *Woollerton and Wilson Ltd* v. *Richard Costain Ltd* [1970] 1 WLR 411, *John Trenberth Ltd* v. *National Westminster Bank Ltd* (1979) 39 P & CR 104, *Lewvest Ltd* v. *Scotia Towers Ltd* (1981) 126 DLR (3d) 239, Nfld SC.

[36] *Boomer* v. *Atlantic Cement Co. Ltd* 257 NE 2d 870 (NYCA, 1970), *Miller* v. *Jackson* [1977] QB 966, CA.

[37] See *Cadbury Schweppes Inc.* v. *FBI Foods Ltd* [1999] 1 SCR 142, 167 DLR (4th) 577 (interest in confidential information not categorized as proprietary, and injunction refused).

[38] [1989] 1 SCR 1367 at 1375.

there might be such an advantage.[39] However, the open-ended nature of a legal rule does not in itself present any particular reason to defer to a judge of first instance; on the contrary, the open-ended nature of a rule may be a very good reason for the appellate court to give guidance and to settle uncertainties.[40] This is true whether or not there is theoretically a 'correct' legal answer.[41] Thus, one favouring (as has the writer) a broad power of relief from contractual liability on grounds of unfairness or unconscionability is not bound also to exclude the appellate courts from settling, defining, and developing the law.

Generally, appellate courts have quite readily undertaken the review of final equitable orders, notwithstanding that they are called 'discretionary'. It has often been affirmed that a judge exercising discretionary powers is not thereby authorized to act on 'caprice',[42] or in a manner that is 'arbitrary or unregulated'.[43] The judge is obliged to apply the law.[44] Moreover, it cannot be credibly maintained, simply because the judge has what is called 'discretion', that one decision is as good as another. In an English case of 1998, for example, the question arose whether a contractual obligation to conduct a business for a period of nineteen years was specifically enforceable.[45] The judge of first instance refused a decree; the Court of Appeal, by a majority, decreed specific performance; and the House of Lords restored the judge's order. The final disposition was the restoration of the judge's order, but not because special deference was due to the judge on this issue – still less because one decision on the question was thought to be as good as another. The question at stake was of high importance, both to the parties in the particular case and to contracting parties generally. Opinions in the legal profession and on the bench differed sharply, as is demonstrated by the division of opinion in the Court of Appeal, and between the majority in the Court of Appeal and the House of Lords. There was every reason for the appellate courts to entertain the question and to determine it.

---

[39] For a fuller account, see S. Waddams, 'Judicial Discretion' (2001) 1 *Oxford University Commonwealth Law Journal* 59. It might be possible in some cases to construe relevant legislation as actually restricting the right of appeal, but this is implausible in *Elsom* v. *Elsom*.

[40] D. Galligan, *Discretionary Powers* (Oxford, 1986), pp. 5–6, 25–6.

[41] R. Dworkin, *Taking Rights Seriously* (Cambridge, Mass., 1978), p. 81, or A. Barak, *Judicial Discretion* (New Haven, 1989), pp. 16, 30.

[42] *Beddow* v. *Beddow* (1878) 9 Ch D 89 at 93.

[43] *Harris* v. *Beauchamp Bros* [1894] 1 QB 801 at 808, Barak, *Judicial Discretion*, p. 118.

[44] R. J. Sharpe, 'Judicial Discretion' [1998] *Advocates' Society Journal* 4.

[45] *Cooperative Insurance Society Ltd* v. *Argyll Stores (Holdings) Ltd* [1998] AC 1, HL.

Other recent decisions are to the same effect. In *Attorney General* v. *Blake*[46] (2000), discussed in an earlier chapter, the House of Lords asserted a power, in exceptional cases, to order an accounting of profits derived from breach of contract. Lord Nicholls said that 'when, exceptionally, a just response to a breach of contract so requires, the court should be able to grant the discretionary remedy of requiring the defendant to account to the plaintiff for the benefits he has received from his breach of contract'.[47] There are of course elements of uncertainty in such a principle, and Lord Nicholls was very careful not to lay down any precise rule. Some have criticized such a principle as too vague, but flexibility is not inconsistent with the court's developing the law on a rational and consistent basis. In calling the remedy 'discretionary' Lord Nicholls evidently did not mean to imply that individual judges should be free to make contradictory decisions, and there was no suggestion that any special deference was due to the judge of first instance, who had refused to order an accounting of the profits. If the facts of the *Blake* case should recur, the result should be the same. Similarly on the question of proprietary estoppel, the legal principle is necessarily very flexible, but this does not mean that the decision of a trial judge is to be preferred to that of an appellate court,[48] nor that indistinguishable facts should lead to differing legal consequences according to the decision at first instance.

One aspect of this question is the long-disputed question of whether proprietary remedies, particularly the constructive trust, can be said to be 'purely remedial'.[49] The question is, does the court give the remedy (constructive trust, or lien) because the plaintiff has a property interest, or does the plaintiff have a property interest because the court gives the remedy? This question has been found to be unanswerable just because it assumes a sharp demarcation between property and obligations that has not in practice existed in Anglo-American law: 'the imposition of a constructive trust can both recognize and create a right of property'.[50] The plaintiff in cases where a constructive trust or lien is imposed practically never has

---

[46] [2001] 1 AC 268, HL.   [47] *Ibid.* at 284–5. See chapter 6 above.
[48] See chapter 4 above, and *Gillett* v. *Holt* [2001] 1 Ch 210, where the Court of Appeal reversed a trial judge who had refused to find a proprietary estoppel.
[49] R. Goode, 'Property and Unjust Enrichment', in A. Burrows (ed.), *Essays on the Law of Restitution* (Oxford, 1991), p. 215 at p. 216.
[50] La Forest J, in *LAC Minerals Ltd* v. *International Corona Resources Ltd* [1989] 1 SCR 579 at 676, 61 DLR (4th) 14, at 50.

a pre-existing property interest in the strict legal sense, for, if she did, equitable remedies would usually be unnecessary. On the other hand, an examination of the actual decisions of the courts does not suggest that the judges have entirely disregarded proprietary considerations – still less that equitable remedies have been awarded on a whim. It is true that the notion of a purely 'remedial' constructive trust, in its extreme form, would be open to the objection that it invited random and unprincipled creation of property rights:[51] there would be reason to object if, in response to a claim on a simple debt, the court created a property interest and attached it to assets that had no connexion with the dispute, for such a process would amount to random confiscation of accretions to value and profits derived from the property, would short-circuit the due process of execution, and would often give the plaintiff an improper priority over other creditors of the defendant.[52] But in practice the constructive trust, whether or not called 'remedial', has usually been employed in cases where the claim is strongly linked with particular assets, such as the domestic property cases,[53] the cases of proprietary estoppel,[54] and the cases of benefits derived from the taking by the defendant of what has been perceived in a general sense to belong to the plaintiff (though not strictly speaking property).[55] The Supreme Court of Canada has said that 'for a constructive trust to arise, the plaintiff must establish a direct link to the property which is the subject of the trust... [T]he notion that one can dispense with a link between the services rendered and the property which is claimed to be subject to the trust is inconsistent with the proprietary nature of the notion of constructive trust.'[56] It is true

---

51 P. Birks, Book Review (1999) 115 *Law Quarterly Review* 681 at 686, P. Birks, 'The Law of Restitution at the End of an Epoch' (1999) 28 *Western Australian Law Review* 13 at 56, 64, P. Birks, 'Three Kinds of Objection to Discretionary Remedialism' (2000) 29 *Western Australian Law Review* 1, and in other writings, G. Virgo, *Principles of the Law of Restitution* (Oxford, 1999), p. 637.

52 John McCamus has suggested the exclusion of 'people who willingly choose to become unsecured creditors', J. McCamus, 'The Restitutionary Remedy of Constructive Trust', in *Law Society of Upper Canada Special Lectures* (Toronto, 1981), p. 122. The converse proposition, suggested in P. Maddaugh and J. McCamus, *The Law of Restitution* (Toronto, 1990), pp. 95–6, that an involuntary creditor *should* enjoy proprietary rights, would be difficult to apply to tort claims unconnected with particular property, e.g., a claim for damages for personal injuries. See D. Paciocco, 'The Remedial Constructive Trust: a Principled Basis for Priority Over Creditors' (1989) 68 *Canadian Bar Review* 315.

53 See chapter 7 above, and compare the civil law concept of community of property.

54 See chapter 4 above.   55 See chapter 6 above.

56 *Peter v. Beblow* [1993] 1 SCR 980 at 996, 101 DLR (4th) 621 at 649–50. Peter Birks, to somewhat similar effect, insists on the need for the claim to have a 'proprietary base', P. Birks, *An Introduction to the Law of Restitution* (Oxford, 1985), pp. 378–85, P. Birks, 'Establishing a Proprietary Base: Re

that the concept of 'direct link' is not very precise, but, as we saw in respect of profits derived from wrongdoing, neither is the question whether the plaintiff's claim can be called proprietary a simple one, nor is it independent of concepts of contract, wrongdoing, unjust enrichment, and public policy. As the Supreme Court of Canada put it in 1997,

> under the broad umbrella of good conscience constructive trusts are recognized both for wrongful acts like fraud or breach of duty of loyalty, as well as to remedy unjust enrichment and corresponding deprivation. While cases often involve both a wrongful act and unjust enrichment, constructive trusts may be imposed on either ground.[57]

It is apparent from these considerations that the interrelation of property and obligation cannot readily be captured by a two-dimensional map or diagram: neither is the one concept subordinate to the other,[58] nor can they be visualized as parallel and completely separate.

The question of the proprietary consequences of breach of fiduciary duty has caused a sharp division of judicial and academic opinion. In *Attorney General for Hong Kong* v. *Reid*[59] the Privy Council, departing from a case that had stood for over a century,[60] held that bribes received by a government official, and traceable proceeds of them, were held on a constructive trust for the government. In *English Private Law* (2001) the *Reid* case is criticized by the author of the chapter on property as illogical and unprincipled,[61] and is said in the chapter on agency to raise 'some problems',[62] but is noted without adverse comment in the chapter on judicial remedies.[63] The Privy Council's conclusion represents the view that the proceeds of the bribes *ought to be treated* as the government's property, and this is not a conclusion that can be derived exclusively from pre-existing rules of property. It was strongly

---

Goldcorp' (1995) 3 *Restitution Law Review* 83. David Paciocco suggests the need 'in general terms' for a 'connexion or nexus between the plaintiff and the property', 'The Remedial Constructive Trust', note 52 above, at 350. That the concept is malleable strengthens the argument in favour of appellate review to preserve stability. See also R. Scane, 'Relationships "Tantamount to Spousal", Unjust Enrichment, and Constructive Trusts' (1991) 70 *Canadian Bar Review* 260 at 279, 288, 305.

[57] *Soulos* v. *Korkontzilas* [1997] 2 SCR 217 at 240, 146 DLR (4th) 214, at 229.

[58] It has been stated that the constructive trust is simply a remedy for unjust enrichment, but this attempt to subordinate the constructive trust to unjust enrichment cannot explain the many cases where constructive trusts have been imposed but the requirements of unjust enrichment (particularly the requirement of a loss corresponding to the enrichment) have not been met.

[59] [1994] 1 AC 324, PC.   [60] *Lister* v. *Stubbs* (1890) 45 Ch D 1, CA.

[61] P. Birks (ed.), *English Private* Law (Oxford, 2001), paras 4.430–4.438.

[62] *Ibid.*, para. 9.141.   [63] *Ibid.*, para. 18.232.

influenced by considerations of public policy expressed in forceful and colourful terms: 'bribery is an evil practice which threatens the foundations of any civilized society... [and the court should prevent the property from being] sold and the proceeds whisked away to some Shangri La which hides bribes...'[64]

It has been said of the constructive trust that it is 'the means by which the conscience of equity finds expression',[65] that it is 'imposed by law whenever justice and good conscience require it',[66] and that it is the 'versatile hand-maiden of equity'.[67] Such language might seem to suggest a radically vague discretion, but if it were said instead that the constructive trust is the form by which equity often has given effect to its conclusions (a statement having much the same effect) this would be generally accepted as a sober and historically accurate account of the practice of Anglo-American courts. There is a link between equity and proprietary remedies, but it is not historically accidental nor in practice has it been arbitrary, because equitable remedies have been generally available in just those cases in which the defendant has been perceived to retain something that, in a general sense, belongs to the plaintiff.

Another kind of claim that mixes proprietary with non-proprietary concepts is tracing, a process that permits the assertion of proprietary claims where one piece of property has in various circumstances been substituted for another. For instance, one who buys property with misappropriated money may be held to be a trustee of the property. Naturally this process has been found difficult to classify in the context of the present enquiry.[68] It has been asserted that 'proprietary interests contingent on tracing... always arise from unjust enrichment',[69] and, on the other hand, that the assertion of a property interest excludes unjust enrichment (because no concept other than property is necessary).[70] Both assertions are true in their own terms, but they each assume a sharp dichotomy between property and unjust enrichment that it has been in practice the very function of

---

[64] [1994] 1 AC at 330, 339.
[65] *Beatty* v. *Guggenheim Exploration Co.* 225 NY 380 (1919) at 386.
[66] *Hussey* v. *Palmer* [1972] 1 WLR 1286 at 1290.
[67] *Re Spears and Levy* (1974) 52 DLR (3d) 146, NS App. Div., at 154.
[68] 'In truth, the exact status of tracing is, today, not easy to discern', G. Samuel, *Law of Obligations and Legal Remedies* (2nd edn, London, 2001), p. 404.
[69] P. Birks, 'Property and Unjust Enrichment: Categorical Truths' [1997] *New Zealand Law Review* 623 at 661.
[70] R. Grantham and C. Rickett, 'Tracing and Property Rights: The Categorical Truth' (2000) 63 *Modern Law Review* 905, *Foskett* v. *McKeown* [2001] 1 AC 102, HL.

the law of tracing to transcend. Tracing permits the assertion of property-like rights in some circumstances against assets in the defendant's hands even though the claimant does not have a full legal property interest. One of the reasons for permitting such a claim has undoubtedly been to avoid unjust enrichment.[71] But a principal reason for recognizing the defendant's enrichment to be unjust has in turn been that the defendant has taken or received something that has been perceived to belong (though not, ex hypothesi, in a strictly legal sense) to the plaintiff.[72] Thus the proprietary overtones cannot be avoided and the concepts of property and unjust enrichment have been intertwined. It is in this light that suggestions are to be understood that a proprietary remedy is appropriate only where there is some kind of pre-existing link, connexion, or nexus between the claim and the property.[73] It has been rightly pointed out that such concepts are 'malleable',[74] but this is not to show that they have been irrelevant or, in the actual practice of the courts, uninfluential.

It has been said that tracing is a process and not a claim or a right or a remedy.[75] This is true in one sense, but tracing is not the mechanical assertion of a simple prior property right,[76] for it is precisely where the claimant does *not* have a simple prior property right that tracing has been found necessary:[77] the law of tracing developed in equity[78] in order to attain a justice between the parties not attainable at law.[79] The reasons of justice have included concepts both of property and of unjust enrichment, and it is

---

[71] Thus R. Goff and G. Jones, *The Law of Restitution* (London, 1966), and P. Maddaugh and J. McCamus, *The Law of Restitution* (Toronto, 1990), include the subject.

[72] See Smith, 'Less than Full Ownership', L. Smith, *Law of Tracing* (Oxford, 1997), pp. 326, 332–3, 337.

[73] See note 56 above.

[74] C. Rotherham, 'Restitution and Property Rites: Reason and Ritual in the Law of Proprietary Remedies' (2000) 1 *Theoretical Inquiries in Law* 205 at 226, C. Rotherham, *Proprietary Remedies in Context* (Oxford, 2002), pp. 330, 336, 338.

[75] *Boscawen* v. *Bajwa* [1996] 1 WLR 328, CA, at 334 (Millett LJ).

[76] S. Worthington, 'Justifying Claims to Secondary Profits', in E. J. H. Schrage (ed.), *Unjust Enrichment and the Law of Contract* (The Hague, 2001), p. 451 at p. 462, Rotherham, *Proprietary Remedies*, pp. 89–126.

[77] L. Smith, *Law of Tracing*, pp. 6–7, usefully distinguishes 'following' a physical object in time and space from 'tracing' into substituted property.

[78] G. Palmer, *The Law of Restitution* (4 vols., Boston, 1978), vol. I, s. 2.14, S. Kurshid and P. Matthews, 'Tracing Confusion' (1979) 95 *Law Quarterly Review* 78, L. Smith, 'Tracing in *Taylor* v. *Plumer*: Equity in the Court of King's Bench' [1995] *Lloyds Maritime and Commercial Law Quarterly* 240, L. Smith, *Law of Tracing*, pp. 168, 278, 326.

[79] See C. Rotherham, 'The Metaphysics of Tracing: Substituted Title and Property Rhetoric' (1996) 34 *Osgoode Hall Law Journal* 321, Rotherham, *Proprietary Remedies*, p. 115.

not possible to choose one of these to the exclusion of the other.[80] There are familiar elements of circularity in the proposition that the claimant has an equitable proprietary interest, for the proposition describes both the effects of tracing and the reason for it: 'when a constructive trust is imposed as a result of successfully tracing a plaintiff's asset into another asset it is indeed debatable which [recognition or creation of a property right] the court is doing'.[81] A unitary law of tracing (by which is usually meant a single concept in law and equity) has the attraction of simplicity, but the categorization of all tracing as the assertion of simple common law property rights would have the effect of defeating the legitimate defences (recognized both in equity and by the law of unjust enrichment)[82] of good faith purchase and change of position,[83] as well as other equitable defences such as election and delay, and it would permit the kind of duplicative claim that has been excluded by the common law of conversion.[84] Lionel Smith has pointed out in this context that against the attractions of 'consistency and logic' must be set the consideration that 'the justification for proprietary rights in traceable proceeds is a sort of proxy version of the cause of action in unjust enrichment'.[85]

Tracing has been largely a creature of equity, and the whole effect of equity has been to cause a blurring of the line between obligation and property. The logic of property is that if a thing belongs to one person it does not simultaneously belong to another. The effect of equity has been to subvert this logic, largely through the concept of use, or trust. Equity, being a supplement to or gloss upon the law and not a self-contained

---

[80] C. Rotherham, 'Trust Property and Unjust Enrichment: Tracing into the Proceeds of Life Insurance Policies' [2000] *Cambridge Law Journal* 440 at 442.

[81] La Forest J in *LAC Minerals Ltd* v. *International Corona Resources Ltd* [1989] 2 SCR 579 at 676, 61 DLR (4th) 14, at 50.

[82] Goff and Jones noted that defences equivalent to bona fide purchase and change of position were recognized in equity, *The Law of Restitution*, pp. 485–6.

[83] P. Birks, 'Property and Unjust Enrichment: Categorical Truths' [1997] *New Zealand Law Review* 623 at 634, points out that the defence, if applicable to a personal claim, must also be available in response to a proprietary claim.

[84] The danger is real. In *Foskett* v. *McKeown*, note 70 above, at 109, and 127, for instance, it was said that there was 'no discretion', and that the plaintiff's claim was a matter of 'hard-nosed property rights'. Following Lord Hope (a civilian judge) all the law lords agreed in excluding the possibility of requiring the claimant to elect between personal and proprietary rights on the ground that these were 'two wholly unrelated remedies', at 117. But see L. Smith, *Law of Tracing*, pp. 378–9, and compare the election required by the common law in conversion, discussed above.

[85] L. Smith, *Law of Tracing*, pp. 384–5.

system,[86] did not flatly contradict the law of property, but the concept of trust enabled it, by imposing a personal obligation on the conscience of the defendant, binding also on all other persons except good faith purchasers for value of the legal title, to create what was *almost equivalent* to a property interest.

Maitland put it in this way:

> 'I can't understand your trust' said Gierke[87] to me. We must ask why this is so. Well, the trust does not fit easily into what they [German lawyers] regard as the necessary scheme of jurisprudence ... Jurists have long tried to make a dichotomy of Private Rights: they are either *in rem* or *in personam*. The types of these two classes are, of the former, *dominium*, ownership; of the latter the benefit of contract – a debt. Now under which head does trust – the right of *cestui que trust* – fall? Not easily under either. It seems to be a little of both. The foreigner asks – where do we place it in our code – under Sachenrecht [property] or under Obligationenrecht [obligations]? The best answer may be that in history, and probably in ultimate analysis, it is *jus in personam*; but that it is so treated (and this for many important purposes) that it is very like *jus in rem*. A right primarily good against *certa persona*, viz the trustee, but so treated as to be almost equivalent to a right good against all – a *dominium*, ownership, which however exists only in equity.[88]

'Almost' equivalent, Maitland said, for the legal title did not vanish, and could, as Maitland repeatedly stressed,[89] be asserted by a good faith purchaser for value without notice of the equitable interest. Milsom, writing in 1969, made the same point in saying that

> equity has proved that from the materials of obligation you can counterfeit almost all the phenomena of property... Your counterfeit will look odd to one brought up on categories of Roman origin, but it will work.[90]

The logic of obligation is that the defendant is bound personally to the plaintiff, usually to pay a money sum, but equity has supplemented the law in many cases both by impeding the enforcement of obligations recognized by law and by creating obligations where the law has not recognized any. Here too equity avoided a direct contradiction of the law. Where the exercise

---

[86] F. Maitland, *Equity, also The Forms of Action at Common Law* (Cambridge, 1910), p. 156.
[87] Otto Friedrich von Gierke, 1841–1921, prominent German scholar and jurist.
[88] Maitland, *Equity*, pp. 23–4.   [89] *Ibid.*, at pp. 84, 85, 119, 143, 169, 281.
[90] S. Milsom, *Historical Foundations of the Common Law* (London, 1969), p. xi.

of a legal right was found to be inequitable, the right was not formally nullified; but the holder of it was prevented (by the common injunction) from exercising it. Where obligations not recognized at law were created, equity did not contradict the law directly by creating a money remedy; but, where the defendant held property closely connected with the claim, equity sometimes declared the defendant a trustee of that property for the plaintiff's benefit. The effect was to create an interest *superior* to that of a simple money obligation by use of a concept (trust) that was *almost equivalent* to a property interest. There is little of strict logic in this. It is an inevitable consequence of these relations between law and equity that the distinction between property and obligation in Anglo-American law has been blurred.[91] Somewhat similar conclusions may be drawn in respect of equitable liens and subrogation.[92] Probably Anglo-American law would have been conceptually simpler with a single idea of property and no separate system of equity. It is possible to argue persuasively on several grounds in favour of such a simplification, but not on the ground that it represents an accurate account of the past.

It is easy in the twenty-first century to be impatient with such historical enquiries, and it is natural to demand a simple restatement of the modern legal position without regard to the past history of law and equity. But this is a demand more easily made than satisfied. If the law of obligations operated as it should, it might be suggested, there would be no need to supplement it with proprietary remedies. It is true that development of the law of obligations may reduce the need for proprietary remedies. Thus, insofar as the law recognizes and enforces a money remedy to reverse unjust enrichment, or to protect reliance, or to prevent the making of profits from wrongs, or to protect the interests of domestic partners, the need to employ proprietary remedies to effect these purposes will be reduced. But those remedies are unlikely to vanish in the classes of case where they have been recognized, and no historical evidence can be adduced in support of the suggestion that they will not be used in the future in new kinds of case.[93]

Attempts to restate the law in simple terms are apt to lead to the assertion of extreme opposite conclusions. Thus it has been asserted that the courts

[91] Rotherham, *Proprietary Remedies*, p. 187.
[92] D. Wright, 'Proprietary Remedies and the Role of Insolvency' (2000) 23 *University of New South Wales Law Journal* 143, Rotherham, *Proprietary Remedies*, p. 250.
[93] Rotherham, *Proprietary Remedies*, gives many recent instances.

always have a discretion to grant a proprietary remedy in response to a personal claim, and, on the other hand, that the courts never have such a discretion. Where one writer sees a welcome flexibility another may discern a dangerous instability. In a rather forceful review (1999) of David Wright's *The Remedial Constructive Trust*, Peter Birks has written:

> He [Wright] takes the view that proprietary rights are trivial constructs, constantly changing and therefore evidently malleable... Consequently he sees no inherent difficulty in a discretionary, retrospective property right... This cavalier attitude to property must be rejected. Property rights cannot be deconstructed... [T]he discretion which the author favours would compel judges to do something for which they are no better qualified than any drinker propping up a bar... Put in plain language it is politically repulsive and intellectually disreputable.[94]

There have been judicial statements also to the effect that equitable property rights are not discretionary. In *Foskett* v. *McKeown*, for example, Lord Browne-Wilkinson said that 'It is a fundamental error to think that because certain property rights are equitable rather than legal, such rights are in some way discretionary.'[95] These comments assume a strict unchanging and unchangeable dichotomy between property and obligation that has not in the past been characteristic of Anglo-American law. The two points of view (that equitable property rights are, and are not, discretionary) are sharply contradictory on the surface, but they can be largely reconciled for, from a historical perspective, each captures a different aspect of the relations between law and equity. Elements of both views could be combined in the following proposition: where there is a close connexion between a personal claim and particular property held by the defendant, and where the claimant has no adequate money remedy, the courts have sometimes imposed a trust or a lien on the property, but they have not defined precisely the circumstances in which they will do so, and have withheld such declarations where they have been likely to operate unfairly against the defendant or against third parties.

---

[94] P. Birks, Book Review (1999) 115 *Law Quarterly Review* 681 at 685–6. Replies are D. Wright, 'Professor Birks and the Demise of the Remedial Constructive Trust' (1999) 7 *Restitution Law Review* 128, and D. Wright, 'Proprietary Remedies and the Role of Insolvency' (2000) 23 *University of New South Wales Law Journal* 143.

[95] [2001] 1 AC 102 at 109. Lord Browne-Wilkinson was well aware of the requirement that the conscience of the trustee should be affected. See his speech in *Westdeutsche Landesbank Girozentrale* v. *Islington London Borough Council* [1996] AC 669, HL.

The deficiencies of an over-simple dichotomy now become apparent. An insistence that rights must be either purely proprietary, or on the other hand, wholly non-proprietary, and that proprietary rights can admit of no element of discretion, cannot derive support from the history of Anglo-American law. Maitland wrote of the divisions of Roman law that

> these famous distinctions [of Justinian's *Institutes*] have at various times attracted English lawyers, and attempts have been made to impose them upon the English materials, attempts which have never been very successful.[96]

Geoffrey Samuel has similarly pointed out that, largely due to equitable concepts, English law 'can seemingly defy the classification system of Justinian's *Institutes*'.[97] Moreover, the insistence that the concept of discretion must be entirely excluded from proprietary rights is likely, in the light of the history of equitable remedies, to be self-defeating. Thus many judges and academic writers have understandably rejected the notion of arbitrary judicial creation of property rights, but curiously enough it is the very concept of discretion that has in practice tended to avert the dangers they fear. The courts of equity, alive to the burdens imposed by the creation of property-like rights, have employed the concept of discretion not to confer unfettered power on individual judges to create arbitrary property rights, but on the contrary to restrict that power by insisting on the *withholding* of equitable remedies where they are likely to operate unfairly against the defendant or against third parties.

The concepts of property and obligation are therefore distinct, but the line between them has been blurred in respect of many issues and over several centuries. Insistence on a sharp demarcation cannot be made consistent with the actual history of Anglo-American law, however desirable it might be on other grounds.

---

[96] Maitland, *Equity*, p. 361.
[97] Samuel, *Law of Obligations and Legal Remedies*, pp. 277–8. See also Samuel, *Foundations of Legal Reasoning*, p. 71.

10

Public interest and private right

Many shades of opinion are to be found among judges and academics on the question of the relation between private law and public policy. Three main strands may be discerned. First is the view that the two are separate; legal rules are to be derived or deduced from legal sources, the function of private law being not the creation of law in the public interest, but the declaration and application of pre-existing law for the prevention and correction of injustice between the individual parties to each dispute. Second, there is the view that when courts are called upon to create a new rule, or to modify an old one, or to extend it to a new situation, they address the question of whether the proposed rule would be, on balance, beneficial to the community; assessment of this question requires the weighing of the costs and benefits of the proposed rule as it will be applied in the future to parties other than the individual litigants in the current case. Third is the view that an element of judgment is frequently involved that includes broad social and political considerations. There are many intervening combinations and shades of opinion.

The three main views correspond broadly with what may, for the sake of convenience, be epitomized as principle, utility, and policy. These have sometimes been presented as competing 'theories', of which the reader is impliedly invited to choose one and reject the other two. But from a historical standpoint they appear rather as complementary strands in a single rope, or different dimensions of a single phenomenon. They merge into each other, because, where a new legal problem presents itself for decision, it has not been possible to consider what would be a just rule for the particular parties without to some extent considering the consequences of the proposed rule in other cases. Principle and policy, though sometimes contrasted, have been in practice inseparable, for principles have been adopted to give effect to policies, and adherence to principle has been itself a policy. Holmes wrote that judges take into account 'what is expedient in the community concerned', adding that 'every important principle which is developed by

litigation is in fact and at bottom the result of more or less definitely understood views of public policy'.[1] In related decisions released on the same day
in 1999, the Supreme Court of Canada said both that 'judicial policy must
yield to legal principle',[2] and that 'the best route to enduring principle may
well lie through policy'.[3] Emphasis has varied from time to time and from
one jurisdiction to another, but elements of all three dimensions have been
consistently present, sometimes on the lips of a single judge in different
cases, or even in the same case.[4] In the important eighteenth-century case
of *Omychund* v. *Barker*[5] (1744), where the issue was the admissibility of
the evidence of a witness who could not take the Christian form of oath, all
three dimensions were evident. Counsel (William Murray, later Lord Mansfield), arguing in favour of admissibility, said that the question was 'whether
upon principles of reason, justice, and convenience this witness ought to
be admitted'.[6] His fellow counsel (Dudley Rider, also, like Murray, a future
Chief Justice of the King's Bench) said that 'trade requires it [admission of
the testimony]; policy requires it'. The Lord Chancellor (Hardwicke) relied
both on the principle of justice between the parties and on the overt policy
consideration that 'if we did not give this credence, courts abroad would
not allow our determinations here to be valid'.[7] This was also the case in
which Murray said, in urging judicial reform of the law, that the common
law 'works itself pure'.[8] The remark has often been quoted out of context to
suggest that Murray favoured a purity of formal legal principle, but it is evident that 'purity' did not, in Murray's mind, or in the Chancellor's, exclude
considerations of utility and policy. All three dimensions (principle, utility,
and policy) can derive support from historical evidence. But from this it
necessarily follows also that historical evidence cannot support a claim of
any one of them to be the *exclusive* explanation of private law.

   Judicial statements purporting to exclude considerations of public policy
have been very frequent. An example often cited is the assertion of Parke B
in *Egerton* v. *Brownlow*[9] (1853) that

---

[1] O. W. Holmes, *The Common Law*, ed. M. D. Howe, (Boston, 1963 [1881]), p. 32, and see p. 2
above.
[2] *Jacobi* v. *Griffiths* [1999] 2 SCR 570 at 593, 174 DLR (4th) 71, at 89 (Binnie J, for a majority).
[3] *Bazley* v. *Curry* [1999] 2 SCR 534 at 551, 174 DLR (4th) 45, at 58 (McLachlin J, for the whole
court).
[4] Dr Lushington, admiralty and ecclesiastical law judge, is a good example. See S. Waddams, *Law,
Politics, and the Church of England: the Career of Stephen Lushington, 1782–1873* (Cambridge,
1992).
[5] (1744) 1 Atk 21.   [6] *Ibid.* at 32.   [7] *Ibid.* at 33.   [8] *Ibid.*   [9] (1853) 4 HLC 1.

It is the province of the judge to expound the law only; the written from the statutes, the unwritten or common law from the decisions of our predecessors and of our existing courts, from text writers of acknowledged authority, and upon the principles to be clearly deduced from them by sound reason and just inference; not to speculate upon what is best, in his opinion, for the advantage of the community. Some of these decisions [past decisions on public policy] may no doubt have been founded upon the prevailing and just opinions of the public good; for instance the illegality of covenants in restraint of marriage or trade. They have become part of the recognized law, and we are therefore bound by them, but we think we are not thereby authorized to establish as law everything which we may think for the public good, and prohibit everything which we think otherwise.[10]

This passage bears some of the marks of its origin as part of a draft collective opinion of the judges summoned to advise the House of Lords. The case was notorious and controversial, the issue being the validity of a provision in a will leaving a large sum of money conditionally on the acquisition of a dukedom, and the fear being that upholding such provisions would lead to corruption. But the judges were not unanimous, and the House of Lords requested their individual opinions.[11] Alderson B spoke even more forcefully in the same sense:

But it is said that these provisoes [the conditional clauses in the will] are illegal, and they may lead to public evil or inconvenience; that, in short, they are contrary to public policy. I think that is a very grave and important question; if by public policy is meant the object and policy of a particular law, then I readily accept it as a rule, for it is a reasonable mode of construing a particular law to look at the object with which it was formed, and the evil it was apparently intended to remove. Again if a proviso be either illegal or impossible, no doubt it is void. But here it seems to be contended that an act, possible and legal, but in the opinion of sensible men not expedient to be done, is for that reason to be void as contrary to public policy. Now I think that this, which is really what is here meant, would altogether destroy the sound and true distinction between judicial and legislative functions and I pray your Lordships to pause before you establish such a precedent as that. By this public policy will be meant the prevailing opinion, from time to time, of wise men (and in saying 'wise men' I give a favourable view of the principle) as to what is for the public good – an excellent principle, no doubt, for legislators to adopt, but a most dangerous one for judges. It is obvious that this would introduce an ever-shifting principle of decision.[12]

The rhetorical and slightly plaintive tone is suggestive of the argument of an advocate expecting to lose, and so it turned out, as we shall see shortly. Similar views to those of Parke and Alderson BB have frequently been expressed by other judges.[13] In refusing relief to a wife complaining in a matrimonial case of cruelty, Dr Lushington said:

> I say nothing of a probability of that peace and happiness which ought to belong to married life. Of such considerations I have no cognizance . . . I may, individually, regret the painful consequences to which my judgment may subject her; but this court is only a mouthpiece to declare the law.[14]

Views of this sort have often been accompanied by rejection of the idea of wide judicial discretion, as appeared in the discussion of proprietary remedies in the last chapter. Dr Lushington in another family law case said: 'I know nothing more painful than to have to exercise a judicial discretion without landmarks to guide the judgment.'[15]

In recent years a formal approach to private law has received the approbation of distinguished academics, including Peter Birks, pressing the logical claims of classification and taxonomy, and Ernest Weinrib, writing from a philosophical standpoint. These writers have reminded us that private law cannot dispense with its own forms and its own framework of thought, for if private law were reduced to a means of effecting some extraneous purpose (social, political, or economic), it would in a sense cease to be law, and become a mere tool of the extraneous purpose.[16] Others have also stressed the need for internal coherence and for adherence to form, but none would claim to have established by historical evidence that these have, in the past, been the *exclusive* approaches of Anglo-American private law. If law is to be taken on its own terms its actual past, not just an idealized version of it, must be consulted. The extent to which judges have, in the past, adhered to principle is difficult to assess, because the results in particular cases depend on the level of generality at which principles are framed. The denial of specific performance in a land sale

---

[12] 4 HLC 106.   [13] See *Harrison* v. *Carswell* [1976] 2 SCR 200.
[14] *Dysart* v. *Dysart* (1844) 3 Not Cas 324, 369, revd 5 Not Cas 194, 1 Rob Ecc 105.
[15] *Anon* (1857) Deane 295 at 298.
[16] E. Weinrib, *The Idea of Private Law* (Cambridge, Mass., 1995).

contract, for example, has been called a 'principled approach'[17] on the premiss that the principle is that specific performance is only available in sales of unique property. But if the principle were stated at a higher level of generality, for example that contracts should be observed, or that sales of land should normally be enforced, the opposite result would equally appear to be principled.

Much evidence supports the view that judges have often been influenced by the perceived probable costs and benefits of legal rules. Lushington himself was certainly no exception, for immediately after the passage last quoted, in which he said that the court was only a mouthpiece to declare the law, he added 'and is forbidden, *for the wisest reasons*, from interfering in matrimonial intercourse save for the protection of personal safety'.[18] In another matrimonial case, where the husband was alleging cruelty, he refused to allow himself 'to be led away, by an anxiety to relieve a hardship upon an individual, to do what might cause an infinitely greater injustice to the interests of the public at large'.[19] He was here giving attention to the costs and benefits, as he perceived them, of the then very narrow rule permitting separation only in case of extreme cruelty. Sir William Scott (later Lord Stowell), of all the ecclesiastical court judges, had spoken most plainly on this point:

> To vindicate the policy of the law is no necessary part of the office of a judge; but if it were, it would not be difficult to shew that the law in this respect has acted with its usual wisdom and humanity, with that true wisdom, and that real humanity, that regards the general interest of mankind. For though in particular cases, the repugnance of the law to dissolve the obligations of matrimonial cohabitation, may operate with great severity upon individuals; yet it must be carefully remembered, that the general happiness of the married life is secured by its indissolubility. When people understand that they *must* live together, except for a very few reasons known to the law, they learn to soften by mutual accommodation that yoke which they know they cannot shake off; they become good husbands and good wives from the necessity of remaining husbands and wives; for necessity is a powerful master in teaching the duties which it imposes. If it were once understood, that upon mutual disgust married persons might be legally separated, many couples, who now pass through the world with mutual comfort, with attention to their common

---

[17] *Domowicz v. Orsa Investments Ltd* (1993) 15 OR (3d) 661 at 683, and see *Semelhago v. Paramedavan* [1996] 2 SCR 415.

[18] 3 Not Cas 369.   [19] *Furlonger v. Furlonger* (1847) 5 Not Cas 422.

offspring and to the moral order of civil society, might have been at this
moment living in a state of the most licentious and unreserved immorality.
In this case, as in many others, the happiness of some individuals must be
sacrificed to the greater and more general good.[20]

The rules governing separation for cruelty were judge-made, and Scott
and Lushington did not doubt the judicial power to relax them. But they
thought relaxation inexpedient. The fact that public and judicial opinion
has changed so radically on this question since their time makes all the
plainer the extent to which the judges' estimate of the social costs and
benefits of the legal rule were influential.

Other judges have addressed these considerations in overtly economic
terms. In *Bamford* v. *Turnley*,[21] for example (1862), Bramwell B said that a
person might be liable to pay damages to those injured by a nuisance even
though the defendant's activity was, on balance, for the public benefit, by
which he meant 'that if all the loss and all the gain were borne and received by
one individual, he on the whole would be a gainer'.[22] But such an individual
still ought to compensate those who had suffered the losses, because if the
activity really were beneficial the defendant could compensate the plaintiff
and still show a profit; if not, the activity was, when its full costs were taken
into account, not truly profitable:

> It is for the public benefit that trains should run, but not unless they pay their
> expenses... [U]nless the defendant's profits are enough to compensate [the
> persons injured] I deny that it is for the public benefit he should do what he
> has done; if they are he ought to compensate.[23]

This is one of the arguments for strict liability considered in an earlier
chapter, and similar arguments, based on 'internalization' of costs, have
been adduced in support of strict liability on other legal issues, for example
vicarious liability for acts of employees and agents, and injury caused by
defective products.[24]

An even better-known economic analysis is that of the law of negligence advanced by Judge Learned Hand in *United States* v. *Carroll Towing
Co*.[25] the defendant was to be adjudged negligent if the costs of averting an

---

[20] *Evans* v. *Evans* (1790) 1 Hagg Con 35, 36–7.
[21] (1862) 3 B & S 62. See chapter 5 above.   [22] 3 B & S 85.   [23] *Ibid.*
[24] See chapter 5 above.   [25] 159 F 2d 169 (2d Cir., 1947).

accident were less than the probable cost of the accident discounted by the improbability of its occurrence; the test was put into algebraic form.[26] Economic analysis may thus be adduced in support both of strict liability and of negligence, but economics does not say how the choice should be made between them. As we saw in chapter 5, there has been no single answer to this question: an element of judgment is needed as to which activities ought to bear their full costs, and to which it is feasible to attribute such costs. If negligence according to the Learned Hand analysis were the only test of liability, it would, as Steve Wexler has pointed out,[27] lead to the curious conclusion that a defendant who subjected a neighbour's property to risk on a deliberate and accurate calculation that the damage to the neighbour would be less than the cost to the defendant of averting the risk would not be liable to make compensation at all, thus in effect expropriating a right without compensation and deriving, at the neighbour's expense, a *greater* profit than that originally calculated.[28]

The purest forms of economic analysis of private law have insisted on a rigorous exclusion of attention to the re-allocation of wealth between the individual parties to the dispute (on the ground that economics is not concerned with the actual distribution of wealth among individuals) and exclusion also of broad considerations of social policy (on the ground that the economic concept of efficiency is a neutral principle independent of social and political considerations). Whatever may be the merits of such rigorous exclusions from an economic point of view, their effect has been to detach this kind of economic analysis from any links with the actual historical institution of Anglo-American private law, for it cannot be effectively denied that the latter has been very materially concerned with the re-allocation of wealth between the individual parties to disputes, and has been concerned also with broad questions of social policy. A more moderate view, held by such influential scholars as Guido Calabresi and Michael Trebilcock, is that economic analysis illuminates the understanding of private law, but does not exclude considerations of justice between the

---

[26] R. Posner, *Economic Analysis of Law* (2nd edn, Boston, 1977), p. 122.
[27] See S. Wexler, 'Do we really need the Hand Formula' (2001) 9 *Tort Law Review* 81. A similar point was made by R. Epstein, 'A Theory of Strict Liability' 2 *Journal of Legal Studies* 151 at 158–9, and 'Defences and Subsequent Pleas in a System of Strict Liability' (1973–4) 3 *Journal of Legal Studies* 165 at 213.
[28] See chapter 5 above.

individual parties nor wider considerations of social policy.[29] Economic
considerations, though influential, have not been in themselves determinative. As Robert Sharpe put it (1983),

> While the pursuit of efficiency is...an important legal goal, it is a pursuit
> qualified by the concept of rights which may not be superseded merely because
> the general social welfare would be advanced[30]

Let us now return to *Egerton* v. *Brownlow*, the case of the bequest conditional on acquisition of a peerage. The views of Parke and Alderson BB,
described above, though held by nine of the eleven common law judges, did
not prevail. Pollock LCB summarized the contrary view of the other two
judges by saying:

> My Lords, it may be that judges are no better able to discern what is for
> the public good than other experienced and enlightened members of the
> community; but that is no reason for their refusing to entertain the question,
> and declining to decide upon it.[31]

He thought that upholding the bequest was likely, not in this case but in
possible future cases, to lead to corruption in the dispensation of peerages,
and the majority of the law lords agreed.[32] This is, in the broadest sense, a
judgment on a question of social policy. Pollock did not hesitate to describe
the court's function as 'political'. Adopting the words of Lord Hardwicke
from a case a century earlier, he said that

> Political arguments, in the fullest sense of the word, as they concern the
> government of a nation, must be, and always have been of great weight in the
> consideration of this Court.[33]

This reference to 'political arguments' was expressly adopted in the House
of Lords by Lord Lyndhurst, who, at the age of eighty-one, gave the leading
speech for the majority.[34] *The Times* praised the result, describing the will
as 'most iniquitous' and saying that the decision 'will be received with

---

[29] Calabresi's best-known article was subtitled *one view of the cathedral*, with reference to the
many dimensions of Rouen cathedral: G. Calabresi and A. Melamed, 'Property Rules, Liability
Rules and Inalienability: One View of the Cathedral' (1972) 85 *Harvard Law Review* 1089;
M. Trebilcock, *The Limits of Freedom of Contract* (Cambridge, Mass., 1991).
[30] R. Sharpe, *Injunctions and Specific Performance* (Toronto, 1983), s. 4.550.
[31] 4 HLC 151.
[32] Lords Lyndhurst, Brougham, Truro and St Leonards (Cranworth LC dissenting).
[33] *Earl of Chesterfield* v. *Janssen* (1751) 2 Ves Sen 125.   [34] 4 HLC 160.

unqualified satisfaction by the public'. The writer of the leading article had some difficulty in describing the proper role of the judges:

> The point has been decided by the House of Lords in a manner contrary to the opinions delivered by the judges of the land. These learned persons had, of course, but one point to consider – what the law was – not what it should be. They are interpreters, not makers of the law, and cannot be charged with its defects or shortcomings.

But this distinction was not helpful to the writer's line of thought because, if true of the common law judges, the same should have been true of the House of Lords in its judicial capacity. The editorial writer was constrained to add, rather lamely, 'We must notice it as a curious fact that this opinion should have been overruled by that of the law Lords in the Upper House.'[35]

Closely related to such cases of wills are questions of public policy in contracts. Contracts are not enforceable if contrary to public policy, nor can restitution of contractual payments be obtained in such cases on grounds of unjust enrichment.[36] As Lord Mansfield recognized in 1775, the consequence is to deprive the plaintiff of a result that justice otherwise would require:

> The objection, that a contract is immoral or illegal as between plaintiff and defendant, sounds at all times very ill in the mouth of the defendant. It is not for his sake, however, that the objection is ever allowed; but it is founded in general principles of policy, which the defendant has the advantage of, contrary to the real justice, as between him and the plaintiff, by accident, if I may so say.[37]

Although at certain periods the courts, in some jurisdictions, have taken a narrow view of the power to declare new heads of public policy,[38] it cannot be doubted that judicial perceptions of public policy have varied from time to time and from place to place: 'public policy is necessarily variable'.[39]

---

[35] *The Times*, 20 Aug. 1853, 8d.

[36] R. Goff and G. Jones, *The Law of Restitution* (5th edn, London, 1998), pp. 67–72, P. Birks, 'Recovery of Value Transferred Under an Illegal Contract' (2000) 1 *Theoretical Inquiries in Law* 155.

[37] *Holman* v. *Johnson* (1775) 1 Cowp 341 at 343.

[38] *Fender* v. *St John Mildmay* [1938] AC 1, HL, at 42.

[39] P. Winfield, 'Public Policy in the English Common Law' (1929) 42 *Harvard Law Review* 76 at 93.

One example of this variability is the changing judicial attitude in the nineteenth century to separation agreements between husband and wife. Of such agreements Sir George Jessel said, in 1879:

> Judicial opinion has varied a great deal... For a great number of years, both ecclesiastical Judges and lay Judges thought it was something very horrible, and against public policy, that the husband and wife should agree to live separate, and it was supposed that a civilized country could no longer exist if such agreements were enforced by Courts of law, whether ecclesiastical or not. But a change came over judicial opinion as to public policy; other considerations arose, and people began to think that after all it might be better and more beneficial for married people to avoid in many cases the expense and the scandal of suits of divorce by settling their differences quietly... and that was the view carried out by the Courts when it became once decided that separation deeds *per se* were not against public policy.[40]

A few years earlier the same judge had in another contractual context, rejected an appeal to *overt* considerations of public policy, but this does not show that public policy had in fact no influence, for the conclusion itself rested on the judge's perception of what public policy required:

> If there is one thing which more than another public policy requires it is that men of full age and competent understanding shall have the utmost liberty of contracting and that their contracts when entered into freely and voluntarily shall be held sacred and shall be enforced by courts of justice.[41]

The context of this last case was restraint of trade, a doctrine that has reflected differing views of the importance of a free market in various commodities and services.[42] There are many other instances of changes in perceptions of public policy. The attitude to racially discriminatory contracts, and similar provisions in wills, clearly enforceable until the middle of the twentieth century,[43] were, by the end of the century just as clearly unenforceable.[44] Contracts of financial support between unmarried

---

[40] *Besant v. Wood* (1879) 12 Ch D 605 at 620. See also *Davies v. Davies* (1886) 36 Ch D 359 at 364 (Kekewich J).

[41] *Printing & Numerical Registering Co. v. Sampson* (1875) LR 9 Eq 462 at 465 (Sir George Jessel, MR).

[42] M. Trebilcock, *The Common Law of Restraint of Trade* (Toronto, 1986), pp. 1–59.

[43] See, for example, *Essex Real Estate Co. v. Holmes* (1930) 37 OWN 392, affd 38 OWN 69, Div Ct, *Re McDougall and Waddell* [1945] 2 DLR 244, *Re Noble and Wolf* [1949] 4 DLR 375, revd on other grounds [1951] SCR 64.

[44] See *Canada Trust Co. v. Ontario Human Rights Commission* (1990) 69 DLR (4th) 321, Ont. CA.

cohabitants, clearly immoral in the nineteenth century,[45] were, by the last quarter of the twentieth century, clearly enforceable in most jurisdictions.[46] In the New Jersey case of *Henningsen* v. *Bloomfield Motors*[47] (1960), a products liability case, the court said:

> Public policy is a term not easily defined. Its significance varies as the habits and needs of a people may vary. It is not static and the field of application is an ever increasing one. A contract or a particular provision therein, valid in one era, may be totally opposed to the public policy of another.[48]

An English judge said a few years later that 'the law relating to public policy cannot remain immutable. It must change with the passage of time. The wind of change blows upon it.'[49]

Legal reasoning is often said to be 'result orientated', by which is meant that internal logic does not in itself determine the result; judgment, in the broad sense mentioned earlier,[50] is also involved. The point was made in an English case of 1892, in a jurisdiction and at a time when formal legal reasoning was highly valued. The question in issue was whether a contractual acceptance sent by mail in reply to an offer delivered by hand was effective on mailing. Earlier cases had held that an acceptance sent by mail in reply to a mailed offer was effective on mailing, one of the reasons adduced being that the mailing of an offer gave the offeree implied authority to reply by the same means. In *Henthorn* v. *Fraser* the court was required to determine whether this reason was crucial to the result. Lord Herschell said that it was not:

> It strikes me as somewhat artificial to speak of the person to whom the offer is made as having the implied authority of the other party to send his acceptance by post. He needs no authority to transmit the acceptance through any particular channel; he may select what means he pleases, the post-office no less than any other. The only effect of the implied authority is to make the acceptance complete as soon as it is posted, and authority will obviously be implied only when the tribunal considers that it is a case in which this result ought to be reached.[51]

---

[45] See *Fender* v. *St John Mildmay*, note 38 above, at 42.
[46] See *Chrispen* v. *Topham* (1986) 28 DLR (4th) 754, affd 39 DLR (4th) 637, Sask. CA.
[47] 32 NJ 358, 121 A 2d 69 (SCNJ, 1960).   [48] *Ibid.* at 121 A 2d 95.
[49] *Nagle* v. *Fielden* [1966] 2 QB 633, CA, at 650 (Danckwerts LJ).
[50] See chapter 1 above.
[51] *Henthorn* v. *Fraser* [1892] 2 Ch 27, CA at 33.

Professor Lon Fuller gave the telling example of a child injured by play-
ing on dangerous machinery left unfenced on the defendant's land. Many
courts, faced with a rule that trespassers on land could not recover compensation for injuries sustained there, reclassified the child as a licensee on the
reasoning that the landowner had impliedly invited children onto its land
by leaving dangerous machinery there that was attractive and accessible
to children.[52] Parallel in some respects was the highly artificial reasoning
used to mitigate the harsh consequences of the common law rule that a
negligently injured person forfeited all right to compensation if the injured
person's own negligence had contributed to the injury. In order to avoid
this result, courts in many jurisdictions held that if the defendant could
be said to have had a 'last opportunity' or 'last clear chance' to avoid the
injury, the plaintiff was entitled to compensation despite his or her own
prior negligence. The desired result (that the injured persons should receive compensation) was evidently influential in both lines of reasoning.
Such fictions and artificialities have often seemed in retrospect illogical,
inelegant, and unnecessary. But a recent (2002) judicial observation on
the 'last opportunity' rule, fifty-seven years after its effective disappearance
from English law, was rather more respectful of past reasoning: 'To say that
it [the rule] was illogical or inelegant seems... neither here nor there. If
it is recognized that the... rule was a development of the common law to
mitigate the rigour of the contributory negligence rule, there was nothing
illogical about it. As for inelegance, it was the best which could be done in the
circumstances.'[53] And as for necessity, open abrogation of the underlying
rule, which might seem in retrospect to have been a preferable alternative,
has not always been practicable for decision makers constrained by precedent, by their own framework of thought, and by the authority of superior
courts. As for the implied superiority of present perspectives, we should
not be too ready to congratulate ourselves on our own emancipation from
fictions, for, as John Baker has shown, it has not proved possible entirely to
avoid fictions at any period of legal history.[54]

Another example of the influence of public policy on the enlargement of
tort liability is vicarious liability for an employee's deliberate wrongdoing.

---

[52] L. Fuller, *Legal Fictions* (Stanford, 1967), pp. 66–8.
[53] *Fairchild* v. *Glenhaven Funeral Services Ltd* [2002] 3 WLR 89, at 126, HL (Lord Hoffmann).
[54] J. H. Baker, *The Law's Two Bodies: Some Evidential Problems in English Legal History* (Oxford, 2001).

Both the Supreme Court of Canada (1999) and the House of Lords (2001) have held an employer liable for sexual assaults committed by an employee in children's residences. These results were not reached by purely logical inference which, indeed, tended in the opposite direction. Both courts relied on broad considerations of public policy, and Lord Steyn, who gave the leading speech in the English case, warned that

> a preoccupation with conceptualistic reasoning may lead to the absurd conclusion that there can only be vicarious liability if the bank carries on business in defrauding its customers [with reference to a case of fraud by a bank clerk]. Ideas divorced from reality have never held much attraction for judges steeped in the tradition that their task is to deliver principled but practical justice. How the courts set the law on a sensible course is a matter to which I now turn.[55]

The words 'absurd', 'reality', and 'sensible', and the rejection of 'conceptualistic' reasons reflect the influence of broad considerations of judgment and policy. The same may be said of *Fairchild* v. *Glenhaven Funeral Services Ltd*[56] (2002), where strict requirements of proof of causation were modified in favour of injured employees who could not prove which of various employers had caused their injuries.

There are many examples of the effect of general policy considerations leading to the denial or abridgement of tort liability. The whole law of defamation has been controlled by considerations of freedom of speech. Liability for negligence has also been controlled by general considerations of public policy.[57] Recent examples of denial of tort liability on public policy grounds include the decision of the House of Lords in the Scottish case of *McFarlane* v. *Tayside Health Board*[58] (1999), where recovery was refused, on general public policy grounds, of compensation for the cost of bringing up a healthy baby conceived as the result of an unsuccessful vasectomy. Lord Steyn said that 'the court must apply positive law', adding, however, 'but judges' sense of the moral answer to a question, or the justice of the case, has been one of the great shaping forces of the common law'.[59] Another recent example is the decision of the Supreme Court of Canada in *Dobson* v.

---

[55] *Lister* v. *Hesley Hall Ltd* [2002] 1 AC 215 at 224.   [56] Note 53 above.

[57] *Anns* v. *Merton London Borough Council* [1978] AC 728, HL, rejected in *Murphy* v. *Brentwood District Council* [1991] 1 AC 398, HL, but followed in Canada; *Kamloops (City)* v. *Nielsen* [1984] 2 SCR 2, *Cooper* v. *Hobart* (2001) 206 DLR (4th) 193.

[58] [2000] 2 AC 59, HL (Sc).   [59] *Ibid.*, at 82.

Dobson (1999).[60] In this case an expectant mother was involved in a car accident allegedly caused by her negligent driving, and the child was born with injuries caused by the accident. The issue was whether the mother, if proved to be negligent, was liable to the child. The Supreme Court of Canada, reversing the two lower courts, held that she was not. In this case formal legal reasoning and internal logic tended to support the claim, as previous decisions had established that an unborn child, if negligently injured and subsequently born alive, could bring an action against the person responsible for the injuries, and this was conceded, in relation to any person other than the mother.[61] Economic considerations might also be said to support the claim, for it would seem that the cost to the mother of driving carefully must have been less than the expected (discounted) cost of the injury. Some policy considerations might also be said to support the claim, in that encouraging careful driving is beneficial to the community, and that one of the purposes of compulsory liability insurance is to secure a fund for the compensation of those negligently injured in road accidents; in fact the mother personally favoured the claim in the particular case.

But all these considerations were overridden in the mind of the majority of the court by the argument that if the mother were held liable in this case pregnant women in the future might be subjected to undue restraints on their freedom. In the words of the majority:

> The determination of whether a duty of care should be imposed must be made by considering the effects of tort liability on the privacy and autonomy interests of women, and upon their families, rather than by reference to a formalistic characterization of the conduct in question... The public policy concerns raised in this case are of such a nature and magnitude that they clearly indicate that a legal duty of care cannot, and should not, be imposed by the courts on a pregnant woman towards her foetus or subsequently born child.[62]

This is a judgment, as in *Egerton* v. *Brownlow*, on a very general question of social policy, and the judgment in both cases was evidently influenced by the social and political climate of the times. The opposite result in *Egerton* v. *Brownlow* could readily have been reached by saying that testators had a

---

60 [1999] 2 SCR 753, 174 DLR (4th) 1.

61 See L. Klar, 'Judicial Activism in Private Law' (2000) 80 *Canadian Bar Review* 215.

62 Note 60 above at 790 and 797 (SCR), 27 and 32 (DLR).

right to dispose of their property as they wished unless Parliament restricted it, and in the *Dobson* case, as the reasoning of the minority demonstrates, by saying that the injured child had a right to compensation according to established legal principles, unless the legislature declared that it should be removed.

To these instances should be added the many cases, discussed throughout this study, where considerations of public policy have played an auxiliary role concurrently with considerations of property, contract, wrongdoing, and unjust enrichment. Together these examples show that judgment, in a broad sense, has played an important part, and sometimes a crucial part, in private law adjudication. On the basis of such evidence it was suggested, in the first half of the twentieth century, by the school of thought known, loosely,[63] as 'American legal realism'[64] that formal legal reasoning was often fictitious, and this line of thinking was taken up in the second half of the twentieth century, and given a powerful political edge, by the school known (again loosely) as 'critical legal studies', and also by writers who have shown that judgment on matters of social policy has often been influenced by disputable assumptions about race and gender. These lines of thinking have drawn attention to an important aspect of the relation between law and policy, and they support the conclusion that judgment on matters of social policy has often played a significant role in adjudication. Attempts to deny this, if they cannot be effectively supported by historical evidence, are likely to encourage a more radical scepticism than they seek to oppose. Peter Birks has said that until there is a sound taxonomy, 'the fundamentalists of the school of critical legal studies will continue to play from a winning hand'.[65] But, assuming the objective of preventing this, it could not be attained by denying the actual complexities of the past.[66] The conclusion that policy has played an important part, however, does not establish that it has been the *exclusive* explanation of private law, or that considerations of principle and utility have not also been important.

---

[63] See W. Twining, *Karl Llewellyn and the Realist Movement* (Norman, Ohio, 1973), pointing out that there was no organized 'movement' and that critics often overstated the case against the realists. Corbin, for example, who was identified as a realist in 1930, was certainly not a radical sceptic, and devoted his life to his great treatise on contract law.

[64] R. Pound, 'The Call for a Realist Jurisprudence' (1931) 44 *Harvard Law Review* 697.

[65] P. Birks, 'Equity in the Modern Law: An Exercise in Taxonomy' (1996) 26 *Western Australian Law Review* 1 at 4.

[66] Compare the treatment of equity by G. Alexander, 'The Transformation of Trusts as a Legal Category, 1800–1914' 5 *Law and History Review* 304 (1987).

The implications of critical legal studies were sometimes taken, both by supporters and by opponents, to include a trivialization or disparagement of legal doctrine and reasoning, but such conclusions were not necessary and were not universally held. In a retrospective account of the critical legal studies school of thought one of its leading figures, Duncan Kennedy, allowed that 'Judges sometimes behave in ways well described as "consistent" and "logical" meaning obedient to a role constraint that requires them to apply rather than make law.'[67]

Closely related to these questions is the capacity of the law to change by judicial decision. This has important implications for the role of the judge and for the relevance, in judicial decision making, of public policy. Judges in civil litigation have had both an adjudicative and a rule-making function. As Joseph Jaconelli put it, 'the adjudicative process in developed legal systems may be said to possess both a private and a public aspect'.[68] Considerations of public policy have been to some degree inescapable, for the court, in making a new rule, has always, implicitly if not expressly, taken into account the probable costs and benefits to potential future litigants of the proposed change. Many judges have been reluctant openly to avow a rule-making function; hence the 'agreeable fiction',[69] or 'fairy tale'[70] that judges only declare and do not make the law. Some would doubt whether the fiction is agreeable, or the tale innocuous, but the judicial reluctance overtly to assume a law-making power has been strongly associated with perceptions of the proper constitutional role of judges and of the need for legal continuity. The relation between the declaratory and law-making functions is complex, for rules may be stated at many different levels of generality, and it is often impossible, even for the decision-maker, to distinguish between the application of an existing rule and the making of a new one, for 'the application of existing law to new circumstances can never be clearly distinguished from the creation of a new rule of law'.[71] There may be good reasons for judges and for advocates to disclaim creativity, but

---

[67] D. Kennedy, *A Critique of Adjudication (Fin de Siècle)* (Cambridge, Mass., 1997), pp. 160, 275–6.
[68] J. Jaconelli, 'Hypothetical disputes, Moot Points of Law, and Advisory Opinions' (1985) 101 *Law Quarterly Review* 587.
[69] Jocularly by A. P. Herbert, *Uncommon Law* (London, 1959), p. 156.
[70] Seriously by Lord Reid, 'The Judge as Law Maker' (1972) 12 *Journal of the Society of Public Teachers of Law (New Series)* 22, *Kleinwort Benson Ltd v. Lincoln City Council* [1999] 2 AC 349, HL, at 358 (Lord Browne-Wilkinson).
[71] R. Cross, *Precedent in English Law* (Oxford, 1961), p. 22.

legal historians, whose function is different from both, cannot always accept such disclaimers at face value.

It cannot be doubted that the courts, particularly at the appellate level, do change the law, and we have seen many examples of this in previous chapters. In 1998 Lord Goff said: 'we all know that in reality, in the common law as in equity, the law is the subject of development by the judges ... It is universally recognized that judicial development of the common law is inevitable.'[72] Nevertheless an element of the 'fiction' (that judges do not make law) has persisted, as the very case shows in which these statements were made. In the 1980s a practice had grown up in England of local government authorities (municipalities) entering into transactions with banks, called 'interest rate swaps' that amounted to a kind of speculation on future interest rates. In 1991 these transactions were held by the House of Lords to be wholly void as beyond the powers of the local authorities. In the aftermath of this decision many disputes arose as to the effect of the earlier transactions. Between 1982 and 1985 the city of Lincoln had entered into some of these transactions, and, the speculation turning out in the city's favour, payments had been made by the bank accordingly. After the 1991 decision the bank sought repayment on the ground that the payments had been made by mistake. When this claim reached the House of Lords in 1998, the House did alter the law by abolishing the former rule that excluded restitution for mistakes of law. This decision had retrospective effect in the sense that it was declared by the court that the parties' rights were to be determined as though relief for mistakes of law had been available when the payments were made. In this sense all judicial decisions that alter the law are retrospective, and Lord Goff thought that this was inevitable in the absence of a system of 'prospective overruling'.[73] But another aspect was the retrospective effect of the 1991 decision. The city argued that the bank had made no mistake in 1985, because it was only in 1991 that the law changed: in 1985 the bank believed that the transactions were valid, and rightly, for that was indeed the law at the time. The majority of the House of Lords (in 1998) held that the decision of 1991, though it made new law, yet had retrospective effect. Lord Goff put it this way:

---

[72] *Kleinwort Benson* v. *Lincoln City Council*, note 70 above, at 377.

[73] I.e., promulgating a rule to come into effect on a stated future date; the propriety of the court's assuming such an overtly legislative role in civil litigation has been questioned. See Jaconelli, 'Hypothetical Opinions', note 68 above, at 618–19.

The historical theory of judicial decision, though it may in the past have served its purpose, was indeed a fiction. But it does mean that, when judges state what the law is, their decisions do, in the sense I have described, have a retrospective effect. That is, I believe, inevitable...To me it is plain that the money was indeed paid over under a mistake, the mistake being a mistake of law. The payer believed, when he paid the money, that he was bound in law to pay it. He is now told that, on the law as held applicable at the date of the payment, he was not bound to pay it. Plainly, therefore, he paid the money under a mistake of law, and accordingly...he is entitled to recover it.[74]

Lord Goff said 'plainly', but the question was a difficult one: two judges dissented, and another (Lord Hoffmann) only changed his opinion (to agree with Lord Goff) after the argument. The minority opinion was that the bank had made no mistake at the time of payment, a proposition that would have been incontrovertible if the change in the law in 1991 had been brought about by legislation.

It has often been said that the role of the court in changing the law has been 'interstitial',[75] or 'incremental',[76] but it is not very clear what this has meant in practice. In *London Drugs Ltd* v. *Kuehne & Nagel International Ltd*[77] (1992) the Supreme Court of Canada held that an employee (though not himself a party to the contract) might take advantage of an agreement limiting liability for accidental damage to goods. The court, in admitting an exception to the rule against enforcement of contracts by third parties, several times described the change as 'incremental', indicating a reluctance to make a 'major change in the common law involving complex and uncertain ramifications'.[78] From one point of view the court created a single limited exception, leaving the rule of privity otherwise intact. But from another point of view the decision made a very radical change, abolishing the rule *as a rule*, and inviting courts in the future to admit new exceptions whenever 'consistent with modern notions of commercial reality and justice'.[79] In subsequent decisions the court has introduced into maritime law the rules of contributory negligence and of contribution among tortfeasors, and a

---

[74] [1999] 2 AC 378–9.

[75] Justice Holmes in *Southern Pacific Co.* v. *Jensen* 244 US 205, 221 (1917).

[76] *Winnipeg Child and Family Services (Northwest Area)* v. *DFG* [1997] 3 SCR 925,152 DLR (4th) 193. See C. R. Sunstein, *One Case at a Time: Judicial Minimalism and the Supreme Court* (Cambridge, Mass., 1999).

[77] [1992] 3 SCR 299.   [78] *Ibid.*, at 453.

[79] *Ibid.*, at 437. See *Fraser River Pile & Dredge, Ltd* v. *Can-Dive Services Ltd* [1999] 3 SCR 108.

scheme of liability to third parties for fatal and non-fatal injuries, including compensation for intangible losses.[80] It may well be thought that these were useful improvements to Canadian maritime law, but most observers would not have described these changes as 'incremental'. It had previously been generally supposed that legislation was necessary to introduce into the law the principle of compensation for fatal accidents, to extend that principle to injury to third parties by non-fatal accidents, to extend it further to cover intangible losses, and to introduce the principles of apportionment for contributory negligence, and of contribution among wrongdoers. Several of these questions have 'complex and uncertain ramifications'. It would appear, therefore, that the assertion by the court that judicial development of the law can only be incremental must be read in the light of a generous interpretation of what is meant by 'incremental'.

A significant factor has been the rise and in some jurisdictions the subsequent decline in the second half of the twentieth century of law reform commissions. If it can be confidently expected that private law will be regularly reviewed and reformed by legislative commissions, there is correspondingly less need for active judicial law reform. This was a factor that influenced the House of Lords in *Beswick* v. *Beswick*[81] to refrain from amending the contractual rule of privity. Eventually (though not until thirty years later) the rule was reformed in England by statute.[82] When this question came before the Supreme Court of Canada in 1980[83] no reforming action was taken, but when it arose again in 1992 the court, as we have seen, did take action to alter the law.[84] By that date it was clear that Canadian legislatures were unlikely to resolve the problem either promptly, or on a uniform basis.[85]

There has been some difference of opinion on the question of whether the courts, in developing the common law, may take into account analogous

---

[80] *Bow Valley Husky (Bermuda) Ltd* v. *Saint John Shipbuilding Ltd* [1997] 3 SCR 1210, *Ordon Estate* v. *Grail* [1998] 3 SCR 437.

[81] [1968] AC 58, HL, at 72: 'If one had to contemplate a further long period of parliamentary procrastination, this House might find it necessary to deal with this matter. But if legislation is probable at an early date I would not deal with it in a case where that is not essential' (Lord Reid).

[82] See chapter 3 above.

[83] *Greenwood Shopping Plaza Ltd* v. *Beatty* [1980] 2 SCR 228.

[84] *London Drugs*, note 77 above.

[85] The Ontario Law Reform Commission had proposed reform in 1987, but no legislative action was pending or probable in Ontario. The rule was, however, altered by statute in New Brunswick by Law Reform Act, SNB 1993 c. L-1.2, s. 4(1).

statutory provisions. Often legislation has been seen as a series of special exceptions leaving the common law intact except insofar as specifically changed by the statutory words, indeed as strengthening the common law because the special legislative exception is taken impliedly to affirm the general common law rule. But the changing needs of society may be addressed both by legislation and by common law, as, for example, in the sphere of domestic relations discussed in chapter 7, and the role of the courts in adapting and altering the law from time to time is now universally acknowledged. There is a strong argument, therefore, in favour of the courts' taking into account the direction of legislative change, and sometimes extending the provisions of legislation to analogous cases.[86] Lord Diplock took this approach in *Erven Warnink Besloten Vennootschap* v. *J Townsend & Sons (Hull) Ltd*:[87]

> Where over a period of years there can be discerned a steady trend in legislation which reflects the view of successive parliaments as to what the public interest demands in a particular field of law, development of the common law in that part of the same field which has been left to it ought to proceed upon a parallel rather than a diverging course.[88]

Lambert JA expressed similar views in *Harry* v. *Kreutziger*[89] on the question of unconscionability in contracts. Having referred to community standards of commercial morality, he added:

> It is also appropriate to seek guidance as to community standards of commercial morality from legislation that embodies those standards in law.[90]

Another aspect of the question is judicial interpretation of statutes. Statutes that amend private law, especially codifying statutes, have often been interpreted so as to accommodate changes in the law. This approach reflects the view that such statutes are rarely amended by the legislature, and the judges have therefore undertaken to keep the statutes 'up to date' and in tune with parallel judicial developments in a way that they have not done, for example, in respect of taxing statutes. An illustration is the treatment of certain provisions in the Sale of Goods Act by the English Court of Appeal

---

[86] J. Landis, 'Statutes and the Sources of Law', [1934] reprinted (1965) 2 *Harvard Journal on Legislation* 7, J. Beatson, 'Has the Common Law a Future?' [1997] *Cambridge Law Journal* 291, J. Beatson, 'The Role of Statute in the Development of Common Law Doctrine' (2001) 117 *Law Quarterly Review* 247.

[87] [1979] AC 731, HL.   [88] *Ibid.*, at 743.

[89] (1978) 95 DLR (3d) 231, BCCA.   [90] *Ibid.*, at 241.

in *Cehave NV* v. *Bremer Handelsgesellschaft mbH*[91] (1976). The question at issue was whether a defect in goods gave the buyer a right to reject them even if the defect did not prevent their commercial use. The Sale of Goods Act had previously been interpreted to mean that every obligation must be classified as at the time of the contract as a condition or a warranty, the former but not the latter giving the buyer the right to reject. The consequence seemed to be that a defect in quality, even if commercially of small practical importance, must (being a breach of condition) give the right to reject. But in the *Cehave* case considerations of commercial fairness, and of parallel developments outside sales law,[92] led the court in the opposite direction. Ormrod LJ said:

> We have all been brought up since our student days to ask the question in the form: 'Is this stipulation a condition or a warranty?' [but] ... the modern form of the question tends to put the cart before the horse ... The law has developed since the Act was passed. It is now accepted as a general principle ... that it is the events resulting from the breach, rather than the breach itself, which may destroy the consideration for the buyer's promise and so enable him to treat the contract as repudiated.[93]

The reference to 'development' of the law since the passing of the statute shows that the 'sound and true distinction between judicial and legislative functions'[94] has often been elusive in practice.

A contrast between private right and public interest has often been supported by references to government power to acquire private property in the public interest, called, in various jurisdictions, expropriation, compulsory purchase, or eminent domain. Thus, in *Goodson* v. *Richardson*[95] (1874), where the court granted an injunction to restrain the laying of water pipes on the plaintiff's land, Lord Selbourne said:

> What Parliament might do, if it were to deal with the question, is, I apprehend, not a matter for our consideration now, as Parliament has not dealt with the question. Parliament is, no doubt, at liberty to take a higher view upon a balance struck between private rights and public interests than this Court can take.

---

[91] [1976] QB 44, CA.
[92] *Hongkong Fir Shipping Co. Ltd* v. *Kawasaki Kisen Kaisha Ltd* [1962] 2 QB 26.
[93] *Cehave*, note 91 above, at 82–3.
[94] Alderson B in *Egerton* v. *Brownlow*, note 11 above, at 106.
[95] (1874) LR 9 Ch App 221 at 224.

The two concepts, however, have not operated in isolation from each other, as is demonstrated by several nineteenth-century English decisions on water rights.

In *Bradford Corporation* v. *Pickles*[96] (1895) the House of Lords held that a landowner was entitled to divert water percolating through his land in order to prevent it reaching his neighbour's land. In this case the 'downstream' neighbouring land was owned by the town of Bradford, which wanted the water for a public supply. The decision is commonly thought to show the isolation of private rights from questions of public interest, and the court's preference for the former. Thus, Brian Simpson has written that

> The decision...seems to me to be a most striking illustration of the persistence, in the common law tradition, of the individualistic conception of property rights... The claims of the public interest surely favoured the Corporation against Edward Pickles. But Pickles' despotic dominion triumphed in spite of the obvious awareness of the judges of the potential consequences of their decision. Let there be sanctity of property even if the heavens fall, or even if the City of Bradford is converted into a howling desert.[97]

There is some force in this point, but the real question was not whether the inhabitants of Bradford would go without water, but how much they would have to pay for it.[98] Had the heavens been in real danger of falling, the decision would probably have been otherwise. As Corbin remarked, 'Fiat justitia ruat coelum [let justice be done though the heavens fall] is a phrase impressive mainly because of its being in Latin and not understandable. When the skies begin to fall, Justice removes the blindfold from her eyes and tilts the scales.'[99]

The courts in *Bradford* v. *Pickles* were fully aware of the public interest, and were not at all averse to the idea that Pickles' water rights should be expropriated by Parliament, as is shown by Simpson's own original and important research on the background of the case and by that of Michael Taggart.[100] The judge at first instance had given an injunction in favour of the town. A few days after argument, while the decision of the Court

[96] [1895] AC 587, HL.
[97] A. W. B. Simpson, *Victorian Law and the Industrial Spirit* (London, 1995), pp. 16–17.
[98] See M. Taggart, *Private Property and Abuse of Rights in Victorian England: The Story of Edward Pickles and the Bradford Water Supply* (Oxford, 2002).
[99] A. L. Corbin, *Corbin on Contracts* (12 vols., St Paul, 1964), vol. I, s. 2.
[100] Note 98 above.

of Appeal was pending, the presiding judge of that court (Lord Herschell) suggested to counsel for the town that the court's decision should be adjourned to allow the town an opportunity to apply for a private Act of Parliament, this being the regular procedure for acquisition of land rights in the public interest, and the deadline for giving notice to Parliament being a week away.[101] The effect of this very unusual suggestion would have been to *continue the injunction* against Pickles until his rights could be expropriated, thereby ensuring the continuity of the public water supply. This shows that the Court of Appeal was very conscious of the public interest – so much so that they were willing to depart from usual etiquette by contacting counsel outside the framework of legal argument,[102] and proposing the continuance of an injunction that they were about to hold had no legal basis. This is a striking instance of a clear and deliberate (though limited) sacrifice of private right to public interest, and strongly supports Corbin's comments on judicial blindfolds. Counsel advised the town to accept this proposal:

> I am disposed to fall in with this suggestion. It indicates that the Court of Appeal are against us, but that they think we ought to have Parliamentary powers, which will not involve any substantial payment to Pickles.[103]

But the town, fearing that the parliamentary route *would* involve substantial payment to Pickles,[104] decided to take its chances instead, for all or nothing, in the judicial system.

The merits of the final decision in *Bradford* v. *Pickles* may be disputed, but the case is hardly persuasive evidence that the courts were oblivious to the public interest. Nor can the contest be characterized as one between property rights and something else: it was a contest between two landowners each asserting competing claims to water rights. If the decision had been in favour of the town its effect would probably have been summarized not as abridging property rights but as creating a new legally protected interest in water (i.e., of a 'downstream' landowner in percolating water even though

---

[101] See, in relation to railroads, R. Kostal, *Law and English Railway Capitalism, 1825–1875* (Oxford, 1994).

[102] Opposing counsel were to be informed, Taggart, *Private Property*, p. 59.

[103] Simpson, *Victorian Law*, p. 15. The date of this letter was 5 Nov. 1894 (Taggart, *Private Property*, p. 60). Argument had concluded on 30 Oct., and the deadline for parliamentary notice was 13 Nov. The decision of the Court of Appeal was announced on 10 Dec. (Simpson, *Victorian Law*, p. 15, and note 12).

[104] Taggart, *Private Property*, pp. 60–61.

not flowing in a defined channel). An important earlier decision, *Chasemore* v. *Richards*[105] (1859), had involved a dispute where the 'upstream' landowner (i.e. the landowner in a position comparable to Pickles') had taken percolating water for public purposes, and the 'downstream' owner had complained of loss of water for private use. The court had there held in favour of the 'upstream' owner on the same principle as was applied in Pickles' case, the court's decision operating on that occasion in favour of the public use. There is certainly room for debate on what is the preferable rule to resolve disputes over percolating water, but that is a small-scale debate about the scope of water rights, not a large-scale debate about the sanctity of property.

There is certainly truth also in the proposition that nineteenth-century judges favoured respect for property rights, but this does not establish that they preferred private to public interests. On the contrary, *Chasemore v. Richards* might plausibly be criticized for giving *too much* preference to the public interest at the expense of the reasonable interests of the private 'downstream' landowner,[106] and Lord Herschell in *Bradford v. Pickles* showed, as we have seen, remarkable concern for the public interest, even to the extent of manipulating the adjudicative process to ensure the continuance of an injunction that lacked legal basis. In general the judges' view was that the public interest was best served by a kind of partnership between the courts and the legislature, with the courts enforcing and defining property rights but leaving redistribution of them to the legislature. The alternative, that the court should allocate and reallocate water rights according to its perception from time to time of the public benefit of particular uses, was not thought to serve the public interest better, especially as, having no taxing power, the court usually[107] lacked the means to pass on the cost of an expropriation to the section of the public that benefited by it. Thus, *Bradford v. Pickles* does not show that considerations of public policy had no influence; it shows the very opposite, both in the willingness of the Court of Appeal to continue the injunction, and in the more general consideration that the desirable relation between the court and the legislature was itself based on

---

[105] (1859) 7 HLC 349.   [106] See Lord Wensleydale's near dissent on this question.

[107] *Spur Industries Inc.* v. *Del E Webb Development Co.* 494 P 2d 700 (Ariz, SC, 1972), where a developer of land for residential housing was granted an injunction to restrain an incompatible use, but only on condition of paying the defendant's costs of relocation, might be regarded as a limited exception.

the court's view of what public policy required; protection of property, like enforcement of contracts, *was* public policy.[108] Public policy has played an important role in all the questions considered in earlier chapters, but in two kinds of case it has operated directly so as actually to impose in litigation between individuals obligations to pay rewards and fines. The law of maritime salvage, though closely associated with unjust enrichment, contains an element that cannot be derived from unjust enrichment, namely reward for the performance of meritorious service. Somewhat analogously, the law of exemplary (punitive) damages permits the imposition of a fine in order to punish and deter conduct that is the reverse of meritorious. Private law concepts, considered alone, do not explain why the reward element in salvage cases should be owed by the defendant, nor why exemplary damages should be payable to the plaintiff.

By admiralty law a reward (salvage) is payable for saving property at sea. Modern English scholars differ sharply on whether or not salvage law should be included in the law of unjust enrichment. Some writers have included it,[109] but others have doubted whether it should be included within the subject, partly because the services are rendered voluntarily, and partly because the measure of recovery is not exclusively based on the defendant's enrichment.[110] Francis Rose has accommodated the opposing views by leaving open the question of whether salvage strictly forms part of the law of unjust enrichment, while adding that 'it is clear that many of the principles which govern restitution [unjust enrichment] also operate within salvage...'.[111]

Salvage law falls within most definitions of private law, and of the law of obligations, in that it imposes legal obligations on private persons for the benefit of other private persons. But there has always been a strong element

---

[108] See pp. 19 and 200 above.

[109] R. Goff and G. Jones, *The Law of Restitution* (London, 1966), ch. 15, D. Steel and F. Rose, *Kennedy's Law of Salvage* (5th edn, London, 1985), ch. 16, G. Klippert, *Unjust Enrichment* (Toronto, 1983), p. 46, A. Burrows, *The Law of Restitution* (London, 1993), pp. 236–8.

[110] Lord Wright, *Legal Essays and Addresses* (Cambridge, 1939), p. 55, noting with approval the omission of the subject from the American Law Institute's *Restatement of Restitution*, P. Birks, *Introduction to the Law of Restitution* (Oxford, 1985), pp. 304–8, G. Virgo, *Principles of the Law of Restitution* (Oxford, 1999), p. 321, A. Burrows, *The Law of Restitution* (London, 1993), pp. 248–9.

[111] F. D. Rose, 'Restitution and Maritime Law' in E. J. H. Schrage (ed.), *Unjust Enrichment and the Law of Contract* (The Hague, 2001), p. 367 at p. 380.

of public policy. Dr Lushington, judge of the High Court of Admiralty from 1838 to 1867, said, citing Justice Story, the American scholar and judge, that salvage is 'a mixed question of private right and public policy'.[112] He said that the reward is given 'not merely to remunerate the effort made to save the ship, cargo, and lives of the persons on board, but also to encourage others to make similar attempts'.[113] 'Say what you will', he said in another case, 'so long as human motives operate on conduct, unless you give a reward, you must take away all incitement to service.'[114] He had no doubt of the beneficial effect of salvage law, describing it as 'of the utmost importance to the safety of shipping',[115] and 'absolutely necessary'.[116]

If public policy were the exclusive source of the obligation then one would expect that merit would be rewarded regardless of success. However, one of the chief characteristics of salvage law has been that merit alone is insufficient:

> However meritorious the exertion of alleged salvors may be, if they are not attended with benefit to the owners they cannot be compensated in this Court; salvage reward is for benefit actually conferred in the preservation of property, not for meritorious exertions alone.[117]

A principal reason was that some property had actually to be in the custody of the court to give it jurisdiction.[118] A further indication that public policy was not the sole consideration is that salvage law, until modified by statute in 1846,[119] allowed no reward for saving of life, unless property was also saved.[120] Moreover the very case in which the most generous award was allowed (traditionally one-half of the value salved) was the case of derelict (property abandoned at sea), where human life was not in danger.

Salvage law cannot be fully explained on contractual principles. No request for the services was necessary,[121] as the case of derelict also shows. Considerations of unjust enrichment were prominent. Lushington spoke

---

[112] *The Albion* (1861) Lush 282 at 284. The reference is probably to *The Henry Ewbank*, 1 Sumn 400, 11 F Cas 1166, 1170 (CA, Mass., 1833) ('mixed question of public policy and private right').

[113] *The William Hannington* (1845) 9 Jur 641.   [114] *The Rosalie* (1853) 1 Sp 188, 189.

[115] *The Albion*, note 112 above.   [116] *The Neptune* (1858) 12 Moo PC 346, 350.

[117] *The India* (1842) 1 W Rob 406, 408.   [118] *The Chieftain* (1846) 2 W Rob 450.

[119] Wreck and Salvage Act, 9 & 10 Vic., c. 90.

[120] See *The Bartley* (1857) Swab 198, *The Fusilier* (1865) Br & Lush 341, *Silver Bullion* (1854) 2 Sp 70, *The Coromandel* (1857) Swab 205.

[121] *The Annapolis* (1861) Lush 355.

often of 'remuneration',[122] recompense,[123] compensation,[124] and 'what the services were worth'.[125] 'Salvage is governed by a due regard to the benefit received', Dr Lushington said, while adding 'combined with a just regard for the general interests of ships and marine commerce'.[126] In giving a large reward for a brief but efficient service Lushington said that 'it is not the mere time occupied; it is not the mere labour, but the real value of the services rendered'.[127]

Many judges have said that salvage is based on principles of natural justice and equity,[128] but this did not mean equity as administered by the Chancery Court, nor did it imply unfettered discretion. The matter might be summed up by saying that salvage law has been influenced principally, but not solely, by considerations of unjust enrichment, and that it cannot be assigned exclusively to any one part of the law of obligations. From one point of view it may be regarded as a kind of imperfect taxation, imposing a surcharge on owners of ships and cargo saved, in order to maintain, in the public interest, a means of inducing seafarers to rescue those in distress. Since salvage law was not part of the common law, and was administered until 1875 by a court entirely separate from the courts of law and of equity, it is scarcely surprising that it does not fit readily into categories derived from the law of obligations.

The primary function of private law has been to correct injustice between the parties, and damages have usually been measured by compensatory principles. 'You do not give damages... *in poenam* [as a penalty]; it is not a paternal correction inflicted by the court, but simply compensation for the loss.'[129] 'Moral indignation is not a factor that is to be used to inflate the calculation of a compensatory award.'[130] But, as we saw in an earlier chapter, awards have sometimes been measured by the defendant's profit,

---

[122] *The Inca* (1858) Swab 371, *The Harriett* (1857) Swab 218, *The Undaunted* (1860) Lush 90.

[123] *The Syrian* (1866) 14 LT 833.

[124] *The Rajasthan* (1856) Swab 171, *The Mary Pleasants* (1857) Swab 224.

[125] *The Mary Pleasants*, note 124 above, *The Africa* (1854) 1 Sp 299 ('reward for services rendered'), *The Otto Herman* (1864) 33 LJPMA 189 (payment for 'services').

[126] *The Fusilier* (1865) Br & Lush 341, 347.

[127] *The General Palmer* (1844) 5 Not Cas 159n.

[128] *The Juliana* (1822) 2 Dods 504, 521 (Lord Stowell), *The Calypso* (1828) 2 Hagg 209, 217 (Sir Christopher Robinson), *The Harriet* (1853) 1 Sp 180, and *Cargo ex Capella* (1867) 1 A & E 356 (Dr Lushington), *The Beaverford* v. *The Kafiristan* [1938] AC 136 at 147 (Lord Wright).

[129] *Williams* v. *Peel River Land & Mineral Co.* (1886) 55 LT 689.

[130] *Cadbury Schweppes Inc.* v. *FBI Foods Ltd* [1999] 1 SCR 142 at 181, 167 DLR 4th 577 at 606 (Binnie J).

and this result has been supported by a mixture of considerations, including public policy and the prevention of profit by wrongdoing.[131]

Punitive and deterrent considerations have also played a part in various rules of damage assessment. For example, it is common for the claimant's burden of proof to be eased by presumptions operating against a wrongdoer. Deliberate mixing of goods has long had penal consequences.[132] Where a wrongdoer has added value to property, for example by extracting minerals belonging to the plaintiff, the courts have been less ready to make an allowance for this factor in the defendant's favour where the wrongdoing was deliberate than where it was accidental.[133] In case of a contract induced by fraudulent misrepresentation the courts have been more ready to allow rescission than where the misrepresentation is innocent:

> A case of innocent misrepresentation may be regarded rather as one of misfortune that as one of moral obliquity. There is no deceit or intention to defraud. The court will be less ready to pull a transaction to pieces where the defendant is innocent, whereas in the case of fraud the court will exercise its jurisdiction to the full in order, if possible, to prevent the defendant from enjoying the benefit of his fraud at the expense of the innocent plaintiff.[134]

Compensatory principles include the requirement that the loss claimed should be proved to have been caused by the defendant's wrong, and that it should not be too remote. In several kinds of case, notably fraud and breach of fiduciary duty, the ordinary principles of causation and remoteness have been set aside in order to supply an additional measure of deterrence and punishment. In *Hodgkinson* v. *Simms*,[135] for example, the Supreme Court of Canada held a financial adviser who had been guilty of a breach of fiduciary duty liable for loss caused by decline in the value of an investment subsequent to the transaction. The court refused to entertain the argument that the loss would probably have occurred in any event. La Forest J, giving the majority judgment, went on to say that 'on the facts of this case... damages in contract follow the principles stated in connection with the equitable breach'.[136] The desirability of mixing compensatory and punitive

---

[131] See chapter 6 above.
[132] W. Blackstone, *Commentaries on the Laws of England* (4 vols., London, 1765–9), vol. II, pp. 404–5.
[133] See *Jegon* v. *Vivian* (1871) LR 6 Ch App 742.
[134] *Spence* v. *Crawford* [1939] 3 All ER 271, HL, at 288.   [135] [1994] 3 SCR 377.
[136] *Ibid.*, at 454.

considerations in this way has been doubted by other courts,[137] and by commentators.[138]

The direct award of exemplary or punitive damages has been a persistent feature of Anglo-American law, but it has been difficult to justify solely in terms of correction of wrong between the individual parties to the dispute. Nor can it readily be justified by the kind of economic analysis usually applied to private law: the proper measure of deterrence, from an economic point of view, has been said to be the amount of the claimant's loss discounted by the improbability of a successful claim.[139] The principal arguments against punitive damages in private law are that punishment and deterrence by penal sanctions are proper functions not of private law but of criminal or penal law. The institution of punitive damages enables the court in the course of civil litigation to create and define penal offences, and then to punish them without many of the protections that penal law usually affords to persons accused of crime.[140] From an administrative point of view ad hoc punishment by civil courts is not an effective means of regulation, and may have the counter-productive effect of punishing conduct that has deliberately been approved in the public interest by a regulatory agency.[141] Where the defendant is a large enterprise or a government agency, the cost of the award will not be borne by any person who is actually guilty of the objectionable conduct, but will in practice be passed on to a large section of the community. There is no reason, from the perspective of private law, why a fine, imposed for purposes of punishment and deterrence in the interest of the community, should go into the plaintiff's pocket. Claims for punitive damages complicate private litigation by making relevant many facts, such as the defendant's motives, overall wealth, and conduct in previous cases, that would normally be irrelevant, and they impede settlement because of the radical uncertainty of the probable amount of the award, especially when this is in the hands of a jury. Lord Reid said in 1972 in a libel case:

---

[137] *Target Holdings Ltd* v. *Redferns* [1996] AC 421, HL.

[138] See J. Berryman, 'Equitable Remedies for Breach by Fact-based Fiduciaries: Tentative Thoughts on Clarifying Remedial Goals' (1999) 31 *Alberta Law Review* 95 at 96, 104.

[139] R. Posner, *Economic Analysis of Law* (Boston, 1972), p. 77. The fifth edition (New York, 1998) appears to allow a wider scope to punitive damages.

[140] Burden of proof, right to remain silent, right to jury trial, right to sentencing by a judge, right to appeal against sentence, protection against double jeopardy.

[141] E.g. a pharmaceutical drug that is beneficial to the community but poses an inevitable risk to a few. There is a strong argument here for compensatory damages to the person injured if the drug is defective (see chapter 5 above), but not for punitive damages.

I think that the objections to allowing juries to go beyond compensatory damages are overwhelming. To allow pure punishment in this way contravenes every principle which has been evolved for the protection of offenders. There is no definition of the offence except that the conduct punished must be oppressive, high-handed, malicious, wanton, or its like – terms far too vague to be admitted to any criminal code worthy of the name. There is no limit to the punishment except that it must not be unreasonable. The punishment is not inflicted by a judge who has experience and at least tries not to be influenced by emotion: it is inflicted by a jury without experience of law or punishment and often swayed by considerations which every judge would put out of his mind. And there is no effective appeal against sentence . . . It is no excuse to say that we need not waste sympathy on people who behave outrageously. Are we wasting sympathy on vicious criminals when we insist on proper legal safeguards for them? . . . I am surprised by the enthusiasm of [supporters of] this form of palm tree justice.[142]

Objections of this sort led the House of Lords in 1963 to limit punitive damages to two kinds of case[143] but not to abolish them entirely.[144] Other Commonwealth jurisdictions have retained and in some cases expanded the scope of punitive damages.[145] American jurisdictions have been notorious for large awards of punitive damages,[146] and, despite some legislative and judicial restrictions introduced in the 1980s and 1990s,[147] they retain an important place in American law. The persistence of deterrent and punitive elements in Anglo-American private law shows that no rigid division has in practice been sustained between corrective and compensatory considerations on the one hand, and punitive, deterrent, and public policy considerations on the other.

---

[142] *Cassell & Co. Ltd* v. *Broome* [1972] AC 1027, HL, at 1087.

[143] Profit made from the wrong, and abuse of government power. A third exception was express statutory provision.

[144] *Rookes* v. *Barnard* [1964] AC 1129, HL, *Thompson* v. *Commissioner of Police of the Metropolis* [1998] QB 498, CA. *Kuddus* v. *Chief Constable of Leicestershire Constabulary* [2002] 2 AC 122, HL, exhibits a comparatively friendly attitude to exemplary damages.

[145] *Uren* v. *John Fairfax & Sons Pty Ltd* (1966) 117 CLR 118, [1969] 1 AC 590, PC, *Donselaar* v. *Donselaar* [1982] 1 NZLR 97, *Hill* v. *Church of Scientology of Toronto* [1995] 2 SCR 1130, *Botiuk* v. *Toronto Free Press Publications Ltd* [1995] 3 SCR 3, *Vorvis* v. *Insurance Corp. of British Columbia* [1989] 1 SCR 1085, *Royal Bank of Canada* v. *W. Gott & Associates Electric Ltd* [1999] 3 SCR 408, *Whiten* v. *Pilot Insurance Co.* (2002) 209 DLR (4th) 257.

[146] E.g. *Grimshaw* v. *Ford Motor Co.* (1981) 174 Cal Rptr 348 ($125m reduced to $3.5m), *Texaco Inc.* v. *Penzoil Co.* 729 SW 2d 768 (Tex CA, 1987) ($3 billion).

[147] *BMW of North America Inc.* v. *Gore* 517 US 559 (1996). State statutes are collected in L. Schlueter and K. Redden, *Punitive Damages*, 4th edn (2 vols., New York, 2000), vol. II, ch. 20.

The evidence establishes that judicial perceptions of public policy have often played an important, and sometimes a decisive, role in Anglo-American private law. It follows that considerations of formal legal logic and internal coherence have not been everything. But it does not follow that they have been nothing. The two most influential American judges of the twentieth century have stressed the simultaneous presence of formal and policy considerations. Holmes' statement, quoted in an earlier chapter, that 'the life of the law has not been logic; it has been experience' has usually been quoted out of its context. Holmes' immediately preceding words were 'it is something to show that the consistency of a system requires a particular result, but it is not all'.[148] Cardozo spoke also of 'the demon of formalism [that] tempts the intellect with the lure of scientific order', but added,

> I do not mean, of course, that judges are commissioned to set aside existing rules at pleasure in favour of any other set of rules which they may hold to be expedient or wise. I mean that when they are called upon to say how far existing rules are to be extended or restricted, they must let the welfare of society fix the path, its direction and its distance.[149]

Cardozo's opinion, like that of Holmes, was that 'logical consistency does not cease to be a good because it is not the supreme good'.[150] Historical evidence supports these opinions: both principle and policy have, in the past, been influential in Anglo-American private law, and so closely interrelated as to be inseparable.

---

[148] Holmes, *The Common Law*, p. 1.
[149] B. Cardozo, *The Nature of the Judicial Process* (New Haven, 1963 [1921]), pp. 66–7.
[150] *Ibid.*, at p. 32.

Conclusion: the concept of legal mapping

The study of any legal question may take as a starting point a legal system, located in time and place, and examine the evidence of what the law has actually been at particular times. Alternatively a legal study may start with an idea adapted, as Charles Addison said in 1847 of contract law, 'to all times and races, and all places and circumstances',[1] and apply the idea to a particular legal system, rejecting what is there found to be incompatible with the idea. Both approaches have had an important place in legal thinking and writing. Their concurrence is to some extent unavoidable, because the assessment of what the law is at the time of assessment, or of what it was at any previous time, is itself a complex process, requiring elements of historical enquiry, of judgment, of synthesis, and of prediction.

It has not been possible, therefore, to maintain a simple dichotomy in legal analysis between description and prescription. However, the concurrence carries the risk of distorting an understanding of the past. There is a danger that the universal idea may be used to excise or to marginalize aspects of the past that do not conform to it, while at the same time implying that the past, conveniently pruned by these means, offers support for the idea. Addison, for instance, found a 'surprising... uniformity' between English and Roman law,[2] but if his universal idea is taken as a starting point the coincidence could not be wholly surprising, for evidence of nonconformity with the idea in both legal systems will have been marginalized by its very nonconformity.

Other writers have denounced aspects of the law as chaotic and disorderly: if only the reader would join in accepting a few simple principles and in discarding a few anomalous decisions (the argument proceeds) order might be achieved. A common method has been to propose a scheme, to invite the reader to infer from a selective use of past decisions that there is

---

[1] C. Addison, *A Treatise on the Law of Contracts and Rights and Liabilities ex contractu* (London, 1847), Preface, p. v.
[2] *Ibid.*, p. iv.

historical support for it, to imply that adoption of the scheme will lead in the future to desirable consequences, and then to 'explain' (as showing the hidden operation of the scheme) those non-conforming decisions where the same result could have been reached on a conforming basis, and to condemn the rest as exceptional or unprincipled. This method has been very common in legal writing, but from a historical perspective it has limitations: it tends to assume what is sought to be proved, to marginalize inconvenient material, and to confuse the assessment of the past with a judgment of what is desirable for the future.

Assertions about the past ought to be capable of being tested by historical evidence, and ought, at some stage, to be so tested. Addison's assertion of uniformity between English and Roman contract law is difficult to test in the absence of particulars of specific legal rules to be compared in the two systems, and of the dates in each at which comparisons are invited. Statements like Addison's have a rhetorical component: he was seeking to persuade his readers that the principles which he had identified as 'fundamental... immutable and eternal' not only had been, but ought to be recognized in English contract law, and (combining the two approaches) that, properly understood, English contract law *must* comprise them. This kind of argument, implicit in much nineteenth- and twentieth-century legal writing, is open to the observations that as an account of the past it cannot be falsified, for contradictory evidence, when properly understood, will always be marginalized, and that as a statement of what is desirable for non-historical reasons it is incomplete, for it omits the reasons. No writer is obliged to make assertions about the past, and an account of law might, as was suggested earlier,[3] possibly rest entirely on non-historical grounds. But then the account could neither describe actual past law (remote or recent), nor derive support from it.

The preceding chapters have drawn attention to a number of issues the resolution of which has not conformed to simple accounts of private law. Proponents of accounts to which they do not conform may call them, and have called them, marginal, insignificant, and exceptional. But, as we have seen, such cases have been neither infrequent, nor, from the point of view of the parties or of the public, insignificant. As William Lucy has said, 'were we to... seek to distinguish between competing accounts of a practice on the grounds that one account fits *significant* aspects of the practice better than

---

[3] See chapter 1 above.

another, then our criteria of significance stand in need of justification'.[4] The reader would indeed have reason to object if the criterion of significance turned out to be compatibility with the proposition that the writer was seeking to prove. The suggestion that a set of past decisions, frequent in fact and significant in effect, has been anomalous and unprincipled would require cogent proof, on grounds independent of history, of the intrinsic merit of the asserted rules or principles with which the decisions are supposed to have been inconsistent. To say that the law *properly understood* conforms or aspires to a particular idea, account, or scheme does not reveal precisely what assertion (if any) is made about the past, and cannot therefore be tested by historical evidence. Neither can the suggestion be tested that an idea has been inherent or immanent but latent, because all evidence tending to contradict the inherence or immanence of the idea will go to show its latency.

An ambiguity, or slippage, on this kind of question has been earlier noticed in relation to the law of torts and the idea of fault. Lord Wright's comment (1938) will be recalled on the proposition that 'there is no liability without *culpa* [fault]':

> That may be regarded as a statement of an ideal of what the law should be, or of the existing law. In the latter sense it is demonstrably inaccurate, whether we look at the old or the modern common law.[5]

Similar comments might be made in respect of the propositions that liability for economic loss requires proof of independent wrongdoing, that promises are not enforceable unless bargained for, that profits derived from wrongdoing have nothing to do with property or unjust enrichment, that property and obligation are completely separate sources of rights, and that private law has nothing to do with utility or policy. All these propositions may be supported and have been supported as desirable on a variety of considerations, but, as we have seen, they are not accurate descriptions of the past.

Increased specialization in law has meant that frequently a legal topic has been so narrowly defined as apparently to avoid the necessity of resolving

---

[4] W. Lucy, 'The Crises of Private Law', in T. Wilhelmsson and S. Hurri (eds.), *From Dissonance to Sense in Welfare State Expectations, Privatism and Private Law* (Dartmouth, 1999), p. 177 at p. 208 (emphasis in original).
[5] Lord Wright of Durley, 'The Northwestern Utilities Case' (1938), reprinted in *Legal Essays and Addresses* (Cambridge, 1939), p. 124. See chapter 5 above.

a conflict with non-conforming cases. An example is the protection given to reliance on gratuitous promises to convey land, discussed in an earlier chapter.[6] Nineteenth-century writers on contract law, espousing the view that only bargains could give rise to contractual liability, faced the problem of how to deal with these cases. To ignore them altogether was unsatisfactory, because they appeared to be exceptions to the bargain principle; to reject them was unsatisfactory also, because they answered to a strong intuitive sense of justice that few writers were prepared to refute; consequently they were displaced to some other branch or area of law, not precisely specified – perhaps property, or equity, or wrongdoing, or unjust enrichment, or some miscellaneous category – at any rate to some area not the immediate concern of the writer or reader. But this method is not only historically weak for the reasons mentioned; it also tends to produce a simplification more apparent than real, for the non-conforming legal issues cannot be made to disappear, and continue to require adjudication and resolution.

Similar techniques have been employed by those seeking complete and exclusive explanations of property, tort, and unjust enrichment. Thus the legal questions of liability for harm inflicted in circumstances of necessity, and of liability to account for profits derived from wrongdoing have been assigned by writers on torts to unjust enrichment, and by writers on unjust enrichment to torts.[7] Family obligations, though private legal obligations in the strictest sense of each of those words, and by all measurable standards very frequent and highly significant (legally, economically, socially, and politically), have been neglected in most accounts of private law. The concepts of property, contracts, torts, and unjust enrichment have all been relevant and often conclusive, but family obligations have usually been excluded from studies of those subjects because they cannot be explained by any one of them considered in isolation from the others.

Legal reasoning, as we have seen, has been a complex process, neither illogical in the sense of unreasoned or badly reasoned, nor reducible to any form of logic recognized outside the law. The concepts of contract, wrongdoing, and unjust enrichment have, at the point of their operation (that is, in the context of particular legal issues), often worked concurrently and cumulatively. They have been mutually complementary in the sense that each has supplemented and filled out the meaning of the others. At higher levels of generality the same complementarity may be observed in

---

[6] Pp. 58–62 above.   [7] See chapters 5 and 6 above.

the relations between obligation and property, and between private right and public policy. Two consequences follow on these complexities: it has not been possible to explain Anglo-American private law in terms of any single concept, nor has any map, scheme, or diagram proved satisfactory in which the concepts are separated from each other, as on a two-dimensional plane. The idea of mapping cannot be entirely discarded, and it owes its attraction partly to the fact that it is understood in many different ways, some of which are essential to the organization of thought. But insofar as it implies a separation of legal concepts from each other, or the assignment of each legal issue to one concept alone, it is apt to distort an understanding of the past, and consequently also of the present.

Blackstone's image of map-making[8] was natural enough, no doubt, for an instructor in any field, and other geographical terms, such as domain, province, realm, sphere, world, planet, field, territory, landscape, area, boundary, heartland, frontier, and borderline, have been commonly used in relation to legal concepts. But the law is not a geographical terrain, and in many respects it is not at all like one. Cartography assumes the comparative stability of the geographical features to be mapped, but law is constantly changing; there is no danger of confusing the map with the terrain, but in law it is often doubtful which is which; there are generally accepted grounds, independent of cartography itself, for assessing the reliability of maps, but there is no such consensus in law; mapping improves over time and with experience, but the understanding of law does not; the way in which maps are used does not itself alter them, but every judicial use of a legal map alters the terrain, and consequently the map too; geographical maps cannot be redrawn according to changing opinion of where tracts of territory ought ideally, logically, or conveniently to be located, but accounts of law often seek to do the equivalent; all competent cartographers tend to produce similar maps, but lawyers do not. Even in cartography there are complexities, and no geographical map can be perfectly accurate, or accurate for all purposes, but the analogy between legal classification and the mapping of geographical territory is imprecise.

Some other metaphors, like mapping, imply divisions that are exhaustive and mutually exclusive.[9] These include organizational diagrams and

---

[8] See chapter 1 above.

[9] Peter Birks has said that 'the classified answer to a question must use categories which are perfectly distinct one from another', P. Birks, 'Unjust Enrichment and Wrongful Enrichment' (2001) 79 *Texas Law Review* 1767 at 1794.

biological classification.[10] The image of biological classification implied by Lord Wright's statement (1943) that remedies for unjust enrichment were 'generically' different from those for contract and tort,[11] has been in use before[12] and since. It has been said, as will be recalled from the discussion of profits derived from wrongdoing, that 'it is no more possible for the selected event to be both an unjust enrichment and a tort than it is for an animal to be both an insect and a mammal'.[13] But the analogy is again imperfect, for in law not only the categories but also the specimens (concepts, reasons, rules, issues, cases, or relevant facts – all themselves interconnected) have been constructs of the human mind. Additions to the contents alter the class, and 'the classification changes as the classification is made'.[14] On this view it is not true of legal classification to say that it is 'exactly the same [as] in the natural world',[15] or that 'taxonomy changes nothing but it promotes understanding'.[16]

An English judge said in 1870 that

> it is a great scandal to the public and the profession generally that there should be a case in which a court of law is not able to determine what the law is. I admit the law is very difficult to determine, but I hope that, by means of improvements, the law will ultimately be reduced into a state that a man of ability, who has devoted his whole life to the subject, may be able to tell a person what the law really is on any one point. That state of things, I hope, may be arrived at; but it is not so now, and will not be so in my time.[17]

This vision of order and precision, quintessentially Victorian in its confident expectation of improvements and of attainable perfection, never came

---

[10] Linnaeus compared his scheme (class, order, genus, species) with territorial subdivisions (province, territory, parish, village), and also with Roman military divisions (naming four). It is the Linnaean scheme that has usually been assumed in legal analogies, ignoring genetic and other complexities in modern biology.

[11] Chapter 1 above.

[12] See R. Pound, 'Classification of Law' (1924) 37 *Harvard Law Review* 933, tracing uses of the metaphor to nineteenth-century logic, and indicating (at 937–8) his own rejection of it. Pound was a trained botanist: P. Sayre, *The Life of Roscoe Pound* (Iowa City, 1948), p. 63. See Justice Cardozo's reference (1921) to the 'lure of scientific order' quoted at p. 221 above.

[13] P. Birks, 'Unjust Enrichment', note 9 above, at 1781, and to similar effect in other writings.

[14] E. Levi, *An Introduction to Legal Reasoning* (Chicago, 1949), p. 3.

[15] P. Birks, 'Equity, Conscience, and Unjust Enrichment' (1999) 23 *Melbourne University Law Review* 1 at 9.

[16] P. Birks, 'Equity in the Modern Law: An Exercise in Taxonomy' (1996) 26 *Western Australian Law Review* 1 at 3.

[17] Lord Romilly MR in *Mullings* v. *Trinder* (1870) LR 10 Eq 449 at 455.

close to realization, and faded in the twentieth century. The vision failed to account for the capacity of the law to change, for the element of general overall judgment in adjudication, and for the complexity of the interrelation between facts and law. All these phenomena attended the dispute between Benjamin Lumley and Frederick Gye for the musical talents of Johanna Wagner, with which this study commenced. The facts of that dispute might be, and often have been, summarized by saying that Wagner proposed to sing for Gye in breach of her contract with Lumley. Those facts, and their anticipated sequel, would have been classified before 1852 as giving rise only to an action against Wagner for damages at common law for breach of contract. Gye, though he had access to the best legal advice,[18] failed to foresee the possibility of a Chancery injunction or of a direct action for damages for inducing breach of contract. The materialization of these possibilities demonstrates the capacity of the law to change, influenced, as we have seen, by very general considerations of judgment.

But the cases also show that there can never be an assurance that an account of any dispute includes all the facts that will be found relevant, and so the question that Lord Romilly supposed, of 'what the law really is on any one point', can never be asked of a practitioner, however learned, in a form that can yield a conclusive answer. Summaries of the opera dispute rarely refer to Lumley's failure to make the advance payment to Wagner as promised, an omission that, though held by three courts for three different and inconsistent reasons to be legally inconclusive, ultimately proved to be crucial at the jury trial as supporting Gye's honest belief in Wagner's right to terminate her contract with Lumley. Many twentieth-century commentators, not knowing of the trial or its result, erroneously supposed that the litigation was resolved in Lumley's favour. To these commentators Lumley's failure to make the advance payment, though plainly recorded and published in the reports of the Chancery proceedings, appeared to be irrelevant to the common law claim. This misunderstanding, not of great significance in itself, nevertheless illuminates an important feature of legal reasoning that usually remains obscure, namely that facts can only be perceived as relevant or irrelevant when it is known how the legal issues are to be identified and framed. This casts doubt on the idea that facts

---

[18] See S. Waddams, 'Johanna Wagner and the Rival Opera Houses' (2001) 117 *Law Quarterly Review* 431.

can themselves be classified for legal purposes. No one could undertake to supply a predictable legal response to all possible events or sets of facts, for the number of these is indeterminate and without limit: any number of facts may be included in the description of a person, or of a sequence of human actions.

The contents of legal categories, unlike natural specimens, cannot be itemized, sorted, or enumerated. Thus it is impossible to determine the comparative size of legal categories, or even to say how such a determination might be made. Pothier wrote that contracts 'are the most frequent source of obligations',[19] but it would be irrelevant, and even pedantic, to ask precisely how contractual and other obligations could be quantified and compared: a long-term employment contract, for example, might be counted as one obligation or as many. Such an expression as Pothier's is conceptual rather than historical, and means something like 'most frequent among the matters that are the writer's present concern' or, as his translator put it, 'the leading subject of the author's attention'.[20] Many of the legal issues considered in this study would, since they do not fit the primary categories, be assigned in a comprehensive scheme to a residual or miscellaneous category of obligations, but it is impossible to determine the size of such a category: the relation between spouses, for example, might be said to give rise to a single obligation on each side or to an infinite number. Varying estimates of size have been given by modern writers. It has been suggested that the miscellaneous category is 'a huge and various assortment of rights',[21] that 'in the law of obligations personal rights *rather rarely* arise from miscellaneous other events',[22] that 'most of' the law of obligations falls into the primary categories,[23] and that 'it is difficult to say whether the residual miscellany is large or small'.[24] The apparent diversity of these statements shows not that any of them is incorrect, but that the analogy between legal analysis and the classification of natural specimens is imperfect. From a historical point of view the last answer of the four is to

---

[19] R. J. Pothier, *Treatise on the Law of Obligations or Contracts*, trans. W. D. Evans (London, 1806), p. 3.
[20] *Ibid.*, Introduction, p. 82.
[21] P. Birks, 'Equity in the Modern Law', note 16 above, 9–10.
[22] P. Birks (ed.), *English Private Law* (Oxford, 2000), p. xlii (emphasis added).
[23] A. Burrows, *Understanding the Law of Obligations* (Oxford, 1998), p. 3.
[24] P. Birks, 'Equity, Conscience, and Unjust Enrichment' (1999) 23 *Melbourne University Law Journal* 1 at 8.

be preferred, for if it is to be imagined that by some incontrovertible decree a rigid classification scheme had been imposed on Anglo-American law, it is impossible to say which obligations would have been rejected, which accommodated under extended definitions of the primary classes, and which assigned to a miscellaneous class.

Other metaphors implying exhaustive and mutually exclusive divisions are common: for example, legal concepts have been called 'branches' (impliedly of a tree) or, on the other hand, 'sources' (impliedly of a river). It has been said that an action 'lies' in contract or in tort. Legal concepts have sometimes been likened to parts of the human body, to parts of a machine, to tools, or to rooms in a house. The law has been called a 'mosaic'.[25] To say that legal concepts are not stored in watertight compartments is ambiguous: though often used uncritically, the metaphor suggests compartments designed to be impermeable. Metaphors of this kind are an essential part of the search for understanding of any complex subject; but they are metaphors, not precise analogies.[26]

Not every metaphor presumes exhaustive and mutually exclusive divisions. Sir Frederick Pollock, who did more than anyone of his generation to bring intellectual order to the law of obligations,[27] warned that

> Ambitious writers have sometimes gone to work as if it were possible to reduce the whole contents of a legal system to a sort of classified catalogue where there would be no repetitions or cross references, and the classification would explain itself. Ambition on that scale is destined to disappointment by the nature of things.[28]

The words 'catalogue' and 'cross-references' suggest bibliographic classification, but the usage there differs from that of biologists. Books cannot be assigned to a single category to the exclusion of all others. A book often has many dimensions, and may be found to touch simultaneously on (let us say) history, politics, law, religion, economics, and philosophy. Six different libraries, each accepting the reality, importance, and distinctiveness of

---

[25] R. Goff, 'The Search for Principle', in W. Swadling and G. Jones (eds.), *The Search for Principle* (Oxford, 1999), pp. 313, 328.

[26] See G. Samuel, 'Can Gaius Really be Compared to Darwin?' (2000) 49 *International and Comparative Law Quarterly* 297.

[27] See P. Birks, 'Definition and Division: A Meditation on *Institutes* 3.13', in P. Birks (ed.), *The Classification of Obligations* (Oxford, 1997), pp. 3–4.

[28] F. Pollock, 'Divisions of Law' (1894) 8 *Harvard Law Review* 187, repeated almost verbatim in *A First Book of Jurisprudence* (London, 1896), p. 80.

these six concepts, might reasonably classify the book in six different ways. This idea of classification is, as applied to law, a different metaphor from that of biological classification of the traditional sort, for a book, unlike a biological specimen, may be in several classes at once. Even so, as we see, Pollock rejected a strict analogy with law.

Some other metaphors also allow for fluidity and intermingling of categories: the well-known metaphor of the 'seamless web', though used first of history,[29] has been frequently applied to the law.[30] To say that an action 'sounds' in tort does not necessarily exclude sympathetic overtones elsewhere. Again, legal concepts might be likened to colours that compose white light – sometimes perceived alone, but often in combination. It would be an error to suppose that one metaphor is 'right' and that the others are 'wrong', and it would equally be an error to suppose that metaphorical language could be dispensed with, for metaphor is often the only way of approaching complex phenomena. The undoubted need for metaphors, and their multiplicity and mutual inconsistency, are signals that the matter sought to be understood is complex. Each metaphor may capture an aspect of the matter, but none is adequate alone, and none must be pressed too far.[31]

A single-minded search for precision in private law tends to be self-defeating as new terminology is devised, and concepts and sub-concepts are multiplied and then further refined, in an attempt to accommodate awkward cases.[32] It has, as we have seen, encountered judicial resistance, and has led to warnings that 'a preoccupation with conceptualistic reasoning' may lead to 'absurd' conclusions.[33] Such warnings do not indicate a rejection of concepts, or of reason, or of classification; they signal a recognition that in law, as elsewhere, strict adherence to principle (admirable in itself) may, 'if relentlessly pursued'[34] in a single dimension of a complex question, ultimately impede, rather than assist, sound judgment.

---

[29] F. Pollock and F. W. Maitland, *History of English Law Before the Time of Edward I* (Cambridge, 1895), p. 1.

[30] G. Samuel, 'Classification of Obligations and the Impact of Constructivist Epistemologies' (1997) 17 *Legal Studies* 448.

[31] See H. Bosmajian, *Metaphor and Reason in Judicial Opinions* (Carbondale, 1992), D. Greschner, 'The Supreme Court, Federalism, and Metaphors of Moderation' (2000) 79 *Canadian Bar Review* 47.

[32] An example is discussed in note 20, p. 111 above.

[33] *Lister* v. *Hesley Hall Ltd* [2002] 1 AC 215, HL, at 224 (Lord Steyn).

[34] *Victoria Laundry Ltd* v. *Newman Industries Ltd* [1949] 2 KB 528, CA, at 539 (Asquith LJ).

Pollock denied that the law was 'reducible to patterns on a blackboard',[35] but he did not advocate the dissolution of conceptual distinctions or of reasoned argument. It is impossible for the law to dispense altogether with geo-spatial and linear imagery, for fundamental concepts in private law have in an important sense been distinct from each other and from other concepts. But these metaphors, like some others commonly applied to law, have a notable demerit: they tend to insulate the concepts from each other, and to suggest that a single conceptual location can be found for each legal issue.

The failure of any scheme to explain the actual decisions of the courts led, in the twentieth century, to scepticism of formal explanations and to the emergence of alternative accounts which, in their extreme forms, tended to reduce law to considerations of policy or utility. These views led in turn to counter-reaction and to a reassertion of formal principle. These approaches have sometimes seemed to be so radically opposed to each other as to open unbridgeable chasms. I do not claim by any means that every view can be reconciled with every other, but I do suggest that, in relation to the issues addressed in this study, the opposing views prominent in the academic debates of the past thirty-five years can be largely synthesized. Each of the approaches mentioned has supplied a valuable corrective of a predecessor, and each may have been justified in its own intellectual context, for sometimes an argument must be overstated a little for it to be heard at all. From the present perspective it can be seen that though considerations of principle, utility, and policy have each played an important part, none, considered alone, supplies a full explanation of the past. It is not so much that various *alternative* approaches are *permissible* (as though in some spirit of agnostic toleration) as that various *complementary* approaches are *necessary* (to the understanding of a complex phenomenon).

The examination of the issues considered in this study has shown that several concepts, including property, contract, wrongdoing, and unjust enrichment, though distinct, and each of fundamental importance, have, in relation to many legal issues, interacted with each other and with public policy. It may justly be said that the law has accommodated a considerable degree of complexity and imprecision, but the use of such stronger and pejorative words as 'incoherent', 'chaotic', 'dysfunctional', or 'a mess' might

---

[35] Pollock to Holmes, 24 Jan 1921, *Holmes–Pollock Letters*, ed. M. D. Howe, (2 vols., Cambridge, Mass., 1941), vol. II, p. 63.

be taken to imply that greater order and precision were attainable without sacrifice of other values, a proposition by no means self-evident. The lack of a single or simple explanation of private law has not excluded reasoned argument or, in practice, a considerable measure of coherence, predictability, and stability. The result has not been perfect order. But it does not follow that it has been chaos.

WORKS CITED

Addison, C., *A Treatise on the Law of Contracts and Rights and Liabilities ex contractu* (London, 1847)

American Law Institute, *Third Restatement of the Law: Torts; Products Liability* (St. Paul, 1998)

Anson, W., *Principles of the English Law of Contract* (Oxford, 1879)

Anson's Law of Contract, ed. J. C. Miles and J. L. Brierly (17th edn, Oxford, 1929)

Anson's Law of Contract, ed. J. Beatson (27th edn, Oxford, 1998)

Atiyah, P. S., *Accidents, Compensation and the Law* (2nd edn, London, 1975)

Atiyah, P. S., *Essays on Contract* (Oxford, 1986)

Atiyah, P. S., *Pragmatism and Theory in English Law* (London, 1987)

Atiyah, P. S., *Promises, Morals, and the Law* (Oxford, 1981)

Atiyah, P. S., *The Rise and Fall of Freedom of Contract* (Oxford, 1979)

Atiyah, P. S., *Vicarious Liability in the Law of Tort* (London, 1967)

Austin, J., *Lectures on Jurisprudence, or the Philosophy of Positive Law* (4th edn, ed. R. Campbell, 1879; repr. Bristol, 1966)

Baker, J. H., *An Introduction to English Legal History* (2nd edn, London, 1979)

Baker, J. H., *The Law's Two Bodies: Some Evidential Problems in English Legal History* (Oxford, 2001)

Band, J., and M. Katoh, *Interfaces on Trial: Intellectual Property and Interoperability in the Global Software Industry* (Boulder, 1995)

Barak, A., *Judicial Discretion* (New Haven, 1989)

Baty, T., *Vicarious Liability* (London, 1916)

Beatson, J., *The Use and Abuse of Unjust Enrichment: Essays on the Law of Restitution* (Oxford, 1991)

Beatson, J., and D. Friedmann (eds.), *Good Faith and Fault in Contract Law* (Oxford, 1995)

Benson, P. (ed.), *The Theory of Contract Law* (Cambridge, 2001)

Bentham, J., *A Comment on the Commentaries and A Fragment on Government*, ed. J. H. Burns and H. L. A. Hart (Oxford, 1977)

Berlioz, H., *Evenings with the Orchestra*, trans. J. Barzun (1956 [1852], repr. Chicago, 1973)

Birks, P., *An Introduction to the Law of Restitution* (Oxford, 1985)

Birks, P., *Restitution – The Future* (Sydney, 1992)

Birks, P. (ed.), *The Classification of Obligations* (Oxford, 1997)

Birks, P. (ed.), *English Private Law* (Oxford, 2000)

Birks, P. (ed.), *Wrongs and Remedies in the Twenty-first Century* (Oxford, 1996)

Bishop, J. P., *Commentaries on the Non-contract Law* (Chicago, 1889)

Blackstone, W., *An Analysis of the Laws of England* (London, 1756)

Blackstone, W., *Commentaries on the Laws of England* (4 vols., London, 1765–9)

Bosmajian, H., *Metaphor and Reason in Judicial Opinions* (Carbondale, 1992)

Buckley, F. H. (ed.), *The Fall and Rise of Freedom of Contract* (Durham, N.C., 1999)

Burrows, A., *The Law of Restitution* (London, 1993)

Burrows, A., *Understanding the Law of Obligations* (Oxford, 1998)

Burrows, A. (ed.), *Essays on the Law of Restitution* (Oxford, 1991)

Cardozo, B., *The Nature of the Judicial Process* (New Haven, 1921, repr. 1963)

Chompre, N., *Commentaires sur les lois anglaises* (Paris, 1822)

Chorley, H. F., *Thirty Years' Musical Recollections* (New York, 1926 [1862])

Colinvaux, R. (ed.), *Carver's Carriage by Sea* (13th edn, London, 1982)

Corbin, A. L., *Corbin on Contracts* (12 vols., St. Paul, 1964)

Cornish, W. R., et al. (eds.), *Restitution, Past, Present, and Future* (Oxford, 1998)

Cross, R., *Precedent in English Law* (Oxford, 1961)

Dietrich, J., *Restitution: A New Perspective* (Sydney, 1998)

Dworkin, R., *Taking Rights Seriously* (Cambridge, Mass., 1978)

Edelman, J., *Gain-Based Damages: Contract, Tort, Equity and Intellectual Property* (Oxford, 2002)

Encyclopaedia Britannica (11th edn, 29 vols., Cambridge, 1910–11)

Encyclopaedia of the Social Sciences (15 vols., New York, 1963)

Farnsworth, E. A., *Contracts* (Boston, 1982)

Feldthusen, B., *Economic Negligence* (4th edn, Toronto, 2000)

Finn, P. D. (ed.), *Essays on Restitution* (Sydney, 1990)

Fleming, J., *The Law of Torts* (Sydney, 1957, 5th edn, 1977, 8th edn, 1992, 9th edn, 1998)

Fuller, L., *Legal Fictions* (Stanford, 1967)

Fuller, L., *The Morality of Law* (New Haven, 1964)

Galligan, D., *Discretionary Powers* (Oxford, 1986)

Gilmore, G., *The Death of Contract* (Columbus, Ohio, 1972)

Girard, P., and J. Phillips (eds.), *Essays in the History of Canadian Law* (Toronto, 1990)

Goff, R., and G. Jones, *The Law of Restitution* (London, 1966, 4th edn, 1993, 5th edn, 1998)

Goldberg, R., *Causation and Risk in the Law of Torts: Scientific Evidence and Medicinal Product Liability* (Oxford, 1999)

Graveson, R. (ed.), *A Century of Family Law* (London, 1957)

Gummow, W. M. C., *Change and Continuity: Statute, Equity and Federalism* (Oxford, 1999)

Gurry, F., *Breach of Confidence* (Oxford, 1984)

Halliwell, M., *Equity and Good Conscience in a Contemporary Context* (London, 1997)

Harris, J., *Property and Justice* (Oxford, 1996)

Hedley, S., *A Critical Introduction to Restitution* (London, 2001)

Hedley, S., *Restitution: Its Division and Ordering* (London, 2001)

Herbert, A. P., *Uncommon Law* (London, 1959)

Hogg, P., *Liability of the Crown* (2nd edn, Toronto, 1989)

Holdsworth, W., *History of English Law* (London, 1903–66, 16 vols.)

Holmes, O. W., *The Common Law* (Boston, 1881), ed. M. D. Howe (Boston, 1963)

Holmes–Pollock Letters: The Correspondence of Mr Justice Holmes and Sir Frederick Pollock 1874–1932, ed. M. D. Howe (2 vols., Cambridge, Mass., 1941)

Ibbetson, D. J., *A Historical Introduction to the Law of Obligations* (Oxford, 1999)

Jaffey, P., *The Nature and Scope of Restitution* (Oxford, 2000)

Jolowicz, J. A., and T. E. Lewis, *Winfield on Tort* (7th edn, London, 1963)

Jones, G., *The Sovereignty of the Law* (Toronto, 1973)

Katz, S. N. and M. L. Inker (eds.), *Fathers, Husbands and Lovers* (1979)

Kennedy, D., *A Critique of Adjudication (Fin de Siecle)* (Cambridge, Mass., 1997)

Klippert, G., *Unjust Enrichment* (Toronto, 1983)

Kostal, R., *Law and English Railway Capitalism, 1825–1875* (Oxford, 1994)

Law Society of Upper Canada, *Special Lectures* (Toronto, 1981)

Lawson, F. H., *A Common Lawyer Looks at the Civil Law* (Ann Arbor, 1955)

Lawson, F. H. A., *Remedies of English Law* (2nd edn, London, 1980)

Levi, E., *An Introduction to Legal Reasoning* (Chicago, 1949)

Lieberman, D., *The Province of Legislation Determined: Legal Theory in Eighteenth-century Britain* (Cambridge, 1989)

Lobban, M., *The Common Law and English Jurisprudence 1760–1850* (Oxford, 1991)

Lumley, B., *Reminiscences of the Opera* (London, 1864)

Maddaugh, P., and J. McCamus, *The Law of Restitution* (Toronto, 1990)

Maine, H., *Ancient Law* (London, 1931 [1861])

Maitland, F., *Equity, also The Forms of Action at Common Law* (Cambridge, 1910)

Megarry, R., and H. Wade, *The Law of Real Property* (2nd edn, London, 1959)

Miller, C. J. (ed.), *Comparative Product Liability*, United Kingdom Comparative Law Series 6 (London, 1986)

Milsom, S., *Historical Foundations of the Common Law* (London, 1969)

Mustill, M., and J. Gilman (eds.), *Arnould's Law of Marine Insurance and Average* (16th edn, London, 1981)

Nalbach, D., *The King's Theatre, 1704–1867: London's First Italian Opera House* (London, 1972)

The New Grove Dictionary of Opera, 4 vols. (London 1992)

Owen D. G. (ed.), *Philosophical Foundations of Tort Law* (Oxford, 1995)

Palmer, G., *The Law of Restitution* (4 vols., Boston, 1978)

Palmer, N., and E. McKendrick (eds.), *Interests in Goods* (2nd edn, London, 1998)

Phillimore, R., *Thoughts on the Law of Divorce in England* (London, 1844)

Pollock, F., *A First Book of Jurisprudence* (London, 1896)

Pollock, F., *The Law of Torts: A Treatise on the Principles of Obligations arising from Civil Wrongs in the Common Law* (London, 1887)

Pollock, F., *Principles of Contract at Law and in Equity* (London, 1876)

Pollock, F., and F. W. Maitland, *History of English Law Before the Time of Edward I* (Cambridge, 1895)

Posner, R., *Economic Analysis of Law* (Boston, 1972, 4th edn, 1992, 5th edn, 1998)

Pothier, R. J., *A Treatise on the Law of Obligations or Contracts*, trans. W. D. Evans (London, 1806)

Powell, J. J., *An Essay upon the Law of Contracts and Agreements* (London, 1790)

Reiter, B., and J. Swan (eds.), *Studies in Contract Law* (Toronto, 1980)

Reynolds, F., *Bowstead and Reynolds on Agency* (16th edn, London, 1996)

Roper, R., *A Treatise of the Law of the Property arising from the Relation between Husband and Wife* (2 vols., London, 1841)

Rosenthal, H., *Two Centuries of Opera at Covent Garden* (London, 1958)

Rotherham, C., *Proprietary Remedies in Context: A Study in the Judicial Redistribution of Property Rights* (Oxford, 2002)

Salmond, J. W., and R. Heuston, *The Law of Torts* (21st edn, London, 1996)

Samuel, G., *The Foundations of Legal Reasoning* (Maastricht, 1994)

Samuel, G., and J. Rinkes, *Law of Obligations and Legal Remedies* (London, 1996, 2nd edn, G. Samuel, 2001)

Sayre, P., *The Life of Roscoe Pound* (Iowa City, 1948)

Schlueter, L., and K. Redden, *Punitive Damages* (4th edn, 2 vols., New York, 2000)

Schrage, E. J. H. (ed.), *Unjust Enrichment and the Law of Contract* (The Hague, 2001)

Scott, A. W., *The Law of Trusts* (Boston, 1939)

Sharpe, R. J., *Injunctions and Specific Performance* (Toronto, 1983, 2nd edn, 1992)

Shelford, L., *A Practical Treatise on the Law of Marriage and Divorce* (London, 1841)

Sheridan, L., *Fraud in Equity* (London, 1956)

Simpson, A. W. B., *Leading Cases in the Common Law* (Oxford, 1995)

Simpson, A. W. B., *Legal Theory and Legal History* (London, 1987)

Simpson, A. W. B., *Victorian Law and the Industrial Spirit* (London, 1995)

Smith, J. W., *A Selection of Leading Cases on Various Branches of the Law* (12th edn, London, 1915, 13th edn, 1929)

Smith, L. *The Law of Tracing* (Oxford, 1997)

Spence, M., *Protecting Reliance: the Emergent Doctrine of Equitable Estoppel* (Oxford, 1999)

Spry, I. C. F., *The Principles of Equitable Remedies* (3rd edn, Sydney, 1984)

Stapleton, J., *Product Liability* (London, 1994)

Steel, D., and F. Rose, *Kennedy's Law of Salvage* (5th edn, London, 1985)

Stein, P., and J. Shand, *Legal Values in Western Society* (Edinburgh, 1974)

Stoljar, S., *The Law of Quasi-Contract* (Sydney, 1964)

Story, J., *Commentaries on Equity Jurisprudence* (13th edn, 2 vols., Boston, 1886)

Sunstein, C. R., *One Case at a Time: Judicial Minimalism and the Supreme Court* (Cambridge, Mass., 1999)

Sutton, K. C. T., *Consideration Reconsidered* (St Lucia, Queensland, 1974)

Swadling, W., and G. Jones (eds.) *The Search for Principle: Essays in Honour of Lord Goff of Chieveley* (Oxford, 1999)

Taggart, M., *Private Property and Abuse of Rights in Victorian England: The Story of Edward Pickles and the Bradford Water Supply* (Oxford, 2002)

Tawney, R. H., *The Acquisitive Society* (New York, 1920)

Trebilcock, M. J., *The Common Law of Restraint of Trade: A Legal and Economic Analysis* (Toronto, 1986)

Trebilcock, M. J., *The Limits of Freedom of Contract* (Cambridge, Mass., 1991)

Treitel, G. H., *The Law of Contract* (10th edn, London, 1999)

Twining, W., *Karl Llewellyn and the Realist Movement* (Norman, Ohio, 1973)

Virgo, G., *The Principles of the Law of Restitution* (Oxford, 1999)

Waddams, S. M., *The Law of Contracts* (4th edn, Toronto, 1999)

Waddams, S. M., *The Law of Damages* (3rd edn, Toronto, 1997)

Waddams, S. M., *Law, Politics, and the Church of England: the Career of Stephen Lushington, 1782–1873* (Cambridge, 1992)

Waddams, S. M., *Products Liability* (4th edn, Toronto, 2002)

Walker, D. (ed.) *The Oxford Companion to Law* (Oxford, 1980)

Waters, D. W. (ed.), *Equity, Fiduciaries and Trusts, 1993* (Toronto, 1993)

Weinrib, E., *The Idea of Private Law* (Cambridge, Mass., 1995)

Weir, J. A., *Economic Torts* (Oxford, 1997)

Wilhelmsson, T., and S. Hurri (eds.), *From Dissonance to Sense in Welfare State Expectations, Privatism and Private Law* (Dartmouth, 1999)

Williams, G., *Liability for Animals* (Cambridge, 1939)

Williston, S., *Selections from Williston's Treatise on the Law of Contracts* (revised edn, New York, 1938)

Wilson, D., and J. Cooke (eds.), *Lowndes and Rudolph, General Average and the York–Antwerp Rules* (11th edn, London, 1990)

Winfield, P. H., *The Province of the Law of Tort* (Cambridge, 1931)

Worthington, S., *Personal Property Law: Text and Materials* (Oxford, 2000)

Worthington, S., *Proprietary Interests in Commercial Transactions* (Oxford, 1996)

Wright of Durley (Lord), *Legal Essays and Addresses* (Cambridge, 1939)

INDEX

accounting of profits, 35, 108, 116, 117, 121, 122
acquiescence, 60
Addison, Charles, 7, 222, 223
Admiralty cases, 151, 152
adultery, 130
advice, reliance on, 52
agency, 46, 72–3, 80–2, 83, 113–14
air pollution, 89–90
Alderson B, 193, 198
alimony, 128–9, 130–1
American Legal Realism school, 205
animals, 95–6
Anson, William, 8–9, 11–12, 31
Atiyah, Patrick, 67, 68

bailment, 46
Baker, John, 202
Beatson, Jack, 69, 133, 166, 169
Bentham, Jeremy, 12
Best J, 6
Berlioz, Hector, 23
Birks, Peter, 4, 16–17, 59, 109–10, 163, 189, 194, 205, 227, 229
Blackburn J, 91, 95
black holes, 44, 46–7, 53–4
Blackstone, William, 1, 3, 4–5, 21, 226
blood contamination, 101
Bramwell B, 88, 89, 93, 96, 101, 196
Brandeis J, 175
breach of confidence, 74–8, 121–3
breach of contract
    accounting of profits, 35, 117, 121
    damages, 153, 167–8
    efficient breach, 120, 144
    engagements, 35
    generally, 8, 9

inducement to, 29, 35, 43
Johanna Wagner dispute, 14–15, 28
personal services, 143, 146
profits from, 114–23, 149–50
promises, 15, 57–61, 64–8, 168–9, 225
remedies, 28, 34–5, 153, 155–6
specific performance, *see* specific performance
substitute performance, 114–16
unjust enrichment, 162–71
without wrong, 146–7
wrongdoing, 17–18, 36, 37, 142–5, 154–5
bribery, 113–14, 183–4
Browne-Wilkinson, Lord, 45, 46
Bruch, Carol, 134
Buckmaster, Lord, 63
building defects, 45–6, 47, 157–62

Calabresi, Guido, 197
Campbell, Lord, 26, 37, 52, 54
Carbone, June, 133
Cardozo, Benjamin (Cardozo J), 19, 64, 74, 115, 221
carriage of goods by sea, 45, 47–8
case law
    legal change through decisions, 206–9
    and statutory law, 12–13, 20, 138
causation, 203
change
    legal change, 12
    public policy attitudes, 200–1
    through legal decisions, 206–9